TERROR
ON
HIGHWAY
59

TERROR ON HIGHWAY 59

by Steve Sellers

★

TexasMonthlyPress

Texas Monthly Press, Inc.
P.O. Box 1569
Austin, Texas 78767

A B C D E F G H

Library of Congress Cataloging in Publication Data

Sellers, Steve, 1952 –
   Terror on highway 59.

   1. Sellers, Steve, 1952 –
2. Journalists – United States – Biography.   3. Sheriffs – Texas – San Jacinto
County.   4. Police corruption – Texas – San Jacinto County.
I. Title.   II. Title: Terror on Highway fifty-nine.
PN4874. S426A37   1984   070'.92'4 [B]   84-17
ISBN   0-932012-86-8

To Marcy and Casey

· ONE ·

The newsroom at the *Austin American-Statesman* was fairly quiet on Monday morning, January 18, 1982, the first day of my second week on the job. From what I could tell from one week's experience, the newsroom stayed quiet most of the time. I think that was one of the things that attracted me to the place. Not that the newspaper's brand-new, $34 million, three-story, glass-and-steel building on the banks of the Colorado River, exactly one mile down Congress Avenue from the Texas capitol, wasn't attractive. It was. There were windows everywhere, each seemingly with a perfect view of the river. Inside were the latest and most modern computer terminals, desks, chairs, and library equipment. The carpets were spotless, the paint was new, the windows were shiny, and the newsroom, incredibly, seemed devoid of cigarette smoke. Everything looked *clean*, which was very strange for a newspaper office. But I particularly liked the peaceful aura that hovered over the newsroom. It wasn't at all like the other newsrooms I knew anything about.

At the *Fort Worth Press*, where I worked as a reporter from 1972 to 1975, the newsroom was loud, dirty, and chaotic—very much like the newsroom depicted in the Walter Matthau–Jack Lemmon movie *The Front Page*. And in Memphis, where I worked as an assistant city editor from 1977 to 1982, the newsroom was clean and organized, but it was loud. There were few places you could go in the newsroom at the *Commercial Appeal* in Memphis where you were out of earshot of the crackling police scanner radio. I could appreciate the quietness of the *American-Statesman*, especially since I had accepted a job as investigative reporter after working on the city desk in Memphis for five years, and I figured the transition from editor to reporter would be better served in a quiet environment.

During my first week on the job, I had renewed contacts with a host of lawyers, businessmen, and politicians with whom I had dealt during the early 1970s while working in Fort Worth. And I had spent some time meeting other reporters and introducing myself to the office's computer system. The latter proved fairly easy, since the *American-Statesman*'s brand-new system was identical to the one I had been using in Memphis. While other reporters were struggling to type their stories on the computer terminals, I fascinated myself by poring through the various files of local, national, and international stories. I felt I was making the transition from editor to reporter, and from Memphis to Austin, very well.

Shortly before noon on this Monday, however, a letter was forwarded to me through our capitol bureau. It was addressed to Texas governor Bill Clements, but it had been passed from Clements' office to the Texas Civil Liberties Union, and from there to the newspaper's capitol reporting staff, and from there to me.

The two-page typed, single-spaced letter was dated December 26, 1981, and it was from a man named J. E. Foley, a resident of Jamestown, Kentucky, who was complaining about a run-in that he, his girlfriend, and his son had had with a sheriff's department along U.S. Highway 59 in a tiny little county just north of Houston.

The roughly written letter was addressed to "Governor, State of Texas, Capitol Building, Austin, Texas." The return address said only "Jamestown, Kentucky." It was hard to tell immediately what the point of the letter was, so confusing was the wording. About all I knew at noon on Monday, January 18, was that no one was very interested in what this letter had to say.

Ed Crowell, my city editor, in handing me the letter, mentioned only that it seemed to complain about a bail bond office that was supposedly located inside some East Texas jail, and he remarked that the allegation was probably worth checking out. "Sheriffs aren't supposed to be in the bond business," he said. But he didn't seem too excited about it, and he said I could check it out later. I skimmed over the letter anyway, just to see what it was about, and I decided to make a couple of quick phone calls to see what state agency was looking into the Kentucky man's complaint.

I placed my first call to John Duncan, executive director of the Texas branch of the American Civil Liberties Union, to find out if he knew whether the governor's office was looking into the matter, or whether his office was doing it. It was an easy call. Basically, no one was looking into it, according to Duncan. His agency wasn't, he explained, because it didn't have the staff to pursue such complaints. Instead, he had referred it to the East Texas Legal Services Office in Bryan, a government-funded agency that provided legal aid to the poor. And that agency, my second telephone call determined, was in the process of returning the letter to Duncan with the brief notation "We no longer are able to

investigate complaints of this nature, due to budgetary considerations."
So within an hour of receiving a letter originally addressed to the governor, I had found that no one was following up on it.

I read back over the letter to see why it was causing so many people
to ignore it:

Dear Sir:

Recently, I visited some friends in Houston, Texas. Upon conclusion of my visit my party started to return to Kentucky in two
cars. About 8:00 P.M., November 28, 1981, on U.S. Highway 59,
two members of the Jacinto County Sheriff's Department stopped
one of our cars. Without issuing any citation and without any
probable cause whatsoever, the officers searched the occupants of
the car and placed them in the police car with the announced
intention of transporting them to jail. The police then proceeded
to search the interior of the car but did not open the trunk. They
found less than two ounces of marijaunna in the car. They—the
police—claim they found the contraband in the floor of the front
seat of the car. The driver of the car admitted that the marijaunna
belonged to him but he claimed the police found it under his seat.
He—the driver—also informed the police that his passenger—a 27
year old woman—had no knowledge of the marijaunna being in
the car and that she was completely innocent. I personally checked
the car just prior to our departure from Houston and there was
nothing in the floor of the car at that time. I did not look under
the seats. It appears that there was no probable cause evidence
which would legalize the search of the car. Further, there was no
reason whatsoever to arrest the passenger who was totally innocent of any wrongdoing. I owned the car and I informed the police
that I would be responsible for it and did not want it towed.
They—the police—ignored me and called a wrecker to tow the car.
I followed the wrecker to Cold Springs. There the car was placed
in an unlit, unguarded parking area in the rear of the jail.

There was a bail bond office inside the jail. This office contained
a credit card imprinting device. Attached to this device was a tab
which read "Cold Springs Resale Shop." A bondsman informed
me that bail for each would be $1,000.00. For a fee of 10% of the
bail—$200.00—he agreed to post the bail. He further stated that
for an additional sum of $210.00 he would plead them guilty to the
charge and pay their fine and they would not have to return to
court to answer the charge. I inquired if he would accept a Master
Charge credit card and he stated that he would. He made out the

Master Charge form to show that I had received a cash advance of $410.00. I received no cash whatsoever.

As to the wrecker service which towed the car, they were from Shepherd, Texas, and I did not talk to any of them. The bonds[man] collected their money for them—$45.00 tow charge plus $2.25 state sales tax. He—the bondsman—filled out the Master Charge form where it showed I had received merchandise —towels, dishes. I did not receive any merchandise at all.

As heretofore stated, the innocent passenger was a 27 year old woman—the mother of two small children—who had never before had any contact with police, jails, etc. and whose personality structure was of a nature which rendered her constitutionally incapable of knowingly violating any law. The only reason she was in the car was to keep the driver company during the long drive back to Kentucky. A few minutes after we left the jail she went into a state of shock. She became disoriented and complained of numbness. Believing her to be near a complete nervous collapse, I stopped at a hospital emergency room in a small town off Highway 59 where she was given sedatives. It took her several hours to regain her composure. The fact that she was made to so suffer cannot be justified either legally or morally. She was completely innocent and the police had no grounds whatsoever to subject her to the humiliation they subjected her to.

I know that several other cars were stopped in the same manner that night by the Jacinto County Sheriff's Department. I can readily assume that the occupants thereof were treated in a similar manner. It was a complete "Dukes of Hazard—Boss Hog" operation.

Hopefully, your office will be able to institute remedial action in the matter and it will not be necessary for me to have to call in the Federal authorities. Further, I have taken steps to have payment of the above amounts stopped by the Master Charge people. If I am not able to do so, I shall certainly institute action designed to compel Jacinto County to refund my money—especially that portion which I was required to spend in order to free a completely innocent person. I am enclosing a copy of the receipts I received during this farce and a list of the officers, etc., to whom I am sending a copy of this letter.

Kindly acknowledge and advise.

Respectfully yours,
J. E. Foley

In a decade of work as a reporter and editor, I had seen dozens of letters like this one—all of them written in a moment of anger following some distasteful encounter with the law. All of them wanted quick, thorough compensation for their wrongs, and all tended to leave out bits and pieces of the story that might shed some illumination on the actions of the official parties. I had learned that all of these letters were right and truthful, on certain points. And all of them were incorrect and downright false on other points. Believing everything in a letter of complaint like this would be like holding a criminal trial and listening to testimony only from the defense. But it was an interesting letter nonetheless.

I thumbed over to the two enclosures that were mentioned in the next-to-last paragraph. They appeared to be copies of two cash receipts and two Master Charge sales slips. The copies were so faded, however, that it was hard to decipher some of the words. Both charge receipts were clearly stamped with the imprint of Coldspring Resale Shop. One was marked "cash advance," as the letter said, and the other contained the description "merchandise, dishes, towels." The former was for $410; the latter for $47.25. One of the cash receipts was signed by Herb Atwood, who apparently was representing a firm by the name of Bail Bonding Company of Coldspring, and it read, "POM-2 Bond $100.00 ea., total $200.00; escrow $105.00 ea., total $210.00." The towing bill was not signed, but it was marked "pd. 11-28-81," and the firm's name was B&B Wrecker of Shepherd.

I had never heard of these towns, although I had lived in Texas twenty-five of my thirty years, and "Jacinto County" sounded completely wrong. I checked the large state highway map on the southeast wall of the newsroom and pinpointed U.S. 59. I traced it north from Houston through Liberty County and Cleveland, Texas, and found the town of Shepherd in tiny print about six miles south of the Trinity River, about seventy miles north of Houston. Coldspring was a mere pinprick on the map eleven miles northwest of Shepherd. And the county's name was San Jacinto County. Those two towns and Lake Livingston were the only landmarks in the county shown on the wall map.

I got back on the telephone and again called the East Texas Legal Services Office in Bryan. I was curious why an agency set up to help people who couldn't afford to help themselves was not interested in allegations that (1) bail bondsmen were entering guilty pleas in court for a fee, (2) credit card imprinting devices for a resale shop were being used interchangeably with a bail bond company, (3) bail bonds were being set without benefit of a court appearance, (4) a bondsman appeared to have accepted a guilty plea in the place of a judge, (5) a bond receipt

was changed to show that merchandise from a resale shop had been purchased, and (6) a "Boss Hogg" relationship appeared to exist between the
law enforcement officers, the bail bonding company, and the wrecker
company. I just wanted to hear an explanation.

Jane Swanson, an official in the legal services office, listened to my
questions and then repeated what she had told me earlier: the agency
"unfortunately isn't taking any new cases at all."

"But," I asked, "does any of this interest you personally?"

After a short pause, she said the letter raised some "interesting allegations." And then she asked if she could talk candidly, and not for publication in the *American-Statesman*. I agreed.

This was not the first complaint she had heard about San Jacinto
County, nor was it unusual for such complaints. Other allegations had
been made about a "protection outfit" that was run by some law enforcement officials over there, but she did not have any details. And Bryan,
she pointed out, was about a hundred miles from Coldspring, and San
Jacinto County, as far as she knew, did not have any attorneys who
were willing to cooperate with her agency, or with the ACLU.

"Let me just say that the reputation for law enforcement in that
county is pretty bad," she said. "People who live in that part of the state
know about it, but I doubt that you'll find many people who will talk
to you about it."

I thanked her for her candor and said I'd be checking back with her
soon. I decided to consult the newspaper's library to find out more
about San Jacinto County.

A dozen state reference books, almanacs, and encyclopedias and
decades of newspaper microfilm held less than two paragraphs of information on that county. I learned that the 1980 population was 11,434,
and that the population of Coldspring, the county seat, was 569. Fully
sixty percent of the county lay inside the Sam Houston National Forest,
and the county's chief administrative officer was county judge K. P.
Bryant. There was no city government in Coldspring, so the county
officials were the only officials. Only three practicing attorneys were listed in a recent legal directory, and one of them was county attorney
Robert Atkins, a member of the State Bar of Texas since 1950. The
sheriff was J. C. Parker, and he had been in office since 1969.

I did a little checking also on the adjoining counties—Montgomery,
Walker, Trinity, Polk, and Liberty—and was struck by the Old West
nature of some of the city names: Cut 'n Shoot, Pointblank, Splendora,
Rural Shade, Dodge, Phelps, Pinehurst, and New Waverly. They had
the ring of provincialism.

But more than that, they had the ring of frontier justice. Or at least
wild-wild-West justice. Since the mid-1970s, with the coming of the

urban cowboy craze, people from all over the country have looked to Texas as the last great outpost on the frontier, the last link with this country's pioneer roots. It has become quite fashionable to dress up like a Texan; cowboy hats and boots are acceptable attire just about everywhere these days. Law officers in most rural Texas areas have dressed that way for decades. You can scarcely drive into an out-of-the-way Texas community without seeing a "cowboy-looking" lawman. The sense of tradition among those people, from what I've seen, is tremendous. They identify with the range-riding marshals of the last century, and some even fancy themselves as direct descendants of the old Texas Rangers—the famous freedom fighters of the 1820s and 1830s who rode the ranges in search of hostile Indians, Mexicans, and anyone else who happened to get in their way. Those nineteenth-century officers brandished incredible power, mostly in the form of rifles and pistols. They didn't have to recite the Miranda "blue card" rights to prisoners, and the right to a speedy trial was taken quite literally. There were few appeals to a higher court on the frontier of South Texas during the pre-statehood and pre-Republic days of the 1820s.

I guess it was out of this freedom-fighting mold that the institution of the Texas sheriff first got its almost mystical aura. Several recent movies and television shows have added to that mystique, often to a ridiculous extreme. But the fact remains that for more than one hundred years sheriffs in Texas have had wide-ranging powers and authority in their counties. They were—and still are—the chief law enforcement officers in the counties, and they are charged by statute with preserving the peace for all residents of a county, including those who live in incorporated areas. They are the guardians and operators of the county jails, and as such have broad discretion to establish penal policy. And they are the chief officers in charge of security in the various state and county courtrooms, as well as the primary servers of criminal and civil papers of all sorts. In some of Texas' rural counties, the sheriff still serves as tax collector. There are even some laws on the books that give Texas sheriffs additional powers and responsibilities to serve as special assistants during elections. It probably goes without saying that from time to time, some of these duties get carried out in some counties in a pretty high-handed manner. But sheriffs have always been powerful people in Texas, and in many parts of the state they are stronger than ever.

Some groups of citizens like it that way. One such group, an obscure right-wing element known as the Posse Comitatus, even takes its name from the power sheriffs and other peace officers still retain to summon citizens to help out in an emergency. These citizens are referred to in Texas statutes as the power of the county, a rough rendering of the Latin phrase *posse comitatus*. Now, the members of the organized group

in Texas that goes by the name Posse Comitatus have not been called
by any sheriff to quell a public disturbance or help out in an emergency,
but they seem to revere the office of the sheriff nevertheless. A few
dozen of them even held their own trial on a Saturday afternoon in the
Travis County Courthouse in Austin to pass judgment on a local Internal Revenue Service official who had the audacity to seize a member's
property for nonpayment of taxes. The trial resulted in a guilty verdict
in absentia for the IRS official, and the posse demanded that Travis
County sheriff Doyne Bailey arrest the man. Bailey demurred, and several posse members wound up getting arrested themselves for carrying
loaded weapons into the courthouse. This happened not in 1882 but in
the broad daylight of 1982. Some of the posse members—who seem to
weave a type of Christian fanaticism into a tapestry of tax protesting
and antifederalism—have made contact with similar groups in other
states, and there have been scattered incidents of bloodshed. And a lot
of their zeal seems to be aimed at organizing local and state governments
totally around the offices of the county sheriffs, which they claim is both
necessary and efficient. A federal official in Austin commented after the
Posse Comitatus "trial" that the posse members "seem to want to take
us back to the good old days of the wild West when everybody who carried a gun made his own laws."

Nevertheless, there seems to be a fringe element in the rural areas of
Texas that would like to see the sheriffs take on even more authority—as
long as the type of authority they assume is consistent with the aims and
goals of the so-called Posse Comitatus: antifederal, pro-individual, pro-
white, antiminority.

Some of this passed through my mind as I read about Cut 'n Shoot
and Pointblank, Texas, the former in Montgomery County and the
latter in San Jacinto County. Colorful names. But what kind of law enforcement did they have? I discovered during my afternoon of research
that timber and oil were the big industries in the rural counties north
of Houston, but per capita income was well below the state average.
Lake Livingston, a large recreational reservoir that takes in parts of four
counties, was the primary tourist attraction; it began filling up behind
a dam on the Trinity River in 1969. U.S. 59 and Interstate 45 were the
only four-lane routes through the area. And a quick glance at population trends over the last fifty years showed that the city of Houston was
headed in that direction at a rapid clip; suburbs of Houston already had
sprung up near Conroe, in Montgomery County.

At 6:30 p.m., as I was driving home from my afternoon in the newspaper library, I was still thinking about Mr. Foley's letter. I probably
would not have been so interested in it except that no one else seemed

to want to help the man out. I decided that early the next morning I would try to track down this Mr. Foley in Jamestown, Kentucky.

That task proved more difficult than it originally appeared. All I had to go on was a post office box number, and the long-distance telephone operator had no listing in a seven-county area for a J. E. Foley. Three other families with the same last name had telephone listings, but when I called they said they had never heard of the man.

About 4:00 p.m., I made contact with state senator Kent Caperton, a Bryan lawyer whose district includes San Jacinto County. I had been told that the legal services office had apprised Caperton of Foley's complaint, but I decided to play dumb. The senator said he had received no such complaint. So I changed direction and asked him what he would do if he received one "like the one I heard about."

He responded, "Generally, what I would do on something like that would be to ask the sheriff to look into it, and see what his response is."

I scratched Caperton's name off my list before he even finished his sentence. It was obvious what type of investigation *he* would do with this complaint.

I spent most of the next few weeks chasing legislative "issues" stories for the city desk, and I was unable to do much more about Foley's letter than make two or three telephone calls during the day and do a little legal research at night. I learned from an assistant attorney general friend of mine that bail bondsmen are not regulated by the state and that county governments can, at their option, set up a Bail Bond Board composed of the sheriff, the district attorney, and state district judges to set up local regulations for bail bondsmen. But it was optional. In most rural Texas counties, the sheriff personally regulates bondsmen. And according to state law, sheriffs can—when courts are not in session and when a judge cannot be located—set reasonable bail bonds for persons arrested in their counties. The law also permits sheriffs to collect such bonds in the absence of a judge.

By February 15, I had maneuvered my schedule so that I was able to put myself full time on the Foley complaint. Most of that effort resulted from an intriguing conversation I had with another lawyer, Lamar Hankins, a former employee of the Texas Civil Liberties Union and currently a staff attorney with the Gulf Coast Legal Foundation in Bryan. Hankins had been around East Texas several years and was familiar with San Jacinto County. But like most of the people I had talked with, he had little concrete information that would be pertinent to Mr. Foley's complaint, and what information he had he was unwilling to divulge for immediate publication.

Nevertheless, Hankins recalled that San Jacinto County in 1977 or 1978 had been involved as a defendant in a federal court lawsuit that charged that the sheriff's department had been planting marijuana in the cars of people who had been stopped on U.S. 59. He said there were some allegations about high fines and drug charges that disappeared, and that some defendants had paid their fines in cash, which was never reported.

While working for the Houston chapter of the ACLU, Hankins had a chance to interview two people who lodged complaints against the county. "They told me the sheriff and his people were pretty good about sniffing out longhairs and beards" on Highway 59, he said. But, he added quickly, it was his understanding that the county "cleaned up its act for good" after the lawsuit was filed. And the lawsuit was dismissed before it went to trial. Of course, he had few details. But I was able to confirm his sketchy account with two other legal contacts in Houston; there had indeed been a lawsuit involving shakedowns on Highway 59.

And that was good enough for me to go on. I decided that Mr. Foley might be onto something, and I persuaded Ed to turn me loose on the story. There were enough suspicions, rumors, and lawyerly concerns to indicate that the story was worth pursuing. I used an old reporter's trick and called the postmaster in Jamestown, Kentucky, gave him J. E. Foley's post office box number, and said I had an urgent message to get to him that couldn't wait much longer. The postmaster gave me Foley's unlisted telephone number.

I reached him at his job at a nursery outside Jamestown shortly before 3:00 p.m. on February 15. We talked for ten minutes, quickly going over his letter, and then he said he had more to tell me, but I would have to call him at his home at 5:00 p.m. I called him back at 5:01.

The arrests on Highway 59 had capped a short vacation to Houston, where Foley, his nineteen-year-old son, Jeffrey, and his twenty-seven-year-old girlfriend, Patsy DeBorde, had gone to visit some friends and relatives. While in Houston, the trio purchased a car, which the elder Foley decided to drive back to Jamestown himself. They left from Houston in two cars—an old 1968 Pontiac with Kentucky plates, driven by Jeffrey, and the newer car, which had Texas plates and registration. Patsy DeBorde rode with the younger Foley. The two cars pulled onto U.S. 59 in Houston about 7:00 p.m. on November 28, 1981, a Saturday night. About an hour later, they passed through Cleveland, stopping at the traffic light at the intersection with State Highway 105 in the middle of town. It was dark by then, and the temperature, which was in the mid-fifties, felt unusually warm to the Kentuckians.

The two-car convoy passed by the half-dozen liquor stores on Highway 59 between Cleveland and Shepherd, traveling at a steady fifty miles per hour. There were no stoplights in Shepherd, only a flashing amber light at the intersection with State Highway 150 and a mileage sign indicating that Coldspring was eleven miles to the northwest. About three miles north of Shepherd on U.S. 59, along a dark stretch in the Trinity River bottoms, in a small community known only by its sign—Urbana—the old Pontiac was stopped by officers of the San Jacinto County Sheriff's Department.

"They said the taillight was out in my old car, the one with the Kentucky plates," Mr. Foley said, his voice rising slightly. "They got my son out of the car first. I didn't know what was going on, but they had a bunch of other cars pulled over that I could see. Then they started to frisk them there on the road, even the girl. They never wrote up a ticket or anything. They started to search the car—the passenger side, under the seats, in the back seat, the glove compartment, the girl's purse. And then they found that small amount of marijuana under the front seat."

He stopped talking for a moment. "I knew my son smoked marijuana, but I can tell you one thing: he wasn't smoking it on this trip. That's why the girl was riding with him, to make sure he didn't. He bought that marijuana in Kentucky, placed it under the seat in Kentucky, and that's where it was going back to, unopened. I don't condone his smoking, but he isn't going to do it around me."

By the time the plastic bag was found, a tow truck was pulling up. A deputy told Mr. Foley that his son and the woman were being arrested for possession of marijuana, and that the car would be towed to the jail in Coldspring.

"I protested the towing. I said I was the owner of the car and would be responsible for taking care of it. They told me to shut up and get back in my car," he said.

Handcuffs were placed on Jeffrey Foley and Patsy DeBorde, and they were placed in the back seat of a patrol car. Before proceeding to Coldspring, however, the deputies stopped about a mile down the highway and picked up another person who had been arrested by another deputy for possession of marijuana, Foley said.

The eleven miles up Highway 150 to Coldspring were traveled in about six or seven minutes, at speeds in excess of eighty miles an hour, he recalled. The winding, two-lane road was not heavily traveled that night.

"A bondsman was waiting for us at the jail, and he set the bond. There was no judge around. He said it would cost us $410 altogether. I was more mad than anything else. I had the cash in my pocket, but I pulled out my credit card. The bondsman called the credit card [telephone] number and cleared the amount, like he's supposed to do when the amount is over $50. He also took payment for the towing. You've got receipts for all that—the cash advance that wasn't no cash advance because I never saw no cash. And the dishes and towels that weren't no dishes and towels because I never saw them. I told the credit card people to stop payment on it and they did. I never heard a word from the bondsman or the police down there. They didn't even write us a ticket.

"I'll tell you what: I bet I never hear from them again. It was a set-up deal. They had a bunch of others brought into the jail on the same deal. Why else would they have wrecker trucks, bondsmen, and all that going on on a Saturday night? It was pocket money to them, pure and simple. Oh, I finally did get a letter back from the governor. He said to take the matter through the courts. I'm still mad about it.

"If the public doesn't stand up for their rights, it'll be just like Hitler and the Nazis. . . . I'd like to look at the police, right in their face, and see what they have to say. And that bondsman can't be going around pleading guilty for people and setting their bonds. Listen, you go to that town and have a look around. I believe you can find enough down there in one trip to put them all away."

After an hour's conversation, I was convinced that this middle-aged maintenance supervisor at a Kentucky nursery was not crazy. He was angry, obviously, but not crazy. And he had a point. I decided I'd better get on over to Coldspring to take a look around.

· TWO ·

On Wednesday, February 17, two days after the lengthy telephone conversation with Mr. Foley, I managed to track down a lawyer in Connecticut who had drafted the 1978 federal court lawsuit against San Jacinto County. I had decided to get as much background on that lawsuit as I could, in addition to finding out the nuts and bolts of Foley's complaint, before I traipsed 180 miles across East Texas to check out the scenery in the Piney Woods.

Matt Horowitz was a law professor at the University of Connecticut, and he was not an easy person to locate. As a matter of fact, I had tried for two weeks to find him, and it had taken a week on top of that to get him on the telephone. The first thing I learned in that late-afternoon conversation was that Horowitz had been the staff attorney in the Houston ACLU office in 1978 and had filed the lawsuit on behalf of that agency. The suit listed nine plaintiffs, all of them contending that the sheriff's department had stopped them on U.S. 59 without probable cause and arrested them without a legitimate reason. The suit was never certified as a class-action matter. Horowitz recalled the allegations: "They seemed to be looking for marijuana. It was a fairly consistent pattern. They would find the marijuana, take the people to jail, let them spend the night there, and the next morning would take them into court.

"At that point the arrestees were advised—or I believe it was explained to them—that bonds were difficult to obtain, or that there were no bondsmen, or that it was very hard to get a lawyer. They were told that the easiest approach was to simply work out their fine, to pay what they could. In a few cases, as far as I could tell, where the people refused to pay the fine, they were returned to jail as further incentive to pay up."

One of the intriguing facts uncovered in the ACLU probe was that the numbers of marijuana arrests in San Jacinto County were far out of proportion with the rest of the state. But Horowitz could not recollect the exact numbers. He had left the ACLU in early 1981 while the lawsuit was in the process of being settled out of court. He did not know what ultimate resolution was reached in the case, but he understood it was dismissed when "a very small amount of money" was paid to the two or three remaining plaintiffs; the other plaintiffs had pulled out of the suit by then.

It was a short but interesting conversation. Several of the people Horowitz had interviewed mentioned the county's "paranoia" about marijuana. They said the deputies working along U.S. 59 were frighteningly zealous in their searches for the weed. I immediately got on the phone to the Texas Department of Public Safety to find out just how many drug arrests were made in that county. I was connected with the Uniform Crime Reporting Bureau.

The numbers were staggering: in 1980, San Jacinto County deputies made 757 arrests on drug charges—arrests that were reported to the state. Travis County law officers, by way of comparison, made 1,370 drug arrests that year. Travis County, with the city of Austin and almost half a million residents, is forty times larger than San Jacinto County, yet it made less than twice as many arrests. I asked for more numbers.

The DPS statistics clerk looked up the figures for counties surrounding San Jacinto County and read them to me. These numbers were even more intriguing. Trinity County, with the same population as San Jacinto, made only 37 drug arrests in 1980; Polk County, with 25,000 residents, made 74; and Liberty County, with almost 50,000 residents, made only 12.

I must have stared at those numbers for an hour. They didn't make sense. Why would San Jacinto County officers make sixty times as many drug arrests as the officers in next-door Liberty County, which had a population four times larger? And why would a neighboring county with the same population, Trinity County, make only 37 drug arrrests, compared to 757 in San Jacinto County? I got up from my desk about 5:45 p.m., walked into Ed's office, and ran those numbers by him. We talked about Mr. Foley's comments, the dropped ACLU lawsuit, and the overall bad reputation that the county had in the legal community. Was there a racket going on? We decided that I would drive over there early the next week to take a look around.

As staff photographer Zach Ryall and I loaded up the green, dented 1979 Ford known rather unaffectionately around the newsroom as Car 1, I began to think how I should approach the story. No one I had talked to during the previous five weeks had said anything nice about law enforcement in San Jacinto County. Of course, no one but Mr. Foley had claimed any firsthand experience with the sheriff's office; the rest of my contacts fell into a category I call secondhand witnesses. At best, they are the truth once removed; at worst, they're pure gossips. I elected to concoct a front for my trip—a reason other than the real one. I decided I was visiting San Jacinto County to do a story on small towns within an hour's drive of Houston and how living in the shadow of a giant city affects the lives of the common folk. It sounded like an innocuous and legitimate story.

While we pulled onto U.S. 290 for the four-and-a-half-hour drive from Austin, I ran my idea by Zach, a slim, young, energetic, clean-cut photographer who had been with the *American-Statesman* several years. He said it sounded all right, but he wondered—as I did—if anyone would believe me. Sure, as Houston was spreading northward by leaps and bounds, the myriad problems of the metropolis were spreading, too. Urban issues such as city taxes, school desegregation orders, zoning and building controls, sprawling subdivisions, and water and sewer services would be proliferating along with the city limits. But how was I going to tie it all into my main objective—to find out what was happening on U.S. 59?

I thought about that for nearly a hundred miles. Then, as we were pulling into a McDonald's outside Brenham for morning coffee, I noticed a Highway Patrol car on the shoulder of U.S. 290. Its lights were on and a pickup truck was stopped in front of it; the truck had Oklahoma license tags, and the back was overflowing with boxes. "They must have made the rounds last night," I joked, referring to the hit-and-run burglary rings that frequently pull jobs in small towns during the night. And suddenly I had my tie-in: Was crime from Houston spilling over into the surrounding counties? What were these counties doing to keep Houston's criminals out? And what were they going to do when Houston's drug traffic started moving northward along U.S. 59 and other arteries? I had my front story, my reason for traveling 180 miles to confront various people about what was going on in San Jacinto County, a county that quite obviously was not used to getting news coverage. But would this phony story convince anyone? I wondered. I decided to take a short nap as Zach maneuvered the creaky company car off U.S. 290 and onto State Highway 105.

My short nap on this day, February 22, lasted only forty-five minutes. We were getting close to Conroe, which meant we were getting close to San Jacinto County. Zach said he wanted me to drive the rest of the way, since it was my story we were chasing, and since neither of us really knew what we were going to find. We bypassed Conroe about 11:00 a.m. and zipped onto Interstate 45 for a quick twenty-mile sprint to New

Waverly. From there, we turned east on State Highway 150 and into the sprawling, beautiful Sam Houston National Forest.

The pine trees were fabulous. They towered up and over the two-lane highway and at times formed a tunnel of branches twenty or more feet above the ground. There was very little traffic in either direction, and most of the houses along the secluded stretch were set far back off the road. The houses were of simple one-story frame and masonry construction, with plenty of shade trees, dirt driveways, screen doors, and what seemed like an overabundance of children. There were so many school-age children playing outside—in nearly every yard—that I speculated that the local schools must have taken the day off. It didn't occur to me that many of those kids might not have been going to school in the first place.

I started watching for some signpost or other marker to tell me where Walker County ended and San Jacinto County began. At exactly 11:33 a.m., by my watch, we rolled across the county line. Zach turned on the computerized police scanner radio in our car and punched in the frequency for the local law enforcement agency, which we had obtained earlier from the Department of Public Safety. It wouldn't hurt to eavesdrop on the sheriff's department radio traffic while we were in the vicinity.

It took almost ten minutes for the first voice to break the silence on the airwaves. "Five-oh-three to Coldspring," the nasal, twangy voice said. "I'll be out of the car for a while. . . ." We waited to see what explanation he gave, or whether he would give his location. "I'm going to lunch." So much for eavesdropping.

We pulled into Coldspring at ten minutes before noon, passing a spate of "Vote for Me" signs, a couple of barbecue stands, gas station–convenience stores, and washaterias, and then, quite unexpectedly, we were in the middle of town. An ancient three-story stone courthouse was staring us smack in the face.

The town square appeared to be about all there was to Coldspring. A couple of churches, a saddle shop, a lawyer's office, a small grocery store, a cafe, a title company, several dozen houses. And there, as we circled the courthouse at a modest fifteen miles an hour, on the north side of the square, across from the courthouse, I first noticed the words "Coldspring Resale Shop" on a tiny storefront business that looked every inch a small-town secondhand shop.

We parked our car in front of the shop and walked across the street to the courthouse, wondering all the time who was watching us and what they were thinking about Zach's cameras and my beard. We climbed up the steps to the north door of the courthouse just as a gray-haired woman in a white sweater and wire-rimmed glasses was walking out the door. "We're closed for lunch," she told us in a friendly but loud voice. "You'll have to come back at 1:00." I had forgotten how small towns operate around dinnertime.

Since we had an hour to kill, I decided I wanted to drive the eleven miles from Coldspring to Shepherd, a straight shot to the southeast on Highway 150. And I wanted to take my first look at U.S. 59, to see if there was any police activity going on there. The drive was as scenic as before. Trees everywhere we looked. Few cars. Small houses. And lots of children playing in front yards.

We made the trip in about fifteen minutes. Shepherd looked to be quite a bit larger than Coldspring, or maybe it was spaced out differently. But the central feature of the two towns was the same—trees. I was impressed.

U.S. 59 was on the far side of Shepherd from Coldspring, and it looked as out of place as a rock guitarist in a string quartet. It was a truck route, pure and simple, complete with dusty shoulders, grassy median strips, and fifty-five-mile-per-hour speed limit signs. We spent the next thirty minutes cruising the highway looking for police officers, and of course we found none. The police radio also had been silent for more than an hour. I was shocked to learn from the car's odometer that U.S. 59 was only a twelve-mile stretch in San Jacinto County. From the way people talked, I had assumed it was much longer, but upon looking at my map, I saw that the highway only slashed through a small corner of the county. I wondered why my perception had been so wrong—so much larger than life. Maybe I was expecting too much.

We stopped at a Dairy Queen on U.S. 59 just north of Shepherd, but this time we didn't feel like we were being watched. Bearded people drove that highway all the time, so surely they wouldn't be that much of an attraction. Or maybe that was what I was there to find out. . . . Anyway, our burgers were greasy and the fries were cold, so we cut our lunch short and headed back to Coldspring. I wanted to meet as many county officials as I could, to see their reaction to my front story, hear their comments about Houston's spreading crime problems, and, oh, yes, what about drug traffic on U.S. 59?

We got back to the courthouse at 1:20 p.m. This time, Zach left his cameras in the car; we both decided we didn't want to intimidate or frighten anyone right off the bat. I stuck my small note pad in my back pocket, hitched up my green pin-striped slacks, straightened my tie, walked up the steps and through the old wooden double doors, and knocked on the door of the first office I saw—that of county attorney Robert Atkins.

The distinguished counselor was a short, slim little man who stood about five four or five five and couldn't have weighed more than 130 or

140 pounds. He had a round face and neatly trimmed white hair. I guessed that he was in his mid-fifties. He was standing behind his desk holding a large green law book of some sort when Zach and I were ushered into the inner office by his secretary. I held out my hand and introduced myself.

"We're over here from Austin to do a little research on the counties north of Houston," I started, then waved Zach forward and introduced him as my photographer.

"We're interested in the way counties like this one are changing in response to Houston's growth. You know, such things as crime." I waited half a second to see if Atkins would respond, and when he didn't, I continued, "Are you experiencing any major changes, as far as your job as county attorney is concerned?"

The little man smiled and made one of those nearly inaudible chuckling sounds that usually mean something like "You're invading my privacy." He remained standing, holding his law book, and he spoke in a very quiet voice. "I don't know what kind of investigation you're doing, but you're going to have to talk to the judge."

I thought I had heard him wrong, so I repeated my question.

"I'm not going to answer any questions. If you're doing some kind of investigation, you're going to have to go see the judge."

I looked at Zach and shrugged my shoulders. I explained again that we weren't really investigating anything, that we merely wanted to see how lifestyles were changing in the rural counties north of Houston.

No response. A thought popped into my mind that perhaps Atkins was too busy to talk right then. If we came back a little later, would he have more time to talk? He shook his head.

At that point I got a bit mad. "Are you the county attorney for this county? Do you handle legal matters for this county?" Another little smile and chuckle, and another "You're going to have to see the judge."

That did it. If this man was not going to answer my question, then I was going to give him something to think about, something to digest along with his lunch. "Did you represent the county in a federal court lawsuit filed in 1978 by the ACLU?"

Atkins kept right on standing, never so much as offering us a place to sit down. The three of us were standing there looking at each other like a group of cautious felines. Finally, Atkins shook his head and said no, he hadn't represented the county in that matter. But before I could say another word, he said I would have to talk to the judge about that lawsuit.

"What judge? And where's his office?" I asked impatiently.

County judge K. P. Bryant, Atkins responded, and the office was down at the other end of the hall, right by the exit sign.

As we left Atkins' office, Zach suggested that the county attorney might not be used to talking to reporters. I agreed but added that the man also seemed to lack confidence in his ability to answer questions—either that, or else he was just plain scared that we might find out something.

Yes, Zach said, but what?

It was not a good beginning for this 180-mile trip. And it certainly was an inauspicious debut for my front story; I had pretty much blown my cover as far as Atkins was concerned.

We walked into Judge Bryant's modestly furnished office at the south end of the courthouse. His secretary asked our names and invited us to have a seat. She offered us some coffee, seeming glad to see us, for some reason. That reason immediately became apparent—her name was Mavis Tanner and she was running for county treasurer. And Judge Bryant, she said, was in a tough race for reelection against the current county treasurer, Kent Morrison. She smiled widely and said the judge would see us in a minute or two; he was on the telephone.

On the phone with Robert Atkins, I thought. Nonetheless, I suddenly had a much better feeling about all this—politics can make people talk to the press when they'd really rather just keep their mouths closed. This tough race with Kent Morrison could be just the type of wedge I needed. At five minutes before 2:00, the white-haired, bespectacled, grandfatherly-looking judge walked out of his office and asked us to come on in. He pointed to a couple of straight-back chairs and motioned for us to sit down.

My front story went over much better this time. The judge was the type of person who loved to hear himself talk, and he talked for almost ninety minutes on a wide variety of topics dealing with his county. He didn't even miss a beat when Zach excused himself to go get his cameras, or when Zach snapped a dozen or so candid frames of him talking. Or when I brought the conversation around to the 1978 ACLU lawsuit.

"That suit had to do with stopping cars on 59," the judge said, "and with the old jail. . . . On Saturday nights, with the lake filling up, we had lots of traffic on 59, good traffic and bad traffic. And really, that old jail was too full sometimes. It was too full even if we had one person in it. I even did something that no judge had ever done here: I heard cases on weekends to clear the jail.

"And that lawsuit? Well, we just had a trap down there in that jail. I wasn't happy with it, the state wasn't happy with it, and the federal government wasn't happy with it."

"Did the ACLU lawsuit deal primarily with the jail?" I asked. "And what ever happened to the suit? Was there a trial?"

Bryant kept right on talking. The lawsuit was settled when the county offered $1,000 to each of the four remaining plaintiffs and agreed to post the telephone number of the Houston bar association on the wall. "And that's all there was. We decided to let a little bit of our pride go, and just go on ahead and settle it. It was cheaper to settle than to keep paying legal fees to that high-priced law firm in Houston."

So Robert Atkins did not represent the county in the suit?

"Well, what is the word for it? Our county attorney is not what you would call authorized to practice in the federal courts."

Bryant said he had been county treasurer himself in 1975 and wanted to get out of county government, but a group of people approached him and pleaded with him to run for county judge. He said he was retired from the Air Force and wanted to enjoy his retirement. But his supporters were too insistent. He said he was elected in 1975 on a good-government platform, in which he vowed to actively seek out state and federal grants for the county and to work hard as a judge and chief administrative officer.

He was so talkative that I ventured a question about drug traffic on U.S. 59 and why the county made so many arrests over there, compared to its neighbors. He suddenly got quiet.

"I don't have anything to do with how many arrests are made. I'm a judge in county court . . . and I can't tell the sheriff what to do or who to arrest. My experience, due to pleas I've had and cases I've tried, is that yes, there is traffic in drugs through there. But all this [the arrests] was started by the State of Texas in 1976 and 1977 with the STEP program. They gave us some money for patrol, and after the grant ran out the violations didn't slow down any. Most of them pleaded guilty anyway."

"But why are the numbers so incredibly out of proportion?" I asked.

"I can't say what's better or tougher," he said slowly. "It just appears to me that the sheriff is on the lookout for it. . . . But I'd also say that if we make as many drug arrests as you're saying, then we probably also make more arrests over there for unlawfully carrying weapons than anywhere in the state."

I took a big chance and asked if there had been many complaints about lack of probable cause for stopping cars or conducting searches.

Very few, he said. As a matter of fact, he pointed out, the sheriff went to great lengths to instruct his deputies on when they legally had a reason to stop a car and search it. He said he had heard many of those lectures.

I asked for an example of a legitimate reason to search a car.

"Let's say they stop the car for having a headlight out, and when the driver opens the door, say there is a pistol laying there on the front seat. Certainly the officer has probable cause to confiscate the pistol. Then let's say there is a bag of marijuana on the seat next to the pistol. The question comes in, do they have probable cause to search the car? Certainly a strong odor of marijuana is probable cause."

Then, almost inexplicably, the judge abruptly stopped talking, looked closely at me, and then at Zach. "Look," he continued very slowly. "I'm very sensitive to what you guys are checking into. . . . What's happening, as I see it, I was getting blamed for the sheriff's department operating on 59. I don't have any say about where the sheriff puts his cars. . . ." I hold court once a week, and all I am is a glorified basketball referee. But I do something probably no other judge in the state of Texas does: I read the legal rights to everyone who comes in here. . . . And I've devised my own trial sheet that I go through point by point with every defendant." He pulled a sample sheet from his desk and began reading from it, talking to us as if we were criminals in his court for almost ten minutes.

I interrupted and asked if he was upset by the amount of drug traffic along U.S. 59, whether he ever thought that some of the cases were bogus arrests or whether he believed San Jacinto County simply cracked the whip harder than other counties.

"It's just a pretty big problem here, all these drugs," Bryant answered. "But I've got all the confidence in the world in our county attorney, in myself, and in the sheriff, who's the one who's got to push these cases through. And I realize that we've got lots of cases. But I talk to the people and I try to be a regular, everyday guy when I talk to them, and the predominant number of people I talk to in court, they do have a problem with drugs and they'd like to get rid of it. The whole country has problems, and the people who complain are the ones who have the problem and don't want to get rid of it."

As if to emphasize his point, he said the FBI made a trip into the county "four years ago, and they checked everything, not just me. They checked the commissioners, everybody, and they didn't find anything wrong. Look, I'm disappointed that we have this reputation, but this county was laughed at for years for a lack of leadership before I took this job. Right now we're respected in Austin and all over the country. We're not perfect, but we're sure trying to be."

It was nearly 3:30, and I got the feeling that Judge Bryant was beginning to preach to me. He was starting to rant against the evils of rampant modernism and for the virtues of the good old days, when everyone carried his fair share and no one complained. It reminded me of something I had read about President Calvin Coolidge; he supposedly said that ninety percent of America's problems would go away if everyone would just sit down and shut up. I figured that I had better stand up and leave while I had the chance. So I did, politely, of course.

While Zach and I were walking down the courthouse steps to our car, I tried to sort out the ninety minutes of dialogue with the judge, to find some way of characterizing it, some way of summing it all up. I thought about the county's awful reputation among legal service officers, defense lawyers, and the ACLU, and also about the rumors, fears, and complaints I had heard from other people. And I thought about Mr. Foley, his son, and his girlfriend. What was going on here? How could I capsulize Judge Bryant's comments in the context of all this other information?

I thought about Bryant's image of San Jacinto County as a hardworking little county trying to stamp out injustices, and I thought about his good-government pledge, about his image of gun-toting juvenile delinquents who openly carried bags of marijuana on their front seats, about his aw-shucks attitude concerning the ACLU lawsuit, about his remarks concerning an FBI investigation that positively cleared the county of any hint of wrongdoing, about his upcoming bid for reelection.

It was confusing.

I made a note to check into the FBI investigation. Everything else— from the warm reception by the secretary to the judge's insistence that he was just a regular guy with the defendants—felt wrong. The answers came too freely, too smoothly. All those arrests and very few complaints? That wasn't the pattern I had seen during my early years as a police reporter. Even the last remark by the judge as we were leaving— "You boys come see me again . . . and be sure and send me a copy of your story"—didn't sound sincere.

And so far I had learned nothing substantive except the disposition of the ACLU lawsuit, if indeed that part of the judge's remarks was true. My stomach was churning rapidly; either I was mad or the Dairy Queen hamburger was starting to take its toll. I don't like being the victim of a mental tap dance, and I felt that the judge had done a nice two-step on me. Zach even said that the old man "seemed to have his act together."

Before we turned the corner from the courthouse onto Highway 150 to take another quick spin around Coldspring, I decided to press the issue. The trip to that point had resulted in little usable information, and I was angry at myself for driving all this way and wasting my time. I really had nothing to lose, so I told Zach to pull the car back into the gravel parking lot on the south side of the courthouse. Just down the block was the sheriff's department, located in a new one-story glass-and-brick building. "Let's go pay a social visit to the sheriff," I said.

· THREE ·

Two gray-haired men wearing oil-stained overalls and dirty cowboy boots were leaning against a pickup truck in front of a small gas station across Highway 150 from the San Jacinto County Courthouse, and they were glaring at Zach and me as we walked the 150 yards from the courthouse to the sheriff's department. For some bizarre reason, I waved to them as we walked by. They didn't wave back. And for some other bizarre reason, I thought that was funny. Maybe they were afraid Zach would take their picture. They looked like something right off the set of *The Last Picture Show*. I figured they were probably as afraid of us as we were of them.

The sheriff's department was housed in a cream-colored, one-story edifice called the Public Safety Building, a block west of the courthouse. It looked precisely like a law enforcement center, with a prominent flagpole and several shade trees in front, a closed garage door on the east side, windows along the west side, and a slew of burned and dilapidated cars on a vacant lot to the south, the back side. The glass double doors faced another vacant lot directly across the small two-lane street, this one containing two late-model brown sedans with police-type light bars on top. Neither car had any other markings—no county seal, star, or insignia—to indicate it was a police car. Both had private license plate numbers, not the state "exempt" plates that most law enforcement agencies use. I guessed the cars must belong to a security guard company, since most of the official vehicles I had encountered in my reporting career were clearly marked as such. These two cars couldn't have been used for undercover work, not with those light bars. I jotted down the license numbers as we walked by.

We walked through the double glass doors into a small reception area. A glass display table was directly to our right, and it contained a large assortment of drug paraphernalia, including various water pipes and clips. A small couch was directly in front of us against a wall that contained old pictures of men wearing badges and cowboy hats. They must have been former sheriffs, I reckoned. To our left was a heavy bolted door that led into the jail area and a glass window with a football-sized hole at the bottom; the window looked into the dispatcher's office. There didn't seem to be anyone at home. To our right, past the display table, was a door with "Sheriff" on it. That was where we headed.

The office was laid out much like the ones in the courthouse, with a small outer office for a secretary and a larger inner office. A plump, middle-aged woman with brownish hair and a round face was behind the desk. I told her who we were and that we would like to visit briefly with the sheriff. She asked us to take a seat back in the reception room. Her desk was a disaster area. There were several open file cabinets nearby. The woman looked and sounded tired.

We waited exactly ten minutes. The secretary stuck her head out into the reception area at precisely 3:55 p.m. and announced, "The sheriff will see you now."

J. C. Parker looked the part of a small-county sheriff. He was in his mid-forties, with a protruding waistline, sagging skin around a large neck, a tanned face with deep-set wrinkles on his forehead, large ears set close to his head, close-cut brown hair with gray sprinkles at the temples, and a stylish wave of hair pushed from right to left on top. He wore a very neat white long-sleeved shirt with a wide striped tie. He had a badge on his left shirt pocket, and his tie was pulled up closely around his neck. He smiled widely, greeted us warmly, and asked us to sit down and make ourselves comfortable.

The chairs in front of his desk were plush, extremely soft, and very modern in style. They were low to the ground and positioned in a semicircle around a small, low coffee table. I was flabbergasted to find that I had to look up at the sheriff seated behind his desk. It reminded me of my studies of the Korean War peace talks, where the North Korean negotiators rigged the table so that the Americans were seated at chairs much lower than the others, forcing the U.S. envoys to look up at their opposite numbers. Parker was sitting down, all right, but he seemed to be a good two feet taller than the two of us.

I explained my front story briefly and mentioned that Judge Bryant had suggested that we talk to him about the crime problem that was moving up from Houston. I specifically asked him whether he had any drug traffic along U.S. 59, seeing as how that was the major arterial connection with the big city.

Parker began talking at an incredible rate, much faster than most Texans. He strung words together at such a speed, and with such a backwoodsy twang, that it was hard at first to decipher his remarks. And he had an annoying habit of adding "you know what I mean?" at the end of every other sentence. U.S. 59, he said, was a trouble spot for him and the county, and most of the trouble came from "kids from Houston who don't think nothing about lighting up [marijuana] and driving on up the road. They figure that where the city ends, so does law enforcement, I guess."

He said his men worked the highway very hard, and that he tried to keep cars on that twelve-mile stretch at all hours. On several occasions, he said, he had experimented with lag-time patrol periods on the highway—periods in which no deputies patrolled the road—but robberies and burglaries increased dramatically during those intervals.

"What we do is if we arrest someone for a traffic offense and find dope, then we don't file the traffic charge, because, let's face it, those kids have enough trouble with just the dope charge. . . . And we do work it a lot harder than anyplace else, because that's where most of our burglaries occur, most of our traffic fatalities, and most of our robberies."

He was talking so rapidly that I was barely able to interject a question about the ACLU lawsuit. Didn't that lawsuit have something to say about those arrests, something about probable cause?

The sheriff smiled and—yes—his eyes twinkled. "I'd say we get one complaint a month about that. I ran two kids on a polygraph a while back, and they passed it. They said they both bought those cars recently, and they passed the test. I dropped the charges." He said he offered a polygraph to anyone who complained.

"Oh," I interrupted, "do you have someone certified to operate a polygraph?" (That would be unusual for such a small county.)

No, he said, he had to call for an operator to come down from Lufkin.

The ACLU, he continued, made some excellent points in the 1978 lawsuit. "They had a good lawsuit over the old jail, which was built back in 1870. It was that lawsuit that got us into this new jail, you know what I mean? Without that lawsuit, we wouldn't have gotten a new jail."

I dropped that line of questioning for the moment and inquired again about the county's apparent problem with marijuana.

"You know, I wish they would just legalize the stuff," he said, remarking that the trend across the country was "headed that way" and that it was "just a matter of time" before full legalization took place. "You get the underworld out of it, and take the money-making out of it . . . it would make my job a lot easier."

Most of his drug arrests, he continued, came from U.S. 59, and most came on weekends. Lake Livingston, he said, was a gigantic attraction to people throughout the Houston area, "and on weekends in the sum-

mer we have close to 200,000 people in here. It gets to be a mess around
here."

But the drug problem all boiled down to this, he said: "It's just a matter of whether we're going to look the other way." He then said that he
got about three complaints a month about arrests being made without
probable cause. (I noted on my pad that he had changed this figure from
his earlier one, when he said he got only one such complaint a month.)
And he said he usually tried to settle as many drug cases as he could
outside of court. "The average juror in here is sixty-two years old, and
they're tough on drugs," he said.

I asked if he had an example of this toughness by jurors, and he said
that two kids "a few years ago" were sentenced by a jury to eight years
in prison for possession of eleven pounds of marijuana. He said he
worked diligently to try to get a new trial, because both were first-time
offenders, but he failed. He said he wanted to help the young people as
much as he could.

At that point, I mentioned the statistics that I had found about drug
arrests in this county and the surrounding ones. Why the big swing in
numbers?

Parker never batted an eye. "None of the other counties work traffic,"
he said. "It's the sheriff's discretion."

He then moaned a few fast-paced sentences about bondsmen, calling
them leeches at one point and saying that they were "in and out of here
at all hours of the day and night."

I ventured a quick question about whether a bondsman had ever set
up an office in his jail. He just laughed. He said some of them would
have if he'd let them, but he spent most of his time running them off.

I asked how many bondsmen the county had, and he named three:
Herb Atwood, bank president Jim Browder, and ABC Bonding from
Houston.

Did any of them ever bring a credit card imprinting device or other
office-type supplies into the jail to do business?

"It's a possibility," he responded, adding that he was not concerned
with how the bondsmen took their money from defendants. His concern was solely with the posting of the bonds.

Did some of the bondsmen ever charge higher than ordinary fees and
say that the extra amount was to enter a plea for the defendant in court?
(By then, I figured, the sheriff undoubtedly knew that I had something
up my sleeve.) I asked specifically about an escrow account.

"Now, they might be holding a little escrow. . . . If they're caught in
the dark, they won't be out all their money [on a bond forfeiture].
They'll have a little something."

Then, unexpectedly, he said that Herb Atwood was "best of all" in trying to help defendants. And he said it was a real problem to post a bond and run the risk of the defendant skipping out on court day, which would mean the bondsman was liable for the face amount of the bond. Atwood, he said, was willing to "go the extra mile" for a defendant. "It's a problem . . . but if we could hold their driver's licenses we'd get a lot more of them back [for trial]."

I asked if Atwood had ever used a credit card device in the jail, and he said he'd never seen him do it. But he said he wasn't in the jail twenty-four hours a day and couldn't say with certainty that the device was never there. But he didn't want those devices in the jail.

We spent ten more minutes talking about the county's policy of towing cars, and Parker insisted that he did everything he could to avoid towing cars from Highway 59 to Coldspring. He said towing was a hassle for everyone, and he instructed his deputies to make sure that the cars were left with the owner whenever possible.

We also talked about Houston's rapidly growing metropolitan area, and Parker said he felt sure the city would be "in our back yard" within ten years. A lot of San Jacinto County residents, he explained, were scared to death of Houston. He gave the impression that he was sympathetic with that type of reasoning. As Houston grew, so did its crime problem. And that, he said, meant that his job as sheriff was going to get still harder and more demanding.

I asked if he was concerned that his department was getting a pretty bad reputation with its policies toward drugs.

He stiffened noticeably, paused, and said, "I instruct my men, 'When you find someone breaking the law, don't jack with them. Arrest them.' . . . We like to think that's a pretty good reputation, the way we work it. There's just no use holding your head in the sand and saying this drug problem doesn't exist. You can either do something about it or do nothing about it. And drugs are the biggest problem we've got here."

He was getting testy, but, remembering the unmarked cars in the parking lot and Jane Swanson's remark about a protection outfit, I decided to chance one more question: did he ever operate a private security agency in San Jacinto County while serving as sheriff? I braced for the answer, just as Zach finished clicking the last of his mug shots.

After a short burst of silence, Parker nodded and said that back in 1971 and 1972 he had worked security for Waterwood, a Horizon Corporation development on Lake Livingston. He said he took the job because no one else wanted it. Before I could follow up with another question, he said that he didn't perceive it as being a conflict of interest, because Waterwood was located entirely on private property and because it was only he and one other person who did the patrolling, on their own time.

"They didn't ask anything from the sheriff's office, and they didn't get anything," he said, pointing out that the patrols lasted only a couple of years and that he severed his ties with the land company because "I just didn't have the time to devote to it." He said his private patrols had ended ten years ago, and Waterwood soon afterward hired its own firm. Not only that, he said, but his company — Parker Security — was handled at the time by his brother, Bud Parker, who was currently head of the security department at Waterwood.

As if to dismiss the topic, the sheriff laughed and said, "They spend more for security out there now than the entire county spends for law enforcement."

I glanced at my watch. It was a few minutes after 5:00. I thanked the sheriff for giving us an hour of his time and said we had some other things to do.

He thanked us profusely for our interest in San Jacinto County. He even asked us to stay a bit longer and have a cup of coffee with him, but I got the feeling that he really didn't mean it. And we needed to leave, anyway; a lot of ground had been covered in two interviews — with Judge Bryant and Sheriff Parker — and I needed to go back over my notes and think about what was said. I decided before walking out of Parker's office that I needed to get back to Austin as soon as possible to do some more checking, some more background work, more digging into East Texas, and more analysis of Mr. Foley's complaint.

We left Coldspring at 5:20 p.m. for one last pass down U.S. 59. The result was the same: No police activity, no tow trucks, no nothing. Only eighteen-wheelers.

At 5:50, we crossed the county line into Montgomery County, stopped at a small liquor store, and bought a six-pack of beer. I called Ed and said we were heading back, that it looked like the story was going to take a good bit more digging to root out what was going on. Ed sounded agreeable.

We sipped on a couple of beers and talked a minute before continuing our trip back to Austin. It was hard to tell who was the more confused, the photographer or the reporter.

· FOUR ·

I arrived at the office at 7:30 a.m. the next day, February 23, and began sorting through my notes. The newsroom was almost empty, except for two or three reporters assigned to daily coverage for the *American-Statesman*'s afternoon edition and a couple of assistant city editors. Most of the reporting staff got to work around 9:30, and I wanted to have a couple of hours of relative peace to sift through the notes from Judge Bryant's interview, the San Jacinto County budget, the stack of campaign literature I had taken from a table in the courthouse, the interview with the sheriff, and all the other notebooks I had assembled from previous interviews.

My first telephone call, though, was placed at 8:05 a.m. to Mrs. Imogene Trapp, the county clerk in San Jacinto County. I told her that I was calling from Austin to check on the date of a court hearing for a client of mine, a Mr. Jeffrey Foley, and that I also needed to know the date the charge was filed by the sheriff's department. I said that this man had been arrested on drug charges on U.S. 59 back on November 28. Mrs. Trapp's voice sounded familiar, and I guessed that she was the same elderly woman who had told us the previous day that the courthouse was shutting down for lunch. She asked me to repeat the name of my client. Either the phone connection was bad on her end or she was a bit hard of hearing.

Mrs. Trapp put me on hold for about five minutes. "He's not on the docket, and I have no record of it in my office," she said. "Are you sure he was arrested in this county?"

I told her I was sure. Was there any other place in Coldspring where the possession charge could have been filed? Any other court? I asked.

"No. It would have to be this office," she replied.

I thanked her for her time and hung up. From previous stories I had done I knew that an eighty-day gap between a misdemeanor arrest and the filing of a charge in court was getting perilously close to the limitations in the state's Speedy Trial Act; after ninety days, the charge would be no good. Of course, if the sheriff's department was running a racket on U.S. 59 and shaking down motorists, then it stood to reason that the charges would never be filed in any court. Why would they want to establish a permanent record of a shakedown by taking the arrest into court? And why would they want to give the shakees an opportunity to contest the arrest and embarrass the county?

I quickly called a lawyer friend and asked what he would think about a situation where a dope possession charge was not filed within eighty-odd days of the arrest. "Either the arresting agency is terribly incompetent," he responded, "or else they never intended to file the charge in the first place."

"What if the person who was arrested paid more than $400 to a bail bondsman the night of the arrest?"

"What judge set the amount of the bail?" he asked me right back.

I told him the person never went before a judge.

"Well, I'd say that doesn't sound altogether kosher," he said.

That gave me even more to think about, but it also raised more questions. The ACLU lawyers had told me on several occasions that defendants had raised allegations about fines being collected and never reported in that county. Was that still going on? Or was the county, as Parker and Bryant contended, trying to stamp out a bad drug problem?

I then called Clema Sanders, executive director of the Texas Board of Private Investigators and Private Security Agencies. The sheriff had said he had been in the security business during 1971 and 1972 but had dissolved the company after working only at Waterwood. I wanted to see whether he'd ever gotten a state license for that.

Parker Security, Sanders said, was not currently licensed to operate in Texas. But her records indicated that the firm's license had been revoked by the state more than four years ago. She would have to pull the old file from the archives and call me back the next day. She said the license was taken out by J. C. "Humpy" Parker. That was the first time I heard the sheriff referred to by his nickname.

The next three hours were spent sorting through notes—comparing Mr. Foley's allegations with the generally vague comments from Bryant and Parker. At a few minutes before noon, an East Texas Legal Services Office employee called and suggested that I get in touch with a former county judge in Walker County and ask him what he knew about the San Jacinto County Sheriff's Department.

So I did. I tracked down Judge Amos Gates in Huntsville about 3:00 p.m. He seemed delighted to have the opportunity to talk to a reporter from Austin. I did as I was told: I asked him what he knew about law enforcement in the county next door to his own.

"I haven't heard a whole lot about them lately," he began. "But they used to be dope-happy over there. They'd always get kids around Shepherd who were coming in there to go to the lake. They'd just go crazy trying to get dope. You take a look at the misdemeanor docket over there and you'll get a good idea of what I'm talking about." He said he'd heard many, many complaints about arrest traps that were set along U.S. 59, and that many people were concerned that they were stopped without probable cause. "It used to be a tough county. They'd get your butt over there."

But Highway 59 wasn't the only target, he said. There was a teenagers' hangout in the north part of San Jacinto County near Oakhurst, between Huntsville and Lake Livingston, that also drew some of the arrest traps.

I asked what he meant by "traps."

"They'd take a bunch of sheriff's cars in there and wait for the kids to come out, and they'd pounce on them. And those bondsmen over there would charge the hell out of them. It's horrible when a person is local and has a driver's license and they still charge him $1,000 bond, where he has to put up $50 or $100 in cash, and then he gets fined again in court. That's like being charged for the same offense twice."

Judge Gates talked for another twenty minutes, but he had no specific names he could pass on to me. "You know, I just don't remember, but you could check with me later on and I might remember some of them," he said.

I asked what he knew about Parker Security, and he started laughing. He said that company had a pretty bad reputation, too, and that there were stories going around about shakedowns that were used to drum up clients. He recalled that the state pulled the license from Parker Security "a year or two ago," but he had no information other than that.

The elderly judge then began talking about a cemetery in San Jacinto County that contained four strange grave markers, including one about a thirteen-year-old girl who died at the hands of an "experimenting doctor" in New Orleans. Another marker was on the grave of the girl's brother, who was shot by a hog thief. The children's father died soon after that, and Gates said his marker claimed he was killed by a broken heart. There was no inscription on the mother's tombstone.

I was almost afraid to ask anything about this, but Gates added that all four deaths occurred more than one hundred years ago. I breathed a sigh of relief. And then I hung up.

Judge Gates was a talkative old man, and I put an asterisk by his name for future reference. Maybe he could help me separate fact from fiction later on. As I was writing a note to myself, the newspaper's switchboard operator called and said I had just received a call from Lamar Hankins in Bryan.

The legal services attorney and former ACLU employee was curious about my trip to San Jacinto County. I told him I was pretty confused at that moment, primarily because the county officials seemed to have their stories together. They came off as being just a bunch of hardworking country people trying to deal with a bad dope problem.

We went over some of the things we had covered in earlier talks, including his ACLU interviews with the people who were arrested on Highway 59. All of them were drug possession cases, but he hadn't been able to come up with any names. He recalled that there were several allegations about planted dope, and that all of them raised probable-cause questions. Hankins traced a little of the county's history, especially over the last twenty years. In the sixties, he said, that area had a near-majority black population, but the filling of Lake Livingston in 1969 brought about a dramatic shift. He talked about the backwoods attitudes of many of the residents, and the widespread distrust of outsiders. He also gave me the name of an organization that might eventually help me ferret out some names of defendants: the Texas Criminal Defense Lawyers Association.

I called the association's Austin number and asked for the names of their members in San Jacinto County. There were none. What about Liberty County? None. Trinity County? None. In a noticeably exasperated tone I asked the association's receptionist, "And you probably don't have any members in Walker County, either, do you?"

She put me on hold briefly, and then said, "I would tell you we don't have any there, but that would be a lie. We have three people in Huntsville."

I devoured the names and telephone numbers and blessed her for her help. It was almost 5:00, and I realized that I hadn't gotten much sleep in the last three days. So that was what I did.

The next morning, Wednesday, February 24, I got to the office about 8:00 with the intention of spending most of the day on the phone, tracking down defense lawyers in Huntsville. I figured that if anyone had names of Highway 59 victims, they would. If anyone had firsthand information about the way San Jacinto County processed bail bonds, fines, and towing fees, they would. But I didn't even get a chance to pick up the phone and start dialing away; the phone was ringing before I got to my desk.

The call was from Clema Sanders, director of the Board of Private Investigators and Private Security Agencies. She had located the old Parker Security file in the archives.

The company had been licensed in April 1973 upon written application by James Cecil "Humpy" Parker. It was listed as a sole proprietorship, which was created and operated by Sheriff Parker for security work of a "general nature, including investigations for insurance companies and private businesses, and for patrol services for businesses and residences."

The state board had filed a complaint against the company on April 27, 1976, for failure to maintain the required liability insurance. A hearing was held, and the license was ordered revoked on August 12, 1976. State statutes governing security firms had been amended in 1975 to increase the limits for liability insurance, and Parker Security never attempted to meet those requirements, Sanders said. "The law was changed to make the insurance coverage pretty strict and a lot of companies just decided to go out of business rather than have to pay the higher premiums for more coverage," she said.

Only two companies currently had licenses to operate in San Jacinto County, and both had been licensed for less than a year. Humpy Parker was not listed in either of them.

A good start for this Wednesday morning. The sheriff, it appeared to me, was having a little trouble with his memory. He said he had been out of the security business for ten years, which was false; that his brother had handled most of the business matters, which appeared to be false; that he went into business in 1971, which was false; that he only went into business to take the Waterwood job, which apparently was false; that he got out of business voluntarily, which also was false.

If his memory was this bad about his own company, what did that tell me about all his other statements? I couldn't wait to pass this bit of news on to Ed.

But before Ed got to work a little before 11:00, I made another big connection—with a Huntsville lawyer by the name of John Wright, a member of the state Criminal Defense Lawyers Association.

Sure enough, he had represented a man several years ago who was arrested for DWI in San Jacinto County—arrested while he was *walking* down one of the narrow farm roads. "This guy had been drinking a little, and he stopped on one of those back roads to relieve himself, and when he got back in the car, it wouldn't start. So he and his companion began walking back to town to get help.

"That's when the officers arrested him for DWI, while he was walking down the road. He may have been intoxicated, but I doubt it. But tell me, what was he driving to merit a charge of driving while intoxicated?"

His client later "copped a plea" for public intoxication, paid a small fine, and the case was dropped, Wright said.

"They make you such a good deal that you can't afford to fight the charge. . . . It's pretty disgusting. You're just better off paying the fine. And when you pay the money, the whole thing just goes away. That's not the way it should be."

I briefly related the key points of Mr. Foley's complaint to Wright and asked him if they sounded unusual for San Jacinto County.

"Not really," he said. "It's such a poor county that they're probably just trying to raise money any way they can. But it's worse there, it seems like, than anywhere else. . . . They make you an offer so attractive that you'd be crazy to contest it — it would wind up costing a lot more."

He said it was his experience that cases were disposed of in such a random manner — some in the sheriff's office, some in the courthouse — that documentation of pleas was a serious problem. The DWI case he handled was settled in such an unusual manner, he added, "that I don't know how to this day they could document it."

Had he heard of any unusual cases involving the sheriff's department? Cases involving harassment or violence?

Indeed he had. There was a lawsuit pending in federal court in Houston that was filed by another Huntsville lawyer, alleging that a San Jacinto constable opened fire on a young motorist without sufficient probable cause. He gave me the lawyer's name. And there were several other incidents he had heard about involving students at Sam Houston State University. He gave me the name of the student legal adviser at the university and suggested I call her for details.

"It's a remote county, and they handle things in a strange manner. Sometimes you're never sure who is accepting pleas. The county judge is the only one authorized to take pleas like the ones we're talking about . . . but I'll tell you this: just about anyone will take a plea over there."

We talked for about ten more minutes, during which I bounced a few names of county officials off him to get his opinion. I never really said precisely what I was looking for in San Jacinto County, because at that point I didn't know myself. All I knew was that a lot of people were saying a lot of bad things about the way justice was administered over there. I asked Wright to keep his eyes and ears open for names and dates of U.S. 59 victims — and any other persons who felt they were treated unfairly — and I would check back with him soon.

The game was getting more interesting every minute. People who worked in the counties around San Jacinto County seemed to know all about the crazy brand of justice used over there. They treated it as common knowledge, as something that was both funny and tragic at the same time. I was mulling that over when the telephone rang.

It was the current staff attorney in the Houston ACLU office, returning my call from the day before. I wanted to double-check the disposition of the 1978 lawsuit with him.

As it turned out, the information I had obtained from Judge Bryant and Matt Horowitz, the former ACLU attorney, was substantially correct. Stefan Presser, the current ACLU lawyer, was not happy about the way the case was settled, however.

"Our clients . . . decided to go for the bucks instead of the principles," he said. There were some very important principles—constitutional ones—involved in that case, and we told our clients that we were not anxious to settle for the dollars.

"When we take a case, since we litigate it for free, our interest is in the principles. But we're at the same time representing a client, and our clients were really adamant about wanting the money. Subsequent to the settlement, we had one or two other complaints about Highway 59, most of them in the nature of cars being stopped without probable cause. Other than that, I'm not aware of any other incidents in that county."

One portion of the settlement as related by Judge Bryant was wrong, though. The telephone number that San Jacinto County agreed to post in the jail was not that of the Houston bar association; it was that of the Houston ACLU office. A minor point.

By the time I finished talking to Presser, Ed was walking toward his office, so I hustled over and spent a few minutes with him, relating the gist of my telephone calls that morning. He was intrigued and encouraging, but there was a minor crisis in the office that day that called for another reporter, and I was both nominated and elected. I spent the remainder of the day working on daily news stories. I wasn't too pleased about that.

The next day, Thursday, February 25, started inauspiciously. As I was walking to my desk, another crisis occurred in the city and the *American-Statesman* desperately needed another reporter to help out. I was the first reporter to arrive who was not already assigned to the afternoon newspaper. So I was again drafted.

I spent most of the morning helping the early police reporter track down odds and ends for a story he was working on. Now, I had done that sort of work for close to ten years, but that's not what I was brought to Austin to do. After all, Ed and other bigwigs at the paper had assured me of their interest in investigative reporting, and my probe into San Jacinto County was shaping up—so far—into a fairly intriguing exercise.

But it was an exercise that was not going to perform itself; someone was going to have to go out and do it. There is an old saying in the reporting business that a blockbuster story never floats in over the transom, and whatever story resulted on San Jacinto County certainly wasn't going to walk up to my desk and ask me to write it. I was both annoyed and peeved.

My anger lasted approximately fifteen minutes. From about 1:15 until 1:30. That's how long it took me to renew an old reportorial friendship with an employee in the U.S. Attorney's Office in Houston, a person I had dealt with while I was a reporter in Fort Worth from 1972 to 1975. I didn't even know if he would remember me; after all, it had been five years since I had spoken with him. He remembered. He even recalled in some detail the last story I had worked on that he helped with.

I figured it was time to find out about the FBI investigation that Judge Bryant said had been conducted in San Jacinto County four years ago, in 1978. Did my contact know anything about that probe? Could he find out about it? I had to explain a little about my work in that county, and the general allegations I had heard about U.S. 59. He said he would check and call me back in an hour.

At 2:45 p.m., he called. The civil rights section of the U.S. Attorney's Office had, indeed, been involved in an investigation of San Jacinto County in 1978. The probe started shortly after the ACLU filed its lawsuit in U.S. district court that summer. A team of FBI agents was sent to San Jacinto County, and they did look over records and take statements from a variety of people.

And then, after no more than two or three months, the investigation ground to a virtual halt. My contact's information was a bit hazy, but he said the probe was abruptly transferred from the civil rights section to the racketeering and organized crime section of the U.S. Attorney's Office. And the effort apparently died there. There were some hard feelings when it ended.

"All I can really say is that the FBI wanted to continue the investigation," my contact related, "but for reasons unrelated to the merits of the case, it was dropped. From what I can tell, they were turning up some pretty interesting stuff—things that appeared to be supportive of the ACLU contentions. And that's really all I can say about it."

Was there something political in all this? My contact wasn't sure. And then I asked him point-blank: from his information, and from what he knew, was I on the right track?

Yes.

Was I going about my investigation in the right way? In the right direction?

A long pause.

Then: "Yes and no."

What should I be doing differently?

Another pause. "You're going about it right, but I'd be more careful if I were you."

What exactly did that mean?

"Maybe you ought to let them think you dropped the story, or you ought not to have any contact with them at all for a while. You might even want to do a little undercover work of your own. Just don't take anything for granted over there."

It was at that point, at exactly 3:15 p.m. on Thursday, February 25, almost six weeks after I had begun working sporadically on this story, that I had my first twinge of fear.

And it was at exactly that point that I decided to make a second trip over there. It was time to track down some victims.

· FIVE ·

Most of the next few days were spent getting all my ducks in a row, as a former city editor of mine in Memphis used to say. I didn't want to make another trip to Coldspring like the first one; I wanted to take every precaution to ensure that my time was well spent. It's much easier to deal with angry ducks when they're lined up nice and straight. The trip was scheduled for Tuesday through Friday, March 2 to March 5.

One of the first persons I wanted to line up before venturing back to the Piney Woods was district attorney J. H. Keeshan, one of two DAs who represented San Jacinto County. It was a peculiar relationship. Keeshan, whose office was in Conroe, actually represented Montgomery County, but for six months out of the year he also took cases originating in San Jacinto County. For the other six months of the year, district attorney Joe Price of Groveton, in Trinity County, was in charge. No single district attorney was based in San Jacinto County, which meant that the local authorities, including the sheriff, had greatly enhanced powers.

I reached Keeshan at his home on Sunday afternoon, February 28. He had been working in his yard, and my telephone call rescued him from his labors. He seemed a friendly sort of fellow, but you never know, so I pretended for the moment that I was doing a simple feature story on the counties north of Houston. I gave no details but said I was getting ready to make a trip over there and I wanted to touch base with some of the county officials beforehand—to see if they could tell me about points of interest, attractions, and things like that. Keeshan was more than helpful.

After fifteen minutes of innocuous chitchat, mostly dealing with the backwoodsy nature of the area, I told him I had heard a lot about the aggressiveness of the San Jacinto County deputies in patrolling U.S. 59, and I asked if this was something I ought to watch out for.

He jumped right in. "The sheriff over there has been active in traffic enforcement, yes, and many of them [traffic patrols] result in arrests of various sorts."

I singled out a "rumor" I had heard about drug arrests.

"Yes, a lot of them result in drug-related arrests, especially on the part that goes through Shepherd. . . . But a lot of those cases go through county court, so I don't ever see them. Some of them go through district court, but they have to be over four ounces [of marijuana] or a controlled substance of some sort."

"Didn't somebody at one time file a lawsuit in federal court about some sort of arrest on Highway 59?" I tried not to sound too interested in it.

"There was a case in which a number of defendants combined together and filed a suit, but I had no involvement in it," he said.

"Didn't it have to do with probable cause, or something like that?"

Yes, that was right.

"Do many people complain about probable cause in San Jacinto County?"

"I have had attorneys tell me on one or two occasions that they claim that probable cause—either what was shown in testimony or in the offense report—was not what was shown at the scene. But I think the whole thing of interest is the sheer numbers of arrests."

It sounded like he really didn't want to talk about probable-cause complaints, but I decided to ask a stupid question: what, in his opinion, would be valid probable cause to stop a car and search for drugs?

"One of the first things I have to look for when I get a case is probable cause. If there is no probable cause, then I have problems."

He hadn't answered my question, but I let him continue.

"From what I receive, it appears that probable cause has generally been there. It's really the numbers that are interesting, though." He said he would prefer not to have to draw any conclusions about the numbers, or about the complaints, because "I have to prosecute their cases."

Before I could ask another question, he interjected, "But you do know that the overwhelming percentage pleads guilty, don't you? Most of the time, these people will plead guilty and afterward they are on good terms with the sheriff."

Enough of this, I thought. I thanked Keeshan for his time and told him I'd look him up when I passed through later in the week. And then I drew a large X by his name on my telephone list.

I just knew that Keeshan was being perfectly frank when he said that most of those folks arrested on Highway 59 plead guilty and then become hard and fast friends with the sheriff. I believed that about like I believed that William Henry Harrison was this country's most famous president. It was such an incredible statement that I wondered why he bothered to make it. I poured myself another cup of lukewarm coffee from the pot in the back of the newsroom and thought about his remark.

If I were a district attorney in a small county like San Jacinto, and a strange reporter from a large city 180 miles away called and asked about probable cause, how would I respond? If the reporter knew enough to ask about probable cause, then he certainly knew about the county's reputation. And if he knew about the county's reputation, he knew there had been other complaints about arrests. And if the reporter knew that much, what would be the one thing I could say—as DA—that would be certain to raise even more questions and doubts in his mind? That would keep him digging into the story? Maybe Keeshan was trying to tell me something without telling me anything. I put a question mark by the X.

I spent the early part of the week, Sunday and Monday, outlining strategy for the second trip and pressing my contacts for the names of people who had been arrested on Highway 59. I was careful not to call someone unless I had dealt with him before, or unless someone I trusted referred me to him. If there was something bizarre going on in San Jacinto County, I didn't want half the state to know I was looking into it. Perhaps I was overly cautious. But I had seen reporters foul up very early in an investigation and wind up losing the story. Once, in Memphis, an inquisitive reporter of mine called the wrong person, who in turn notified the subject under investigation, who in turn called a press conference to rebut charges that had never been made. It was embarrassing for everyone.

The result of those two days of work: no names, lots of promises, lots of speculation, lots of gossip. Zero, in other words. By Monday night, hours before I was to leave, I had made several decisions: first, I was going to leave my three-piece suit at home; second, I was going to book myself into a motel in Livingston, in Polk County off U.S. 59; third, I was going to make frequent sorties into San Jacinto County to watch for police activity; fourth, I was going alone, without a photographer; and fifth, I was going to be especially careful.

So at 7:00 the next morning I climbed into another company car—unmarked, undented Car 8, a white 1979 Ford—and headed due east.

The Sam Houston National Forest begins just to the east of Huntsville, and since this was only the second time in my life that I had been in the forest, I thought I ought to see the sights. Not only that, but I just flat didn't trust those woods. I had heard all my life about "backwoods justice," bootleggers, forest-dwelling hermits, weird furry animals, the Ku Klux Klan, and mysterious cults of tree worshipers. And some people were trying to tell me that all of these resided in San Jacinto County.

Actually, the real reason I drove slowly was the statement made by former judge Amos Gates about San Jacinto County's roadblocks around a youth hangout in Oakhurst, a tiny community off U.S. 190. I wanted to make sure I spotted the youth club, which was supposed to have a sign on Highway 190 with an arrow pointing to it. From what I'd been told, the club was a converted high school gymnasium, and I had no idea what that would look like. I didn't want to miss it.

U.S. 190 was identical to State Highway 150, the winding, tree-infested thoroughfare that crosses the middle of San Jacinto County and bisects Coldspring some fifteen or twenty miles to the south. Only there seemed to be more traffic along 190. A quick look at my road map showed why: Highway 150 goes from I-45 to nowhere (actually, to Coldspring), while Highway 190 goes from the interstate to Lake Livingston. Highway 190 is the main road between Huntsville and the lake. And it seemed to be paved fairly well, for a forest road.

Exactly ten miles east of Huntsville, however, the road changed dramatically from a smooth, even surface to one filled with potholes and asphalt patches. Out of the corner of my eye I noticed a small white signpost up against a group of pine trees; the sign announced the end of Walker County and the beginning of San Jacinto County.

Soon I passed a small brick post office with the word "Oakhurst" on the front. I slowed down even more and began looking for nightclub signs.

The whole community of Oakhurst (population: 200) seemed to converge at the intersection of Highway 190 and Farm to Market Road 946. In fact, that intersection was all there was to Oakhurst, except for a small convenience store, a couple of tiny secondhand shops, and, just down the road, the post office. Of course, the trees were so thick that it was impossible to see what was more than a hundred feet or so off the road. I did notice a couple of churches and two dozen small frame houses. And then, right off Highway 190, on the north side of the road at the FM 946 junction, there was a portable sign with metallic letters: "Our Place." There was an arrow across the top that pointed down FM 946, a southerly route that my map said would lead eventually to Coldspring.

I veered onto the farm road and was taken aback by how narrow it was. Or perhaps it was the closeness of the trees that made it appear so narrow. I couldn't tell. The road made a gentle semicircle through a little residential and church district. At least it seemed to be a church district, seeing as how there was a church for every six or seven houses, by my count. But again, my vision was blocked by the trees, and I couldn't see more than a few hundred feet in any direction. About halfway through the semicircle I noticed another yellow Our Place sign like the one on 190; this sign pointed down a dirt road, which looked like a parking lot for a tiny church called the Full Gospel Church. A teenage hangout in a church parking lot? I certainly couldn't see anything that looked like a converted gym.

I wasn't looking far enough. The dirt road turned out to be a tiny residential street that proceeded about two blocks into the trees, past a half-dozen neat brick houses and dozens of No Parking signs. The street passed over a cattle guard into a large dirt parking area in front of a cream-colored, windowless, prefabricated edifice with a glass-and-wood entrance. Two signs hung over the entrance: "No Mixers" and "No Styrofoam Ice Chests." This must be Our Place. It seemed to be well maintained and was hardly the "dump" I had been told it was.

The parking lot looked as though it could hold two hundred or more vehicles, but the dirt was the type that gets pretty messy during bad weather. Several houses along the dirt street had For Sale signs out front. The yellow sign on FM 946 said there was a live country band every Saturday night, and since this was the middle of the week there was—of course—no one around.

The front door to the club was locked, but I could see into a foyer, where dozens of posters of musicians were hung on the walls. I couldn't see into the gym. I knocked several times, thinking there might be a cleaning person around, but no one answered. But as I climbed back into Car 8, I saw a mobile home around back with boxes and lawn chairs lying around, so I decided to drive back there and check. I got out and knocked, but again there was no answer. Curtains, a fifty-gallon barrel filled with trash and beer cans, and a couple of potted plants were sure signs of human habitation, in my estimation.

I thought I saw some movement behind a curtain, so I knocked again and shouted, "Hello!" Still nothing. It was at that moment that I wished I had brought my old Dodge van instead of my official-looking company car, with its government-white color and conspicuous lack of markings. Hell, it looked like a detective's car. Maybe my tan jeans and blue pullover shirt were being offset by a car that looked like an undercover vehicle.

I knocked a third time, with the same result. Damn. I really wanted to talk to someone here about those roadblocks.

I climbed back into the car and drove the two hundred or so yards back down the dirt road to the Full Gospel Church, a funny-looking little building that wasn't much larger than a two-bedroom frame house. What a peculiar spot for a church. Right at the entrance to a nightclub. Maybe someone at the church would have information about the type of people who frequented the club, and the sheriff's activity on party nights.

But the church was as deserted as the club. No cars. No people. Not even any fifty-gallon barrels or potted plants. Only a sign that said services were at 7:30 p.m. on Wednesdays. A couple of very small frame houses were off in the woods nearby, and one of them had a pickup in front, so I elected to take a chance: I made up another front story on the spot and hiked through the trees to knock on a few doors.

This time, I decided, I would be myself—or, at least, I would be a visitor from Austin who was interested in buying a house in the area, maybe one of the houses for sale up the road. But I wanted to know whether the nightclub was causing any problems for the residents.

The first house I came to brought an elderly man to the door. He was wearing overalls and was slightly hard of hearing, and he didn't seem too interested in chatting with strangers. But I explained my interest in buying a house around there, and I said I wanted to know about Our Place.

The old guy chuckled. "They're just a bunch of kids," he mumbled. "They make a little noise racing up and down the road, but they don't bother me and I don't bother them."

"Do the police help out when the kids start racing?"

"Nah. The sheriff's people don't come in here at all. They stay away." He paused about fifteen seconds before continuing, "But they get 'em on down the road a piece."

"They do what down the road?"

"They set up down at 946 and 156, at the Y—and they stop 'em and tow their cars off."

"You mean they arrest the kids?"

"They just set up their cars and wrecker trucks down there and pick 'em all up, get a little money from 'em, tow their cars in. That's all."

"Do they do this often?"

"Yep."

The old man took a step closer to the screen door and looked closely at my beard. I sensed he was tired of talking to me, and I didn't want to sound overly interested in what they were doing down at the Y intersection. I thanked him and hiked on off. I had found out one thing I needed to know.

I added "roadblock at 946 and 156" to my list of things to check on this trip, and I pointed Car 8 back onto Highway 190 for the remaining thirty miles to Livingston.

At five minutes after 2:00, I checked into the Holiday Inn on U.S. 59 in Livingston. I had a lot of work to do this time.

· SIX ·

The first thing I unpacked at the Holiday Inn–Livingston was my already sizable stack of notebooks and telephone lists. I picked up the hotel room telephone no later than ten minutes after entering the sterile, one-bed "McHotel room," and I was prepared to spend the next three hours setting up interviews and tracking down rumors. I wanted to get my hands on people who had firsthand, eyewitness information about this alleged operation along U.S. 59. And what better place to set up headquarters than at a motel on U.S. 59 . . . in an adjoining county, of course.

Judge Gates and another former Huntsville official had encouraged me to track down lawyers who lived in San Jacinto County because, in their opinion, those folks were probably incensed by the goings-on there. I wasn't so sure about that. And I had already learned that there weren't many lawyers to choose from in San Jacinto County. Only three, to be exact, and one of them was county attorney Robert Atkins. The other two, James and Hildegard Faulkner, had been mentioned by name by Sheriff Parker during our talk the week before, so I didn't even attempt to contact them.

Nevertheless, after half an hour of retracing my steps over the telephone and renewing contacts with legal services workers in two nearby cities, I came up with the names of two retired lawyers who now resided in San Jacinto County, Beatrice Hightower and Lawrence Cowart. Perhaps they had some defendants who wanted to do a little talking . . . or maybe they were close friends with the sheriff. I called them anyway.

Hightower was the first one I reached, but she really didn't want to say anything about the county. I told her I was running a check on some complaints about the sheriff's department, and that I just wanted to touch base with a couple of local lawyers before I proceeded. I gave the impression that I knew nothing, not even the exact location of San Jacinto County.

She explained that she had lived there about three years, and that she no longer practiced law. And she was very interested to know how I got her name and telephone number. I dodged her question with a you-know-how-reporters-are answer, and I quickly asked if she had heard anything unusual about the way laws were enforced along U.S. 59.

A long pause.

"Let me just say that this is an unusual county to live in," she replied finally.

Another question: what did she mean by "unusual"?

The same answer.

And that was it. Nothing specific, just "unusual." I asked why she was reluctant to discuss anything with me, and I explained that I was not going to use anything she said in any story I might write for the newspaper.

Her answer: "I've got to live here."

Before pulling the plug on the conversation, I asked one more question: is there anything about U.S. 59 worth pursuing?

Yes.

I thanked her—why, I don't know, because she hadn't been much help—and then I hung up.

Why should a retired lawyer be reluctant to talk? Most of the old barristers I had run into would bend your ear just as long as you plied them with booze or compliments. Something must really be amiss.

Lawrence Cowart proved to be much more talkative. I corralled him about an hour later. He said he'd heard quite a lot about the sheriff, and about the way the department operated; he had been called on numerous occasions by defendants who wanted someone to represent them, but he had turned them down. He said he was very serious about his retirement. He also said he lived in Oakhurst.

"All I know is just what I've heard," he said. "They just spend most of their time picking up young people with beards who are coming through. I've had people call me about it, and I've heard a lot of complaints."

But no names.

Had he heard any complaints about Our Place?

He had. "You see, it's a dry area, and those kids bring their own bottles over there. I don't really know what's going on, but it's a honky-tonk type of place."

Any complaints about sheriff's roadblocks around Oakhurst?

None that he knew of, but he pointed out that if there were any roadblocks, they'd probably be on the south side of the club.

"Where would that be, exactly?" I asked. "Near 946 and 156?"

Yep.

He knew more than he was saying, but I let it drop. Instead, I asked if he knew of anything unusual in the way the sheriff enforced the laws in San Jacinto County.

As a matter of fact, he did. He said he had served on a grand jury there for a six-month period, and that Sheriff Parker on more than one occasion had shown up and bragged about the fine money his department was bringing in from U.S. 59. "He said his department wasn't costing the county any money at all, because of all those arrests on 59. He was proud of it. I thought it was sort of strange."

I asked if most of the people who were arrested were young kids.

"I think that's true," he replied quickly. "The sheriff seems to be down on the young folk, sort of like they can't do anything right." He stopped abruptly; he seemed to be weighing his words with care. "But you know, I haven't been at all impressed with that sheriff when I've seen him. Not impressed at all."

We talked a few more minutes. Cowart sounded very much like a conscientious person who was enjoying his retirement. He had no firsthand knowledge at all, except for his stint on the grand jury, but I figured he would come in handy later on, so I put a little star by his name on my phone list.

I made a couple more calls—one of them to the city desk to tell them where I was staying, and another to my wife, same reason.

And then I placed another call to J. H. Keeshan, the district attorney, who just happened to be in his office and available for a short talk. Maybe he knew something about Our Place.

He did. He said the place had a terrible reputation.

"It has been my wish, and the wish of a lot of people in Conroe, that that Oakhurst place be more tightly controlled. It was our experience that a lot of juveniles went up there and drank and danced. There was a lot of unsupervised drinking."

He pointed out that Our Place did not have a liquor permit from the Texas Alcoholic Beverage Commission, which meant that the Liquor Control Board of the ABC could not move in and close it down. As long as the club did not sell booze, or make it available in other ways to underage kids, the ABC could do nothing—short of picking up the kids who were caught drinking.

Part of his strong feelings, Keeshan explained, stemmed from a recent incident in which a boy from Conroe was killed in a two-car crash while driving home from Oakhurst. The driver of the other vehicle was charged with involuntary manslaughter and driving while intoxicated. The boy was a high school student, and the death was so tragic in the eyes of Conroe residents, Keeshan said, that he personally "would be very sympathetic with more extensive law enforcement of that establishment."

I decided it was time to shift gears. Had he heard anything lately about Sheriff Parker's security business? (It was a gamble on my part to ask this, but perhaps the DA would say something if he thought I knew a lot about Parker Security.)

Keeshan didn't even hesitate. He said he knew "as a matter of general information" that the sheriff at one time had operated a private security agency in San Jacinto County, but he had not heard any complaints about it. "It's just one of the things you hear about Humpy Parker . . . that he makes money from some of the developments on the lake."

He tossed that line out as nonchalantly as I used to throw my curve ball on a three-two count. Makes money from the developments on Lake Livingston? The sheriff? I fumbled with words a minute before deciding it was a good time to start winding this conversation to a close—before Keeshan ran out of these one-liners, and before he found out that I knew a lot less than he thought I did.

But he wasn't ready to stop talking. He jumped back to Our Place and said the club had a large following of fourteen- to sixteen-year-olds whose parents ought to have better control over them. And then he said he was not at all sympathetic with the people who were arrested for drug possession on U.S. 59. And then he mentioned the 1978 FBI investigation and how the agents stopped off at his office for a courtesy call. Over the next fifteen minutes, he confirmed every scrap of information I had about that federal probe. He even gave me the names of the FBI agents who visited him. But he said he had no firsthand information about the FBI probe, that all of his knowledge was hearsay. I didn't say anything.

Keeshan went back over the comments he had made to me earlier about his reluctance to make substantive remarks because he had to represent the sheriff in criminal cases arising in that county. I still kept quiet. Then he started singling out county officials in San Jacinto County and making general comments about them. I could tell he was running down.

First of all, he said, he "wanted to commend" county attorney Robert Atkins for being "reliable, knowledgeable, and a straight arrow." And then he wanted to say a few kind words about Judge Bryant, the county judge, whom he called "very knowledgeable and very understanding" about the problems and issues facing county residents. Those two men, he said, were credits to their jobs, and the people of San Jacinto County should be proud of them. And then he stopped.

Not one word about Sheriff Parker. Not one commendation. Not one word of praise. Not one "very reliable," "very knowledgeable," or "straight arrow." The omission was glaring. I got his message. Again.

By that time, it was quite apparent that Keeshan wanted to help me in any way he could, short of risking his job and alienating his constituents. I put another star by his name, thanked him, and told him I'd call him back later in the week.

It was nearly 5:00 p.m. on this Tuesday—time to go prowling.

My first stop was less than a hundred feet from my motel room—the motel bar. The quickest way to find out things about a strange town is to visit a few local bars during happy hour. People have a tendency to talk more freely when they've had a few drinks, and they'll tell you things in a dark barroom that they wouldn't dare say in the bright sunshine. Sometimes they say unusual things to each other in a bar—and from my years of covering beer joint fights in Fort Worth I knew that there was some danger in the formula drinks plus dark bar plus candid comments. I'd done enough stories about fights, and I sure didn't want to be a participant in one.

The Holiday Inn bar went by the name of the Red Horse Saloon, and it was one of those private clubs that cater primarily to hotel guests. Polk County, I discovered, was dry, as are many counties in East Texas. The bar was almost empty when I walked in at a few minutes after 5:00. The decor was what I'd call modern beer joint, with a deejay's booth at one end, a small dance floor, a dozen or so tables, a revolving disco light over the dance floor, and a bar at the other end. The only person there, other than a young woman bartender, was an elderly man in a three-piece suit. He was semi-slumped over a martini, and I guessed that he wouldn't make for great conversation. I walked to the far end of the bar and sat down.

I ordered a beer and—after I went back out and got a guest card from the registration desk to prove that I was a motel patron—struck up a conversation with the bartender. Again, I proceeded cautiously. Bartenders can be a great help if you don't tick them off; some of them have police-type friends, and others hate cops. I had to see which type this one was. From her appearance—long dark hair, heavy makeup, gaunt and pale countenance—she could have been anywhere from nineteen to thirty-five years old. I guessed nineteen. Female bartenders seldom look younger than they really are; most look a great deal older.

I asked what all the one-dollar bills were doing pasted all over the wall behind the bar.

Oh, those, she said, were placed there by people who had visited the bar. All of them had autographs on them. I looked closer and saw that she was right.

Who was the most famous visitor?

Without hesitating, she pointed to a greenback with the name of Dan Pastorini, the former quarterback for the Houston Oilers, who was well known throughout South Texas for his long passes to Ken Burrough, his handoffs to Earl Campbell, and his interesting lifestyle (not necessarily in that order).

Any other famous visitors?

She mentioned a couple of names, but I had never heard of them. I nodded as if I had, however.

I sipped my Budweiser and said I doubted that I would qualify for barroom stardom; I was just a hardworking reporter from Austin who was trying to find out a few things about San Jacinto County.

I stopped to see what her reaction would be. Either she would curl up in a defensive posture and say something like "What types of things?" or she would nod knowingly and mention something specific about the county and its weird ways.

She chose the latter, much to my relief. "Oh, yeah, you mean the deal they've got going on 59, don't you?" She knew a little about it. Lots of folks had come into the bar with angry stories to tell about being stopped and searched on the highway for no apparent reason; some had been arrested and had their cars towed. All of them were mad. She said the deputies down there drove around in unmarked cars and pickups, and some didn't even wear badges or uniforms. All they had were guns.

I didn't know that, but I acted casual and said I had heard some pretty weird stories.

She had, too, and she said I could come into the bar almost any night and find a couple of people who had been picked up a time or two while passing through the county.

She was starting to attract my attention. Any night? I asked. About what time would be best? I was a little reluctant to ask for names and addresses; that, I thought, would be coming on a bit too strong.

Oh, almost any night around 10:00, she said.

I finished sipping my beer, and we continued talking in general terms about the "deal" on U.S. 59. She said the deputies only picked on people from other counties and visitors from other states. A "guaranteed stop" in San Jacinto County, she said, was a vehicle with out-of-state plates. (Like Mr. Foley, I thought.)

Yeah, I nodded sympathetically. And I'd heard a lot about young kids getting stopped. . . .

Before I could finish the sentence, she related a tale about a carful of young people who were stopped and strip-searched right on the highway shoulder. The deputies, she said, made the kids stand there with their pants down for more than fifteen minutes—in full view of passing motorists.

And did I know that the sheriff's son was a deputy? I told her I didn't. She laughed. Gary Parker, she said in a sort of half-chuckle, made more arrests in that county than any other deputy.

I made a mental note and started to ask about drug traffic along 59, but a half-dozen cowboys walked in and sat down. And they were followed by another half-dozen cowboys. All of them were loud, thirsty, and dusty. Must be quittin' time, I thought.

It was. These grimy-looking creatures were oil field workers, and they had been loading and hauling equipment at a well site since 6:30 that morning. They began devouring pitchers of beer at a phenomenal rate, almost as fast as the participants in a slow-pitch softball league I played in a time or two in Memphis. I was glad I had abandoned my three-piece suit in favor of some grimy-looking clothes of my own.

After they had consumed their first round of pitchers, I motioned to the bartender. Were any of these guys regular customers of the San Jacinto County sheriff? I asked.

No, they were just in Livingston for a few days of work, she said. But I could probably catch some regular patrons later that night. I finished my beer and left.

It was about 6:00 p.m. and already starting to get dark. I nosed Car 8 onto U.S. 59 and started in a southerly direction toward San Jacinto County. I didn't really know what I was looking for, but I convinced myself that I'd know it if I found it.

Basically, I was looking for anything out of the ordinary—a group of police cars, a crowd of people, kids sitting in a parking lot, hitchhikers, wrecker trucks along the highway. Anything. I had my camera and note pad, but I put them under the front seat. Nothing attracts more attention than they do, and I didn't want to attract *too* much attention. I also made damn sure that I drove a steady fifty miles an hour in the fifty-five-mile-per-hour speed zone.

About twenty minutes later I pulled into the Dairy Queen in Shepherd, about five miles inside San Jacinto County. I had seen absolutely nothing so far—only eighteen-wheelers. That stretch of 59 north from Shepherd to the San Jacinto–Polk county line was about as dreary and deserted as any I'd ever seen. It was also the same area where the sheriff's department was supposed to be making all its arrests. Naturally, there were no cop cars this time.

Two teenage boys were sitting in an old white pickup in the DQ parking lot, sipping soft drinks and munching french fries. I parked my car a few spaces away, walked in and bought a small Dr Pepper to go, and then paced slowly over to their truck. I put on my best good-ol'-boy accent and tried to act like a certified East Texas redneck.

"You guys know a guy by the name of Donnie Gentry who's supposed to live somewhere around here?" I asked, making up a name and a story to see what these kids knew and how they'd react to a stranger asking for information. Like the bartender in Livingston, they had two ways to respond. They could get defensive and brush me off or they could attempt to be helpful to a stranger. Either way, I had nothing to lose.

I got lucky again. They said they didn't know anyone by that name, but they asked me where he was supposed to live. They were trying to help.

Gentry, I explained to them, supposedly lived somewhere just north of Shepherd. He was going to meet me here at the DQ at 6:30; it was 6:30 and he wasn't here. I explained that Gentry and I had played a little semi-pro baseball together in Dallas and Fort Worth a few years ago and had gotten to be pretty good friends. I hadn't heard from him in about a year until he called me last week and said he'd gotten himself arrested on Highway 59 and needed someone to go to court with him to be a character witness. The court day was supposed to be tomorrow—Wednesday—in Coldspring. He had sounded pretty bad over the telephone and I was a little worried.

The two kids swallowed my story. They began tossing out names of people that sounded like "Donnie" or "Gentry," and they compared notes on the people they knew who lived north of Shepherd. Both of them were from Cleveland, but they knew most of the high-school-aged kids in the area.

Gentry, I said, was twenty-five years old and had lived there only about a year. (I hoped they wouldn't get too inquisitive about him, because I was making this up as I went along.) He didn't have a telephone and I thought he lived with his uncle, whose name I didn't know.

They exhausted their inventory of names, and I finally said that I'd just wait around until he showed up. And they they asked me why he'd been arrested . . . just the question I was waiting for.

Some sheriff's deputies had stopped him on 59 south of Urbana—somewhere near the Trinity River—and arrested him for DWI. Gentry had told me something about how the deputies pulled all the seats out of his car and strip-searched him on the side of the road. It sounded pretty scary to me, I said.

"So they got him, too," one of the kids said with a little laugh. "You oughta be out here on a Saturday night and watch what happens." The two boys said strip searches of people and energetic searches of cars were commonplace on weekend nights along 59, and that they knew of kids who had been dragged across the ground by their hair for talking back to the deputies.

"It's a good thing they didn't find any dope on him," one of the boys remarked, as the other nodded. "When they're hunting for dope, they usually find it."

Both of them laughed.

"You mean the deputies do all this stuff and no one ever complains?" I asked.

Oh, the ones who complained usually got locked up, they said. Or roughed up a little. The worst thing to do was to complain. It was a lot better just to give them whatever money you had, or have someone bring them some money as soon as possible. Then they'd let you go and you'd never hear anything more about it. Most of the times, they said, the arrests never went on your record if you did that.

Really? I said in amazement, not all of it faked. How did you know that the arrest stayed off your record?

Because that was what the deputies told you when you paid them your money, the kids said almost in unison.

I shook my head and thanked them for their help. As I was turning to walk away, I stopped and asked, as if on the spur of the moment, "Oh, by the way, do you know the names of anyone who's gone through this just like Gentry? Maybe if I let them talk to Gentry he'll decide not to fight it."

They thought a minute and said that I ought to go up to the high schools in Shepherd and Coldspring, because "just about every kid there" knew someone who'd been arrested. I sensed that the kids were getting tired of answering questions, and I didn't want to blow my new cover story. As a matter of fact, I kind of liked it. I climbed back into Car 8 and headed into Shepherd to find someone else to try it out on.

I spent the next hour or so cruising around the southern part of San Jacinto County and the northern part of Liberty County looking for young kids congregating at a public place—a restaurant, fast-food joint, parking lot, school, or church. I stopped once at a Baptist church in Cleveland and talked to some young adults (three men and two women in their early twenties), but their information mostly duplicated what I'd just heard in the parking lot of the Dairy Queen. They had no names for me. But my new cover story was working beautifully.

Everyone wanted to help me find Donnie Gentry. And everyone confirmed indirectly the fictitious events that happened to Gentry along Highway 59. They sympathized with him and said they would advise him not to contest the DWI charge. Everyone knew that the best way to handle an arrest in San Jacinto County was just pay up, shut up, and get out.

As I was driving out of Cleveland on 59 about 7:45 p.m., I stopped at a small barbecue restaurant with a gravel parking lot. Two cars filled with teenagers were pulled up next to each other, and there seemed to be a lot of talking going on. Maybe they'd talk to me. I parked a respectable distance away and walked over.

Do any of you know Donnie Gentry? I asked.

They just started laughing and kept on talking to each other—in Spanish!

Now, I'd had three years of Spanish in college, but that was ten years ago, and I certainly couldn't think fast enough on my feet to ask my questions in Spanish. I fumbled around for a minute.

The kids thought my predicament was funny. I knew—and they knew I knew—that they could speak English, but they were at an age where it is considered great sport to give grownups a hard time. They weren't about to converse in English with this bumbling, bearded Anglo. I walked back to Car 8, started the engine, and decided it was time to head back to the Holiday Inn bar in Livingston.

The thirty-minute drive from Cleveland to Livingston—once again—was peaceful. It was after 8:00 and dark when I passed through Shepherd, and the absence of law enforcement vehicles began to make me wonder just when the sheriff's department patrolled U.S. 59. I'd certainly never seen one of their cars on that twelve-mile stretch of highway. Or maybe I just didn't recognize their cars. The bartender said they drove unmarked cars and pickups. That would explain a lot.

I got back to the motel about 8:30, and there were quite a few more cars in the lot. I checked the desk—there were no messages—and then proceeded directly to the bar. It was unbelievably crowded for a Tuesday night, I thought, especially for this Bible-thumping area of the country where Tuesday nights are supposed to be spent in prayerful contemplation and preparation for Wednesday night church services.

There were several couples on the dance floor, and the country music was blaring from the deejay's booth. Most of the tables were filled, and the dozen or so oil field workers who had gotten there about 5:15 were leaning against each other at a couple of them. They were in that passive and subdued state of drunkenness that is one step away from being stone cold passed out. Two of them staggered out the side door just as I took a seat at the bar.

The bartender at first didn't remember me, but I jogged her memory with a comment about my interest in San Jacinto County. She brought me my beer and pointed to a middle-aged man at the other end of the bar. "You oughta go talk to him," she said loudly, trying to pierce the pulsating Kenny Rogers song and the even louder talking.

There was a vacant stool next to him, and I hustled over, sat down, and introduced myself. I told him I'd been talking to the bartender about Highway 59 in San Jacinto County and was looking for people who had firsthand information about the harassment and illegal arrests.

The wiry, tall, stubble-cheeked man set down his drink and looked directly at me. "You investigating them?" he asked.

I nodded.

"You think what they're doing is wrong?"

I nodded again.

"You think you can do any good?"

A third nod.

"Well," he drawled between sips, "you won't believe what those bastards did to me."

· SEVEN ·

Darrell Johnson was not what you would call an average, run-of-the-mill citizen. At age thirty-seven, he bounced around doing odd jobs in the oil fields between Livingston and Houston. He drove a pickup truck with a police scanner radio, and he liked to have a few beers with the boys at night. He looked a good bit older than his years, too.

The Holiday Inn bar in Livingston was a good place to get lost in a crowd of people who were trying to get lost in one crowd or another. Johnson had spent most of his adult life losing himself in a crowd, but his crowd was considered by many to be composed almost entirely of down-and-outers, people who wandered from job to job, town to town, oil field to oil field, people who always had plans for something better just down the road, some piece of action that was compelling and—at the same time—just out of reach. I was entranced by this man, and we sat and talked for almost two hours.

He spoke quietly, often barely penetrating the laughter and screams from the forty or so people congregating in the bar on this Tuesday night. A few couples danced most of the night, and one white-headed old man in a snap-button shirt and cowboy hat seemed to have the two-step down to a science. The old guy was fabulous, and he went through dance partners as fast as a hungry priest goes through fried chicken at a Sunday afternoon picnic. He danced every time the deejay put on a record, pausing only to down large gulps of beer. Johnson said the guy was at the bar almost every night.

This thin, tall cowboy knew a lot about the San Jacinto County Sheriff's Department. He knew enough to stay away from that county on weekends, and he knew enough to listen to the deputies' chatter on his police scanner. He grew up in Livingston and had lived in that part of East Texas most of his life. But as he explained softly over his highball glass, "sooner or later they're gonna get you."

They had gotten Johnson about three weeks earlier on U.S. 190, in the northern part of the county near Lake Livingston. As a Hank Williams tearjerker played appropriately over the stereo system, Johnson related a tale that began with his broken marriage and continued with his reputation as a "semi-outlaw," his inability to keep a job, and his arrest in early February by Gary Parker, son of San Jacinto County sheriff Humpy Parker.

As he told it, he had stopped off at Junior's, a redneck club on 190 about a mile from the Lake Livingston bridge and about a mile inside San Jacinto County. It was a Saturday night and—he admitted this was unusual for him—he had *not* been drinking. At Junior's, he had three beers before deciding to call it a night. He climbed into his pickup, turned on the scanner, and pulled out of the gravel parking lot onto two-lane 190 for the twenty-minute drive to his house. He didn't get far.

Before he got out of sight of the club, perhaps a block away, the flashing lights of a sheriff's vehicle attracted his attention and caused him to pull over. It was a bit unusual, Johnson said, because he had driven only a block and was not yet up to the speed limit. He said he was doing about forty.

"I climbed out of my truck and was standing there holding my driver's license in my hand when this wrecker truck pulls up and starts backing up to hook on to my pickup. I didn't get to say one word to him. He just said, 'Mr. Johnson, it looks like you been doing a little drinking. You're gonna have to come with me.' I mean, before I even handed him my license, he was telling me this, and that wrecker was backing up to my truck.

"He handcuffed me and drove me to the jail. The bail bondsman was there waiting and it cost me $300 to get out. They said I was DWI. That kid searched my truck and looked through some boxes I had in the back 'cause I was moving. They're just flat pickin' on the poor folks over there."

I asked him who the bondsman was.

Herb Atwood, he said.

And the wrecker company?

B&B Wrecker, out of Shepherd.

The same combination that was involved in the arrests four months earlier of Mr. Foley's son and girlfriend.

Did Johnson know anything about that particular combination— bondsman Herb Atwood and B&B Wrecker?

He started to laugh but stopped suddenly. There was really nothing at all funny about this. He said he had heard a few things, but he paused again. The old guy doing the two-step had found a vivacious young dance partner, and they were going absolutely bananas on the dance floor. After a few minutes, Johnson continued, "I don't know, but I can tell you for sure that they're doing a number on people in that county.

"That kind of stuff makes me mad. I'd just better not run into one of them somewhere outside that county. . . ."

Had he heard anything more from Atwood or the county? Had a court date been set?

He laughed again. "What do you think?" he replied.

We talked awhile longer about the types of people who live in these rural counties in the woods north of Houston—about their paranoia about big cities, their distrust of outsiders, and their reluctance to share their feelings with people they didn't know. He said it was out of character for him to be sitting there at the bar talking to me, a strange reporter from Austin.

Again he asked me what exactly I thought I could do about San Jacinto County, and again I told him I wasn't sure, except that I was going to expose anything they were doing that was illegal, unethical, or immoral. I couldn't promise anything, but I was going to do everything I could to track down more people like him, people who had been arrested and, apparently, shaken down in the jail.

Johnson looked tired. His eyes were heavy and the stubble on his cheeks was thick, making him look almost sinister in the dim barroom light. I figured that he always looked this way—tired and sort of beaten down, beaten down by circumstances partly of his own making, partly out of his control. Beaten down by life in the Piney Woods. The $300 he paid to get out of jail, I guessed, was an unbelievably large amount of money to him. He was not the type of person, though, who was going to run down to Houston and hire a high-priced lawyer to come up and contest the arrest. It looked like a safe arrest for San Jacinto County. Quick. Painless. And no repercussions.

Johnson left about half an hour before midnight. I sat there thinking about what he had said, comparing it with the events related to me by Mr. Foley. The similarities were uncanny: the unexpected stopping of the cars; the quick arrival of the tow trucks; the diligent searches; the handcuffs; the high-speed rides back to the jail in Coldspring; the waiting bail bondsman; the setting of get-out-of-jail-now fees on the spot; the absence of a judge to set the bond, or fee, or whatever it was; the finality of the whole transaction, including no further contact from the county or the bondsman; the arrogance of the deputies; the feelings of the victims, who all felt as though they had been raped, violated, cheated.

I got back to my room about midnight and thought for a minute about making a pass back down Highway 59 into San Jacinto County. I actually got as far as opening the door of Car 8 and starting the engine before I thought better of the idea. I don't belong to the Geraldo Rivera school of journalism (Rivera is the enterprising ABC-TV reporter who tries to get himself arrested to expose corruption).

I was up and about a little after 7:00 the next morning, Wednesday, March 3. I had an appointment at 8:30 with the principal of Coldspring High School, James Boyce. It was time to find out what types of kids went to the school, what their parents did, what people did for fun and recreation, and—oh, by the way—was there a drug problem among the local kids?

Boyce got a slightly different version of my earliest front story. I was again doing research on the counties north of Houston, but this version had it that I was primarily looking at the young people, their interests, hobbies, activities, recreational pursuits, and overall lifestyles. In short, what was it like to grow up in the backwoods an hour or so from one of the world's largest and busiest cities? It sounded convincing, and to tell the truth, I *was* interested in it. So many people had told me conflicting stories about the kids—drugs were being used openly in the schools, only outsiders who used hard drugs were arrested by the sheriff, none of the locals used illicit drugs—that I had to check it out myself. Even the sheriff himself had made a few contradictory remarks about the local kids during my interview with him the previous week. At one point he had decried the open and notorious usage of narcotics in the schools; at another point he had said most of the drug problems came from Houston, from outsiders bringing their drugs into San Jacinto County. Which was correct?

The Coldspring school was situated on a hill northeast of the town square. A series of old-style white brick buldings—and the usual spread of trees—made up the complex. The parking lot was gravel, and it seemed to be filled with pickup trucks this bright March morning. A dozen or so students, both black and white, congregated around a few cars, listening to music and smoking cigarettes.

The principal turned out to be a jovial, round-faced, dark-haired man who liked to hear himself talk. I spent almost two hours in his office, covering a wide range of topics that included (1) the school's pressure from the growth problem in Houston, (2) the school's extensive outdoor recreational program, (3) his problems in hiring qualified math teachers, and (4) the relative contentment on the part of the students, all of whom were happy and pleased to live in San Jacinto County. And we talked about drugs and Our Place, but not in any significant detail. Boyce appeared reluctant to go beyond a few cursory comments.

But he could talk your ear off about the overall merits of backwoods living.

"The lake is a huge drawing card for us. We get at least 35,000 hunters in here every weekend, and that's three times the entire population of the county. And we get a lot more fishermen than that. It's one of the finest fishing places anywhere in the state. When you consider all of this, you'd have to say that we are a recreational-based community. But at the same time, it's only a one-hour drive from this school to the International Airport in Houston. That's an amazing thing to consider . . . and especially when you realize that Houston is growing this way at an incredible rate. We're hoping that the national forest serves as a buffer, to keep Houston from swallowing us up.

"Our young kids are like any young kids, except that they have more outdoor recreation. There's very little in the way of indoor activities here. In Houston, they have the Dairy Queen and Pizza Hut syndrome, but there's really not a lot like that around here for the students to choose from."

He said the high school had four hundred students with a racial breakdown of thirty percent black and seventy percent white. However, in 1967—before the lake opened—the school had been seventy-two percent black and twenty-eight percent white. He called it a "complete flip-flop in only fifteen years." He said he could state the 1967 figures with a great degree of accuracy because that was the year he started teaching in the Coldspring system. He had been principal only a few years and I guessed that he was about forty.

Gradually I turned the conversation to drugs. "Just how bad a problem is drug usage in the school?" I asked.

"Ninety-nine percent of the people arrested for drugs in this county," he said without hesitation, "are from Houston. I'd say that we have less of a problem with that than ninety-five percent of your schools. Of course, we get some pretty wild kids through here from Houston, but we don't really have a problem with our own. We're a lot stricter and a lot more conservative than schools in Houston. And I'd say that we have probably one of the better-disciplined schools in East Texas. We have good kids, excellent kids. And we have extremely low turnover. Out of thirty-eight teachers, there is only one vacancy this year. People just like to come up here to teach."

Had the rather sudden shift from a mostly black district to one that was predominantly white caused any unusual racial problems?

He answered quickly. "In fifteen years, we've had one racial fight. We just don't have racial problems here. As a matter of fact, we have two black members of the school board. So far as racial tensions, we just don't have any."

What about Our Place? What problems had been caused by it, or by law enforcement activity around it? (I worded my questions carefully. I didn't want to fall into the trap of leading the witness.)

"Now, Our Place does generate a problem for us," Boyce said, explaining that the problem stemmed from "outsiders" who came from the lake to the club, and not from high school students in Coldspring. "Unfortunately, those people who go up there and do all the drinking have to drive on the same highways that we do when they leave the place. But we still have to deal with the problem. And from what I hear, it's a real law enforcement problem."

That was about all he wanted to say about Our Place, so I shifted the conversation to Waterwood – the Horizon Corporation development on Lake Livingston. Boyce perked up.

"You know that's one of the largest subdivisions in the state? It takes in 24,000 acres in the northern end of the county. It borders right there on the lake. At one time, before the lake opened up, this was an extremely poor county; but the lake made some people instant millionaires. And it is the primary reason that the racial population of the county shifted so dramatically. In a little more than ten years, this county has changed dramatically; it's a much more affluent population now. Who knows what ten more years will bring? . . . We're just trying to hang on to as much of our local color as we can. I just don't know how long we'll be able to do it."

It was getting close to 10:15 by then, and I felt like the judge of a high school essay contest: Why I Love San Jacinto County (in 25,000 words or more) . . . Why Our High School Kids Are the World's Best . . . Why This School Is Better Than Any Other . . . Why We Don't Have Racial or Drug Problems . . . Why Houston Is Evil and Coldspring Isn't. The whole spiel probably would have nauseated me except that I had been prepared for it. I thanked Boyce for his time and left as quickly as I could. I wanted to hustle on over to county court to see what types of criminals were appearing before the Honorable Judge K. P. Bryant on this Wednesday morning – court day in San Jacinto County.

Judge Bryant almost fell out of his chair when he saw me. He was sitting at the top end of a horseshoe-shaped table in the county commissioners' meeting room, which was serving as his courtroom. I smiled and nodded. It was obvious that I was the last person he had expected to see. But what better place would there be for me to find victims of the Highway 59 operation? I sat down and listened.

The table was the type that was designed for legislative meetings, not judicial proceedings. There was a much larger courtroom, used mainly by the circuit-riding district judges, on the second floor. Bryant was wearing a three-piece suit, and he was seated at precisely the top of the horseshoe; at his left was Imogene Trapp, the county clerk, who was indeed the elderly woman I had run into on the steps of the courthouse the week before. The sheriff's secretary was seated at the judge's right. Two young men had just walked out when I entered, and the judge was preparing to call another case.

The next four docket numbers that Bryant called were no-shows. On each, he instructed the sheriff's secretary, whom he called Mrs. Yarbrough, to go to the door and call the names three times, apparently to see if the defendants were standing in the hall. It looked to me as if this was the first time the secretary had done this, and Bryant finally asked that someone go to a telephone and "get Humpy over here." I felt honored. I was going to see how the sheriff and the judge operated together in court. But where was Robert Atkins, the county attorney? Who was prosecuting these cases, anyway? The sheriff's secretary? The judge? The clerk? This looked odd even for a rural county.

A few minutes later, Sheriff Parker walked in, and a case was called involving three teenagers from Longview who had been arrested for possession of marijuana on Highway 59. Bryant explained the charge against them and—as he had told me he would—he read them their rights, which turned out to be the Miranda warning: you have the right to remain silent, and so forth. Parker leaned over and whispered something to the judge, and I noticed that there was no court reporter; these proceedings were being held off the record, as it were. That wasn't unusual for small counties.

The judge summoned all three teenagers—two girls and a boy—to the front of the table, inside the horseshoe, and asked them how they wanted to plead: guilty, not guilty, or no contest. He said that only one of the three was actually in possession of marijuana at the time of the arrest, and the amount was less than two ounces, so he would probably dismiss the charges against the other two. Both of them quickly pleaded not guilty. The other girl, the one who Bryant said had had the dope, quietly pleaded guilty. It seemed odd for the judge simply to state that only one of them was actually in possession of marijuana; I thought that was what witnesses and evidence were supposed to be for. Anyway, the young girl looked terrified.

After a few minutes of rambling monologue, Bryant announced that he was "going to do something a little different" with the girl who pleaded guilty, even though it was her first offense. He then sentenced her to sixty days in jail and fined her $300 plus $71 court costs. All three defendants started crying.

"But this is the first time I've ever been arrested," the young girl pleaded, sobbing loudly.

Bryant interrupted. "Let me finish," he said. He then said he was pro-bating her jail sentence for six months with the stipulation that she be treated for venereal disease.

The three defendants, who had come to court without a lawyer, looked stunned. "Why?" they asked in unison.

Bryant said he was also ordering the other two—the ones who pleaded not guilty—to be tested and treated for VD. He said he would not dismiss the charges against them until he received a note from a doctor about the tests.

I had never seen anything like that. Once a defendant enters a plea, it is up to the judge to act upon it. But Bryant proclaimed that he would do nothing until the VD tests were made and reported to him.

The young girl who was sentenced to jail did not understand what had happened. She continued to cry, apparently thinking that she was going to have to go to jail. The other two wanted to change their pleas to guilty, too. "If she's going to jail, we're all going," the young boy said, still sobbing.

Bryant explained that the girl would not go to jail unless she got into trouble during the term of her probation, six months, or unless she refused to be tested and treated for VD. At that point, the sheriff left the room. As the $371 in fines and costs was being paid to Mrs. Trapp, the clerk, Bryant announced that this was the last case on the docket. He got up and walked out, and I followed him.

Wasn't all this a bit unusual? I asked him as we walked down the hall.

He said it was, but something had to be done about the awful problem with VD in the country. He made a rather crude remark about what he suspected those kids had been doing, and he said one of the trusties in the jail had overheard "one of the kids" saying something about VD. He said he had been reading about the epidemic proportions of VD and just decided to do something about it.

I walked away a bit dazed by his reasoning. I huddled briefly with the teenagers, who were walking into the probation office, and they were more confused than I was. All they knew was that none of them was going to jail, and they were just glad to be getting out of San Jacinto County.

Their arrest was similar to Jeffrey Foley's and Darrell Johnson's: They were stopped on U.S. 59 for no apparent reason (they said they were never given a reason), and they were searched vigorously. When a small bag of marijuana was found in one of the purses, all three were arrested, handcuffed, and taken to jail at a high rate of speed. All three had to pay $100 to a bail bondsman to get out of jail the same night. They were never taken before a judge, at least until the appearance before Judge Bryant a few minutes before.

"Who set the amounts of the bonds?" I asked.

They didn't know.

At that point, they walked into the probation office.

The only difference between this case and the other two I knew something about was that these three people were notified of their court date. But when they showed up, they wound up listening to one of the weirdest sentences I had ever heard. Or was it a sentence? It was actually an order that all three undergo VD tests—sort of an extralegal command. Or maybe it was the main condition of the guilty girl's probation. But what about the two who had pleaded not guilty? How could Bryant order them to do anything without disposing of their pleas one way or the other? How could a county court judge issue such an ultimatum? I sat down at a bench in the hallway and jotted a few notes to myself. I wasn't at all familiar with this sort of justice.

Then I walked down the hall to the clerk's office and looked in the criminal docket books for records of any charges that were filed against Jeffrey Foley or Darrell Johnson. As I expected, there were none. As far as the official record-keeping body in San Jacinto County was concerned, the Foleys and Mr. Johnson simply did not exist.

I then checked the fine reports and receipts that the sheriff turned over to the county clerk each month to see if the $410 paid by Foley or the $300 paid by Johnson—those get-out-of-jail-quick fees—had been reported. They hadn't. The money just wasn't on the books. Either this was some of the sloppiest bookkeeping on record or someone—in some office—was siphoning it off. Someone was making a profit from all these arrests, and it sure didn't seem to be the San Jacinto County Clerk's Office.

One of the deputy clerks walked over and asked if she could help me find something. I asked if there was any other place in that office, or in any office in the county, where criminal charges of marijuana possession and DWI would be filed.

None that she knew of.

I walked back to Bryant's office and asked him to check his docket lists for Foley and Johnson. He was perturbed but checked anyway, since I was standing there with my note pad and pen poised to record his response. Again, nothing. "Are you sure they were even arrested in this county?" he asked. "You know how folks can get mixed up sometimes."

"Yeah, I know." I walked off absolutely haunted by the three crying teenagers and Bryant's explicit remarks to me in the hallway. I decided it was time to go talk to Humpy Parker about the Foleys and Johnson. After all, the sheriff had seen me sitting in court, and I was sure he would be disappointed if I didn't drop by.

I got there about noon and asked him directly about the November

28, 1981, arrests of Jeffrey Foley and Patsy DeBorde, and about their contention that they had been stopped without probable cause, searched illegally, arrested without cause, and shaken down in the jail. The sheriff jotted down the names and walked out to check his files. He came back and said he could find nothing on them.

Then I asked him about Darrell Johnson. He left again, looked through his files. Same result.

And then he went into a few remarks about his trouble keeping secretaries, and about how two deputies had been off the job with injuries. In a nutshell, he said, his filing system had gone to hell.

How many full-time deputies did he have right then? I asked.

Four, he answered, but that didn't count the two who were injured and not working.

And how many reserve deputies (those part-time officers who work without pay)?

About twenty, he said, and all of them got 103 hours of schooling before they were allowed to go to work.

And what about Deputy Gary Parker, his son?

"He used to be a reserve, but he resigned to run for Democratic party chairman in the election next month." The sheriff seemed a bit nervous about answering questions about his son, but I had a few more that I wanted to ask.

How long did his son work as a deputy?

"Shit, he worked around here all his life," the sheriff said, "through elementary, junior high, and high school, dispatching on weekends and doing things like that. Hell, he grew up around here from the time he was six or seven years old."

And how old was he now?

Twenty-three.

When exactly had he resigned his commission to run for office?

Not sure, but a couple of months ago, Parker said quickly.

I changed the subject just as quickly. Was it unusual to have wrecker trucks sitting out on the highway with his patrol cars? Or was that standard policy?

"They're usually somewhere nearby," he said, "but we don't let them sit out there with us. Hell, we don't want them around. It looks bad."

How many wrecker companies were there in the county?

Five, he said, two in Coldspring, two in Pointblank, one in Shepherd.

Who did most of the towing?

"When we tow someone, we just ask [over the radio] for any available wrecker. We could care less who it is. All are bonded to us in case something gets torn up."

I looked at my watch and said I had to be somewhere else pretty quick, that I had just happened to be passing through and wanted to stop by.

He smiled broadly and asked me to stay and have a cup of coffee. It was one of those I-always-want-to-help-in-any-way-I-can smiles. Nevertheless, I got the feeling that he wanted me to get the heck out of there.

And so I did. I made a quick stop by the courthouse to see if the Longview teenagers had left, and they had. But I had their names, phone numbers, and addresses, and I made myself a note to call them as soon as I could . . . after they'd had a little time to reflect on the events of Wednesday morning, March 3.

I cruised around Coldspring until 1:00, when the courthouse opened up after lunch, and I walked back into the county clerk's office. I got the criminal docket books and began copying down names of people who had been charged with possession of marijuana. The numbers—as the 1980 statistics from the Department of Public Safety had indicated— were staggering. And if what I had been told was accurate, most of those arrests came from Highway 59. I bet all of them had a story to tell about their visits to San Jacinto County by way of U.S. 59 and the county jail. And I wanted to give all of them a chance to talk.

But there was something unusual about the docket books. They were those big, old, clumsy books that most counties stopped using about 1920; all the notations were written by hand in tiny spaces in the books. And all that was listed was the name of the defendant, the docket number, the charge, and the disposition of the charge. Very few of the marijuana possession arrests showed any disposition at all. Most were left "open" or "pending." And—this was odd—there were no addresses, home towns, or telephone numbers for the defendants.

I walked over to Mrs. Trapp and asked where the charging documents—the affidavits sworn by the arresting officers—were kept. She led me back into the cavernlike document room and pointed them out. They were all filed by docket number, she said.

I pulled down two files and began sifting through the contents. The outside covers looked familiar: the State of Texas and County of San Jacinto versus so-and-so. I opened them up and found that all were sworn and attested by Doris Yarbrough, the sheriff's secretary, not by the arresting officers. And the narrative sections on the ones I checked were almost blank. No probable cause was listed. No details of the events leading to the arrests. County attorney Robert Atkins had affixed his signature to all of them.

And then I noticed that only the names of the defendants were listed. No addresses. No home towns. No telephone numbers. No nothing.

Someone didn't want to make it easy to track down these people, I thought. In fact, someone wanted to make it very hard to contact these people, these victims of Highway 59.

And that was just like waving a red flag in front of a pissed-off bull.

· EIGHT ·

The Red Horse Saloon at the Holiday Inn–Livingston began filling up a little before 7:00 p.m. on Wednesday, March 3. It was one of only a handful of places in that dry county where a thirsty oil field worker, or anybody else, could go to match his drinking and dancing skills with those of his peers. Drinking seemed to be winning out over dancing by the time I walked in. For a church night in the Bible Belt, this private watering hole seemed to be doing an extraordinary business.

I felt like doing a little drinking myself. The day had been inordinately hectic, starting with the lengthy session with the high school principal and proceeding to the bizarre county court session, the strange interviews with Sheriff Parker and Judge Bryant, and the hour-long session in the county clerk's office. After finding no records on file to document the arrests of, charges against, and money collected from the Foleys and Darrell Johnson, and after wading through the sketchy affidavits on file against a dozen or more other arrestees, I had left the clerk's dungeon about 2:30 in an awful state of mind. How was I going to prove that the civil rights of Foley and Johnson had been violated when county officials had no documents to show that they were ever there in the first place? As Judge Bryant said, how did I know that they were actually stopped in San Jacinto County? You know how easily some people get mixed up.

Fortunately, I had Mr. Foley's Xerox copies of the bond receipt from Herb Atwood and the towing bill from B&B Wrecker of Shepherd. For Darrell Johnson, I had nothing but his word, which he himself said was the word of a "semi-outlaw." I needed more names, more proof, more information—a lot more, as much as I could get. If I wanted to expose what appeared to be a shakedown operation that involved deputies, bondsmen, and wrecker companies, I was going to have to get on the telephone and track down a heck of a lot more victims. And the records in the county clerk's office were not making my job any easier. How could I possibly find a John Q. Smith who was arrested on November 10 on Highway 59 for having two ounces of marijuana in his possession?

And maybe that wasn't the story anyway. Of all the people who were listed in the criminal docket, how many would complain that their rights were violated? How many had pleaded guilty just to get the heck out of there? How many innocent people are there in the jails and prisons of the world? From my experience, I knew that everyone who was convicted of a crime had a story to tell; there were always extenuating circumstances, alibis, reasons, sudden bursts of insanity, blackouts, drug problems, booze problems, women problems. There was always *something* behind the crime. Maybe the real story of San Jacinto County would lie in people like the Foleys and Johnson, people who were arrested and shaken down but never charged, never contacted, never given a chance for a court hearing. How many people would I find like that? How would I ever find any more people like that?

One way or another, I was going to have to come up with the addresses and phone numbers of people whose addresses and phone numbers were nowhere to be found.

I made my first telephone call about 3:30, to my contact in the U.S. Attorney's Office in Houston. I really needed someone to give me a little boost about then, but my source was too busy to talk more than a few minutes. I told him about the lack of records in San Jacinto County to document the arrests of Foley and Johnson, and he seemed mildly interested. Get a couple dozen like that and call him back, he said, and maybe his office would be interested in taking another look up there. The 1978 federal investigation after the ACLU lawsuit had left some bitter feelings in the U.S. Attorney's Office, and it was going to take an act of God to get them reinterested in that rinky-dink county.

I hung up the phone thinking I was the only person in the world who was excited by this story. I made my second call to Ed Crowell, my city editor, and he seemed to be losing interest, too. He wanted me to come back to Austin early the next day. There were a few local things going on around Austin that he wanted me to help out with. And he wanted me also to start working more or less regularly on Sundays, handling breaking news and other general assignments to bolster the weekend coverage.

Was I being pulled off this story? I asked.

Of course not, he said; there were just some other things that needed to be done locally. I could get back on San Jacinto County later. And at any rate, no one else was working the story.

I hung up the telephone feeling about as dejected as I'd felt in a long time. Was this not a legitimate story? Was Ed starting to show a little impatience? God, I was working this thing as fast as I could, as fast as I dared. I thought he knew that investigative reporting sometimes took a little time. What was I supposed to do, wait until some other news-paper started working on the story, too? Maybe I could call the *Houston Chronicle* and tell them what was going on; if they started investigating, would that make Ed feel any better? Or was it even Ed who was getting impatient? Was he getting pressure from upper management to get some daily-type stories from this high-priced investigative reporter with the long string of writing and editing awards? Maybe the *American-Statesman* wanted me to use all my experience to cover purse snatchings in downtown Austin, or rock concerts on Sundays. The more I thought about Ed's comments the more depressed I became.

I sat there in the middle of my hotel room staring at the telephone. Should I make more calls? Should I bust my butt trying to track down the names of more victims? Did anyone care? My depression slowly changed to anger. I thought about the wars I had waged with top management in Memphis to buy more time for my reporters to in-vestigate stories that I felt had possibilities. Why was Ed becoming impa-tient? Was it money? The *American-Statesman* had a monopoly in Austin, and each day's editions, morning and afternoon, were sixty per-cent or more advertising! Surely that wasn't it.

That damn telephone and I stared at each other for the better part of an hour. It didn't say anything, and neither did I. For one of the few times in my life, I started to feel that I was being used by my boss. City editors, as a rule, are pretty strange people, and their jobs are not easy ones. They have to serve as go-betweens for reporters and top manage-ment, and most of the ones I had worked for tended to side more often with the reporters.

In Fort Worth, at the old *Press*, Mary Crutcher was the city editor, and she was the meanest, roughest, feistiest old woman I had ever seen . . . when it came to getting the news into the newspaper. She got into some of the most gosh-awful arguments, and nearly every time she came firmly down on the side of her reporters. I was one of her reporters for more than two years, and my desk in the newsroom was right next to hers, so I knew what she did and why she did it. News was first with Mary, and diplomacy, timidity, and politics could all just go to hell.

In Memphis, my first city editor was E. B. Blackburn—Ben, as I called him; Blackie, as everyone else called him. He was made right in the Mary Crutcher mold—salty, profane, loud, and interested in getting the news any way he could get it. I became an assistant city editor under Ben in January 1979, and I worked side by side with him until he was promoted by Scripps-Howard to managing editor of the *Rocky Mountain News* in Denver in late 1980. I saw a side of Ben that most reporters never knew existed, and I heard most of his tirades against "goddamn politicians who masquerade as newspapermen." If anyone ever had printer's ink in his blood, Ben did.

Charles Cavagnaro became city editor in Memphis after Ben moved to Colorado, and Charlie moved right in without missing a beat. Where Ben was a student of the English language, and an excellent writer, Charlie was more interested in shuffling reporters around and keeping something going all the time — and damn the language. But he wanted news, and he got it.

All three of my former city editors were hard-news fanatics, and they lived to see their newspaper dig up some bit of corruption or tomfoolery that no other newspaper had. That was their job, and no one could convince them otherwise.

I thought Ed Crowell was the same way, except that he was more soft-spoken, more laid-back. He seemed to be an easygoing person who, nevertheless, expressed an undying interest in getting stories that none of the other media had. He had impressed me from the first time I talked with him over the telephone.

But what was going on now? I had explained to Ed what I had found out, and what I suspected was happening along Highway 59, and what I thought it would take to get the story into print. And he said he needed me back in the office to help out with a bunch of nickel-and-dime stories that any rookie reporter could do. Oh, he never disavowed interest in San Jacinto County and Highway 59 . . . but all that could wait. That highway wasn't going anywhere.

Not going anywhere indeed! And just how the hell many more people were going to be stopped, searched, arrested, harassed, and shaken down while I sat on the story? Did Ed realize that there were real, live people involved in this?

Highway 59 was to all appearances a monstrosity of justice, a back-woods arrest trap of the worst measure. It had survived one civil rights lawsuit and one federal investigation and seemed to be thriving as well as ever. The entire judicial system of this obscure county admittedly was based on that four-lane, twelve-mile stretch of roadway, and that apparently was where most of the sheriff's income came from, from a departmental standpoint. Was I supposed to back off now and let it continue?

I finally worked up enough energy to walk into the Red Horse Saloon a little before 7:00. I ordered a Budweiser and slumped over the bar.

It wasn't long before another Hank Williams song was pounding away.

Thursday morning crashed into me like a freight train without brakes. I guess I must have tipped more than my usual two or three beers. And not only that, but my morning sinus congestion—which I have had about as long as I have been breathing—was operating at 150 percent efficiency. Since I was going to be driving most of the day, I ruled out taking any sinus medicine; that was a surefire way to spend a couple of hours in a deep slumber. Instead, I suffered magnificently.

At least it took my mind off my anger of the previous night. And it gave me a few hours to gather my thoughts while I was blowing my nose. I decided to make a few more telephone calls before packing up Car 8 and heading back to Austin.

There was no way I was going to let go of this story, even if it meant working on my own time to come up with some compelling piece of evidence—or overwhelming numbers of victims—to convince Ed that this was a produceable story, and one that wasn't going to take four years to complete. No one has ever accused me of dragging my feet on an investigation. I don't like wasting time, and I don't like having my time wasted on meaningless assignments. It was no wonder the *American-Statesman* had not won a single substantive investigative or public service award in recent memory. Each year during contest time, the two Dallas newspapers raked in the honors, and that was quite a sore spot among *American-Statesman* staff members, even though the newspaper's editor, Ray Mariotti, had said on several occasions that he was not interested in winning contests, only with covering the news. During my five years in Memphis, I had been used to winning contests *and* covering the news. The two went hand in hand, in my opinion.

I picked up the telephone and called a couple of lawyers in Huntsville, mainly to pick their brains a minute about old cases they might recall in San Jacinto County. Those two telephone calls kept me occupied for almost an hour, but they produced nothing really new, nothing that I could follow up on.

I called a couple of legal services workers, for the same reason. And I got the same result. Everybody knew that something fishy was happening in San Jacinto County, but no one had any real, live, breathing, firsthand evidence. My knowledge of the laws in Texas was limited to what I had seen and observed—not like the law school degree and license to practice law that my wife had—but I knew one thing for certain: you couldn't convict someone, not even a county, on reputation alone. You have to have that firsthand evidence. I had a little bit of firsthand evidence—from the Foleys and Johnson, and from the three Longview teenagers—and I had a whole heck of a lot of gossip and hearsay. In order to establish a pattern of civil rights violations, or a pattern of anything, I was going to need much more.

Finally, about 11:30 a.m., just about the time I had planned to leave
Livingston for one more pass through San Jacinto County and the long
trek home, I finally jarred something loose in the mind of a young legal
services worker whom I had talked with half a dozen times before. I
guess it must have been the pleading tone of voice I used, or my repeated
exhortations, or my fear of losing the story. But the young caseworker
finally remembered something that might help me. She wasn't sure
about any of the details, but she seemed to recall that a couple of years
ago a whole bunch of college students from Huntsville—band members,
a fraternity, or some other organized group—had been involved in a
mass arrest of some sort in San Jacinto County.

Perhaps it was nothing, she said, but she recalled that something
about the arrests was a little unusual—the way the cars were stopped,
the way the charges were handled, the way the cases were disposed.
Something. Something about the arrests was fishy.

"What year?" I asked. "Just give me a date. . . ."

"Sorry. It was a few years ago but could have been as long as five or
six years ago."

"Are you certain they were college kids from Huntsville?"

"Pretty sure."

"Sam Houston State?"

"I think so."

"What were they doing in San Jacinto County?"

"I really don't remember. It was some sort of school function, a party
or something like that."

"At Lake Livingston, maybe?"

"Yeah, I think so."

And then I asked the clincher: "How many students were arrested?"

"Gosh, I think it was about fifteen or twenty."

Now I was excited again. If there was something fishy about a mass
arrest like that, and there were fifteen or twenty eyewitnesses, then I
had my case—rather, my story. But I had one more question to ask
before severing the shaky connection: was the mass arrest reported in
any newspaper, or by radio or TV, after it happened?"

"Are you kidding?" she laughed. "They don't report nothing over
there."

I owed her one, I said.

I thumbed through my Huntsville telephone directory, which I carried in my briefcase along with five or six small-town directories and a
huge stack of notebooks, and turned quickly to Sam Houston State
University. The first number I found for a fraternity house, I called.

I introduced myself to the young man who answered and told him
that I was a newspaper reporter, and that I was trying to track down

an incident a few years back in San Jacinto County in which a bunch of Sam Houston students, possibly fraternity kids, were harassed and arrested by sheriff's deputies. (I embellished a little, hoping to jar his memory.)

He paused and said he'd ask around if I'd hold on for a minute or so.

"Heck, I don't mind at all," I replied quickly.

A little while later, he got back on the phone. "Yeah, there was some kind of bust over at Waterwood sometime last year, but we weren't in it. And no one here knows much about it."

I told him there were fifteen or more students involved.

"I think that's about right," he said. "You ought to check with the Interfraternity Council; they'd know which fraternity was involved."

"Oh, then it definitely was a fraternity?" I asked.

"Oh, yeah, no question about that."

I felt as though I'd just drawn an inside straight. Now I had something to pursue that would give me some victims. Hell, maybe even twenty victims of the same arrest! And if they were all shaken down and harassed. . . .

All I had to do was persuade Ed to let me continue with my investigation.

· NINE ·

The month of March 1982 was one of the most frustrating I have ever spent on a newspaper. I spent the entire month trying to jump off a monotonous and aggravating treadmill of daily stories imposed on me by the city desk. Everyone at the newspaper agreed that Highway 59 was shaping up into a blockbuster story, and I could certainly start back working on it just as soon as I finished whatever fill-in-the-blank story had just been assigned. I covered festivals in parks, shootings, uncountable meetings of the Travis County Commissioners' Court, state court hearings, rugby tournaments, city council sessions, and other assorted minutiae. And I prepared a number of two-phone-call feature stories on religious nuts, faith healers, interstate bicycle riders, and other offbeat subjects. I felt like I had become the "Ripley's Believe It or Not" reporter for the *American-Statesman*. And it was all because I stayed at my desk and tried to track down the names of victims of the Highway 59 operation in San Jacinto County. Every time some oddball walked into the newsroom with a hot news item, Ed or one of his assistants would look up and see me sitting at my desk, usually talking on the telephone; and since I was not working on a story for tomorrow's paper, I obviously could break loose from what I was doing for a few minutes to handle this or that crisis.

I spent most of the month breaking loose for a few minutes. About twice a week I approached Ed about this almost daily ritual, and each time he indicated that it would soon stop. There was always—always—some sort of crisis in the newsroom. Not a week went by when everything proceeded normally, even normally for newspapers, which at their best are usually semichaotic.

But this was the most chaotic type of management I had ever seen. I even coined a phrase for it—management by crisis. It was the old wait-until-something-happens-and-then-react-to-it philosophy. The reporters were griping and whispering much worse than any I had ever seen or heard. With no real competition from newspapers in a fifty-mile radius, the *American-Statesman* had started to degenerate. The most glaring sign was the inordinate number of "team reporting" assignments, in which groups of reporters were pulled aside and given an area to work on: the parole system, growth, the judicial system, legislative issues, and so on. Ed and Maggie Balough, the assistant managing editor, took active roles in these team projects, and the result was pure disorganization. Ed and Maggie wanted reporters to give them outlines, lists of questions, interview dates, and the like. And of course, each reporter was still called on to respond to the regular run of daily crises.

I find it almost miraculous that I was able to do any work at all on San Jacinto County. But I did. Most of it was done either early in the morning or late at night, before Ed got to work or after he left. I did a lot of work at my home, too, much to the displeasure of my family. But doggone it, I was not going to uncover the names of victims while looking through Austin Police Department arrest reports on a Sunday afternoon, or while "covering" a crowd of people at a Zilker Park festival.

At least once a day I made a series of calls to legal service workers, attorneys, and others I had talked with about San Jacinto County. Some of them got a little tired of my repeated calls, and my nagging questions, and my daily pleadings for more and more information. But I had to do it. For one thing, I was afraid that one of the Houston or Dallas newspapers would pick up on the story; I mean, there are honest-to-goodness competing daily newspapers in those two cities, and competition by its very nature makes newspapers more energetic and eager for scoops. I almost hoped that one of those papers would get the story so I could rub the *American-Statesman*'s nose in it, but quite frankly, it would have destroyed me to see this story get away. And I was going to do everything in my power, including making those pesky calls each day, to keep it.

At 2:30 p.m. on March 18, a Thursday, I received a funny telephone call from the editor of the *San Jacinto News-Times*, a woman by the name of Martha Charrey. I was a bit taken aback, especially when she introduced herself and asked me when I was going to be doing my story about the large numbers of marijuana arrests in her county. I didn't know whether to laugh or get angry.

"What makes you think I'm doing a story?" I asked.

Oh, she explained, she had been talking to Sheriff Parker and Judge Bryant and they said I'd been over there a few times asking questions about marijuana arrests.

And?

Well, they had said I was going to write a story, and she just wanted to know when it was going to run and what exactly it was going to say.

I finally burst into laughter. This editor wasn't for real. Or was she? I'd never seen a newspaper, even a weekly like this one, that was so rinky-dink that it would run a story about another newspaper's reporter. I mean, what was there to write? That I'd been over there asking questions? That I'd pulled a few files in the clerk's office? That I'd eaten half of a greasy hamburger at the Dairy Queen? That I had inadvertently tried to talk to someone during the sacred lunch hour? The possibilities were too ludicrous to consider. No newspaper was that hard up for stories.

I decided to pump her for information. It couldn't hurt. So I talked with Martha Charrey for almost an hour, and she turned out to be an intelligent, conscientious person who was running a one-person operation on the little weekly newspaper. She said she had seen a lot of bizarre things going on, but she didn't know how to approach them, much less write about them. And even if she tried to write about them, she said, her publisher might not run them. In a nutshell, she wanted to help me any way she could.

I promised to keep in touch, but I didn't volunteer any information about what I was doing. You never know when someone who calls out of the blue like that is actually trying to undermine your efforts. For all I knew, Sheriff Parker had told Martha to call and pump me for information . . . or try to steer me in the wrong direction.

But there was something about her tone of voice, her willingness to answer general questions about her county, her eagerness to voice opinions about county officials, that made me believe she was sincere. I took down her office and home telephone numbers and put a star by them. At a later date I planned to test her to see where her loyalties stood, with the news or with the county. Some small-town reporters can be very defensive when outside newsmen come waltzing into their territory. I had seen plenty of them, and most were just "good news" reporters who wrote about weddings and civic meetings and high school football games, and never looked beneath the surface on any issue. Was Martha Charrey one of them? I had to wait to find out.

By the end of March, I had pieced together enough information to know that at least eight members of a fraternity at Sam Houston State had been arrested in November 1980 during a formal party at Waterwood, the massive Horizon Corporation development on Lake Livingston. I had reason to believe that the fraternity was Pi Kappa Alpha, and from what I could learn during sporadic telephone calls, there was something strange about the arrests. A roadblock of some sort had been set up, and only the members of that fraternity had been arrested. Other motorists, including the members of other fraternities, were allowed to pass. My information wasn't firsthand, but it was solid enough to convince me that the incident had happened, and that a lot of people were still upset about it. And, of course, there had been no news coverage of the arrests.

There was more. I had learned from several citizens of neighboring counties that San Jacinto deputies often fired shots at cars to get them to stop, and that one such episode had led to a federal court lawsuit in Houston. Again, I had no details, but the reports themselves came to me from several different people, none of whom knew the others, and I thought there was probably something to them. I knew that a policeman who fired shots at a citizen without probable cause, and without good reasons for using deadly force, could be charged with assault to murder. That, in my judgment, was a serious offense. And if it occurred with some regularity, then my story was going to be better than I had thought.

Even Ed couldn't argue with that. I believe he was finally starting to realize that there was more to this story than just a bail bond office that someone said was operating inside the jail. When I mentioned the various reports of deputies shooting at innocent people, Ed seemed to awake from his slumber:

"Don't you think it's about time to go back over there?" he asked.

I was back in the ball game again. And it had taken only three and a half weeks.

On Thursday, April 1, as I was making plans to journey over to East Texas for the third time, I got another phone call, this one from a preacher I had talked with on more than one occasion about Highway 59. The preacher, who had a fairly large church in the general area of San Jacinto County, had been very sympathetic toward my story and my efforts to obtain information where no information was readily obtainable. He wanted to help me in any way he could, short of running afoul of county officials and deputies who belonged to his church. He had talked on numerous occasions with worried young people who had been the victims of shakedowns and other illicit shenanigans that were staged by deputies and other law enforcement officers. He was troubled by what he saw in and around the Public Safety Building in Coldspring.

He called me a little after 4:00 p.m. in an agitated state. The sheriff's Highway 59 operation was out of control, he said, and people were being arrested and shaken down at a rate that defied belief. As a minister and leader in the community, he was offended. "Something has got to be done about this," he said. But that wasn't the real reason he called. He hadn't heard from me in several weeks and was worried that I had dropped my investigation.

"I'm afraid where this whole thing is going to lead if someone doesn't do something," he said. "Those of us who live and work here are extremely unhappy, but there's not a lot we can do. We see things going on that make us sick, and we realize that they can enforce the laws any way they want . . . as long as no one pulls the curtain down on them."

"I'll be over there the first of next week," I promised.

Less than thirty minutes later, I finally made connection with the student legal adviser at Sam Houston State. I had been trying to track down Adele Simpson for at least three weeks—between daily assignments for the city desk and team reporting assignments for Ed and Maggie. When I finally reached her in her office, she seemed a trifle reluctant to talk, a bit apprehensive about my questions.

I explained carefully that I was looking into some complaints about the sheriff's department in San Jacinto County, and that I had heard reports that a number of Sam Houston students had been on the receiving end of some questionable arrests.

She hesitated before answering, and then, with a slight chuckle, said, "I guess you know it's open season over there on college students. The story around here is that it's worse than the law west of the Pecos."

Could she be more specific? Any specific incidents?

Another pregnant pause. She explained that she had to represent a lot of those kids, and the information she had taken from them could not be divulged because of the attorney-client relationship.

What about the Pi Kappa Alpha arrests in November 1980?

"Yes, that happened," she said. "They arrested about seventeen or eighteen of them at the entrance to Waterwood on Highway 190. It was a fraternity party."

Was there anything unusual about the arrests?

Silence.

Anything specific about them that would be of interest to a reporter looking into that county?

"I'd really rather not go into any detail about that. All I know is that a couple of my clients, and the parents of one or two of them, were very irate, and they indicated that they might be filing a lawsuit at some point. I don't know if they ever filed it."

She was a stickler about attorney-client privilege, but I asked if she could simply give me some names of students who were involved in the mass arrest.

Another pause.

"Look, all I really want is names," I said.

She finally agreed to call up a few of the students "at a later date" and see if they wanted to talk to me. If they did, she would give them my number.

Well, that ended that. I thanked her for her time and "trouble," and I looked in my Huntsville directory for the address of the Pi Kappa Alpha house. I jotted it down and placed it at the top of the itinerary for my third trip.

And then I did something that I hadn't done in the more than two months I had been at the *American-Statesman*, and the eleven weeks I'd been working on San Jacinto County: I left the office before 6:00, drove straight home, popped open a cold beer, deposited myself in front of the television set, and took the next three days off.

The trip was on for Monday, April 5. I wanted to have a few days to gather my thoughts for what I hoped would be my last trip to that part of the state, at least on this story. If I could nail down the fraternity bust and pinpoint a couple of unjustified shootings by deputies, I'd just about have my ducks in a row, and then I could start shooting them down in print. Even Ed agreed.

I left the office a few minutes after 6:30 a.m. on Monday, April 5. I was in a great frame of mind. Nothing was going to spoil this trip for me, nothing was going to intrude, interrupt, or otherwise detract from my two primary goals: to talk to every fraternity person arrested in the Waterwood incident, and to come up with at least two incidents in which deputies opened fire on motorists without probable cause. Perhaps I was optimistic in believing I could do both in one trip; but after all, the two previous trips to Coldspring had been fishing expeditions. This time was different. I had done all the preliminary work that needed to be done. I had the names and details of three bizarre arrests in that county—the Foleys, Darrell Johnson, and the three Longview teenagers. And I could establish a pattern of harassment and civil rights violations, of sorts, from those incidents and from the previous ACLU action and the investigations by the FBI and the U.S. attorney. And, last *and* least, I had bucketfuls of secondhand information from lawyers, legal services workers, county residents, prosecutors, preachers, and others.

What more could I want? How about a couple of trigger-happy deputies? Or a mass shakedown of college students? Yeah, this trip was going to be a good one, and I'd wrap it up in three or four days, cruise back to the office, and write a dynamite story.

I made excellent time. I passed through Navasota about 9:00, and I zipped past Conroe about thirty minutes later. My destination again was the Holiday Inn–Livingston, and I estimated that I'd be checking in by 11:00. But I was wrong. I signed in at the motel at exactly 11:07 a.m. I never was any good at time estimates. Anyway, I had the whole rest of the day to set up interviews with fraternity kids, check in with all my contacts, touch base with Mr. Foley, Darrell Johnson, and the Longview teenagers, call the worried preacher, cruise around Huntsville, pass by the courthouse in Coldspring, jot down more names from the docket books, say hello to Judge Bryant and the gang, and still get back to the Holiday Inn before dark.

But the first call I made was to an attorney in Huntsville by the name of Harry Walsh, a former assistant state attorney general who was now in private practice. According to several sources, Walsh was handling at least one federal court lawsuit involving San Jacinto County, and he was supposed to be extremely knowledgeable about what was going on over there. I had been trying for two weeks to track him down—again, between daily stories for the city desk and team projects for Ed and Maggie. I got lucky; I reached Walsh almost immediately.

He was a pleasant-sounding man who was aware of the fact that I had been trying to contact him. It was no big mystery how he found out: I had dropped enough hints to other Huntsville lawyers who were sympathetic with my efforts to find out everything I could about San Jacinto County. Walsh, according to just about everyone, was the man to talk to. Everyone was right.

Walsh was indeed representing a man who had been terrorized by the law west of the Pecos as practiced north of Houston. And he had filed a civil rights lawsuit in federal court in Houston in late 1981. The suit was filed against Rathell Denson, a constable in Precinct 4 in San Jacinto County. The plaintiff, Walsh's client, was currently a first-year law student at Texas Tech University in Lubbock; at the time of his arrest, he had been a student at Sam Houston State. The incident occurred at approximately 10:30 p.m. on December 13, 1980, as the young student, Don Rhodes, was driving west on U.S. 190 from Lake Livingston.

"Rhodes was coming back to Huntsville on 190 when he crested a hill and saw a car stopped in the middle of the highway," Walsh said. "He swerved and barely avoided having a collision. Denson got out of the other car, which was unmarked and had its lights off, and Denson himself was not wearing any type of uniform and did not attempt to identify himself. He made some belligerent statements to my client and was walking over to my client's car with something in his hand, apparently a pistol.

"Rhodes decided at that point that he was in the clutches of a crazy man and drove away as quickly as he could."

The constable, according to Walsh and the lawsuit, then fired several gunshots at the college student's pickup while chasing it at high speeds in his own vehicle. The chase crossed the county line into Walker County, where Rhodes crashed his vehicle into a car parked off the roadway at a house. The student, who had been shot at several times during the chase, jumped out of his pickup, ran to the house, pounded on the door, and told the woman who answered to call the police, that someone was trying to kill him. "The woman in the house got so terrified that she became sick," Walsh said.

Several highway patrolmen, Walker County sheriff's officers, and Huntsville police officers arrived within minutes—along with officers from San Jacinto County. After the officers determined that Denson was himself a deputy, they decided to charge Rhodes with evading arrest and with passing on the wrong side of the road. The passing charge was thrown out almost immediately by a justice of the peace, Walsh said, and the resisting-arrest charge was dismissed several weeks later. When the two criminal charges against Rhodes were dropped, Walsh added, he filed the civil rights suit in U.S. district court in Houston.

Had San Jacinto County responded to that lawsuit? I asked.

It had. The response was filed in November 1981.

What was the response?

"Basically, they said that Denson was performing his duties as a police officer. And they said that my client pleaded guilty to the charges, which is absolutely ridiculous."

What was the current status of the suit?

"We're attempting right now to try to get together for depositions. Both the FBI and Walker County investigated the handling of the case, and they wanted to know why Denson didn't radio for help, if he was doing his duties as an officer. I understand he said his radio was broken."

I jotted down the docket number of the lawsuit and made a note to check it out in the U.S. district court clerk's office in Houston. And since I had Walsh on the line, I decided to question him about his knowledge of the judicial system in San Jacinto County. Had he heard many complaints about the way the laws were enforced, or not enforced, over there?

Like so many others I'd talked with, Walsh gave a slight laugh. He said he had represented several people who were upset about the way they were treated by the San Jacinto County Sheriff's Department. He said he could not give me any names yet because of possible further legal action on his part, but some of the things he had heard "would make you sick."

While he was working for the attorney general's office, had he had any contact with San Jacinto County? Was he aware of the 1978 FBI investigation?

Yes to both questions. He knew that the FBI had been in San Jacinto County at one time, but he said that investigation was "a complete joke" as far as he could tell.

What made him say that? I asked.

He explained that the FBI agents, before talking to one person in the county, printed a little notice in the *San Jacinto News-Times* announcing that they were going to be in the county to investigate wrongdoing in the sheriff's office. And the notice said the agents would use as their base of operations an office in the Bank of San Jacinto County, which, of course, was located across the street from the courthouse. Anyone with a complaint or gripe could just come on over to the bank, which was run by former state representative Jim Browder, a bail bondsman who, according to Walsh, was a friend of the sheriff's. "That's why I say it was a complete joke, and as a consequence, they never got any significant information," he said.

What about his own personal ideas about the sheriff?

Well, he said, while he was employed by the attorney general, he and several other lawyers had been in Huntsville working on a major case and decided to drive out to Waterwood for lunch one weekend. They hopped into a car with the words "Attorney General" on the side and exempt license plates on the front and back. When they got to the restaurant, there apparently was a big bingo game going on, and a San Jacinto County deputy was standing out in the road directing traffic. "The deputy asked us, 'Are you folks here to gamble or to eat?' It was pretty incredible. He could see that we were from the AG's office. It was just his attitude, the idea. They are just so open and notorious about everything they do over there."

Was he aware of any incidents involving Sam Houston students?

He was. He said there were several reports that fraternities who went into that county on organized outings would wind up arrested for little or no reason, hauled off to jail, and forced to post bond to get out.

Anything specific?

Possibly, he said, but he'd have to check further.

I changed the subject and asked if he knew anything about the drug problem in that county.

"You mean the marijuana plantations?" he asked.

What?

"This is just from what I have heard from several reliable and knowl-edgeable people, but there are supposed to be some very large marijuana fields on the west bank of the Trinity River, or in the river bottoms around there. There is a creek by the name of Huffman Creek that is supposed to run through part of the land. . . . It would take a helicopter to spot it, but if you fly over that area—and this is reliable information—you'll find some open areas with some strange-looking crops."

I must have sounded like a sputtering four-cylinder engine about then. But if I could prove what Walsh was saying, then I'd have an even bigger story than I already had. I coughed a few words of thanks and asked if he minded if I checked back with him periodically.

No problem, he said.

I hung up the phone and began pacing nervously. If there were large dope fields—plantations—then someone else had to know about them. Maybe a lot of people knew about them. But did the sheriff's office know? Was there any connection between these so-called marijuana plantations and the huge numbers of dope arrests on Highway 59? What in the heck was going on over there?

I got back on the telephone and called a private investigator whom Walsh had recommended, a Huntsville man by the name of Lee Mackey. According to Walsh, Mackey probably had a great deal of information about the arrests of fraternity kids in San Jacinto County. I reached Mackey a few minutes before 1:00 p.m. and explained that I'd been talking with Walsh about San Jacinto County, and that Walsh had indicated he might have some information about an arrest involving a group of kids at a fraternity party.

"Which one? Several fraternities and sororities from Sam Houston have had problems over there. You could pick any one and check on them." He explained that he worked with students occasionally as part of his job as a private investigator, and that he knew from experience that "they flat don't like outsiders in that county."

He said a game warden had recently stopped a group of college kids coming out of Waterwood in a pickup with a gun rack, and a shotgun in the rack. The truck had a spotlight under the front seat. "Now, this was in the middle of the day, but the game warden stopped them, searched the car, found the spotlight, and nailed them for hunting at night. . . . That kind of stuff goes on day and night over there. It's pret-ty disgusting," he said.

Did he know about the mass arrest involving students from Pi Kappa Alpha?

"Oh, yeah. They actually had a roadblock set up in that one, and they were pulling people and cars left and right. You did know, didn't you, that the sheriff's department dispatcher over there also dispatches for the towing companies? They even use the same radio frequency."

I didn't know that. But what about the Pi Kappa Alpha arrests?

"Just go over to the frat house and ask around," he said. "That way you'd be getting it straight from the horse's mouth."

Next, I decided to see how helpful Martha Charrey, the newspaper editor, wanted to be. I called her around 1:45 and asked point-blank if she knew about any incidents in which deputies opened fire on motorists, and I specifically mentioned the lawsuit involving Rathell Denson.

She wasn't aware of the suit, but. . . . She paused a few seconds and said she recalled a couple of incidents: one, which she said happened "a few years ago," involved a deputy who was chasing three young kids in an unmarked vehicle. She said the deputy fired several shots, one of which struck his own vehicle. The other incident, she said, involved Bud Parker, the sheriff's brother, the head of security at Waterwood. She said Parker "a while back" shot at a car filled with high school students, and even put holes in their car before they stopped. In both of those cases, she said, the kids were not aware that they were being pursued by law officers.

That was similar to the Denson case, I said. Did she write stories on them?

"No, I couldn't," she said. "No information was ever released on them."

Any other incidents of violence involving deputies? What about suspicious shootings, beatings, things like that?

She paused another five or ten seconds. "Oh, we have had a little problem over the last five or six years with several young boys being found dead along the side of the road—"

I interrupted. "Dead? What do you mean, dead?"

"It was a big thing for a couple of years. These boys were found dead on the side of the roads late at night and nothing was ever done about them—"

Again I interrupted. "Nothing was ever done? What do you mean?"

"Well, all of them were found on the side of the road. One of them had his head run over. All of them were killed by cars, or hit-and-run drivers, but there were never any arrests, and there were never any clues. And all of them happened late at night. There was never a great deal of information released about them, either."

How many young boys were killed this way?

"At least five . . . one of them was Charles Hogue. He was found up on 946 near Oakhurst. His mother works right here in Coldspring in the county clerk's office. The Hogue boy was a high school student."

So they were all killed mysteriously by hit-and-run drivers, no arrests, no clues, no information—and all late at night, and all were young boys. . . . "What else do you know about them?" I asked.

"Only the fact that the sheriff said all of them had drug problems."

· TEN ·

My investigation of the San Jacinto County Sheriff's Department—
exactly eleven weeks old on April 5—had suddenly changed course.
And one phone call had done it. After three months, three lengthy
forays into the forests of Southeast Texas, fifty or more interviews, hundreds of telephone calls, an endless string of sleepless nights and tension
headaches, I unexpectedly found myself staring at the specter of dead
bodies. Suddenly the harassment of motorists along Highway 59 no
longer seemed so earth-shattering. Suddenly the reports of deputies
shooting at motorists no longer appeared so dramatic. Suddenly the
story about the marijuana plantations along the Trinity River no longer
sent chill bumps down my back. Suddenly I was apprehensive—"scared"
is a better word. All I had was the word of a small-town weekly newspaper editor, who said she herself was quite disturbed by the mysterious
deaths of young boys in her county. But what disturbed her more was
the quick connection with drugs that the sheriff's department made
with each death—and the use of that dope connection to soft-pedal the
official investigations, if indeed there were any official investigations.
Martha Charrey seemed genuinely upset by it all. And so was I.

The first thing I did after hanging up the telephone, and pacing
around the motel room, was to call the city desk and ask to speak with
Ed. This was not the kind of information a reporter should sit on, hoping to develop it later.

I explained my information in detail, down to the last syllable of my
conversation with Martha Charrey. "I think I may have a whole
different ball game over here," I said.

Ed agreed, but he wasn't quite sure what he wanted me to do.

I suggested that I stick around Livingston for at least another day,
nailing down the mass arrest of the Sam Houston fraternity boys and
perhaps checking more on the reports of unjustified shootings by

deputies. But I said I was not prepared at that point to start nosing around in piles of death certificates, car accident reports, or anything of that nature. All of those reports would be kept either in the county clerk's office or at the sheriff's department in Coldspring. I didn't want to be poking my nose in places where people could see what I was looking at. As a matter of fact, I didn't even want to go back into Coldspring, at least not yet. It's better to be overcautious than foolhardy.

Ed absolutely agreed with me. He advised me to proceed with extreme caution, to check out the fraternity bust and then head back to Austin, and then we'd sit down and figure out how to investigate the mysterious deaths.

I had an idea about how I might be able to sound out a reliable source about the mysterious deaths without tipping off someone who didn't need to be tipped off. I told Ed I'd call him back later in the day. It was about 2:30 p.m. I'd been in Livingston three and a half hours and already I felt like the Highway 59 story was mushrooming right before my eyes. My earlier plans for a quick trip, a quick cleanup investigation, and a quick exit had dissolved. So had my great frame of mind.

My very next call was to Harry Walsh. If he knew enough to talk about reports of marijuana plantations near the Trinity River, then maybe he had heard a wild rumor or two about some strange hit-and-run deaths late at night on the twisting back roads of San Jacinto County.

I apologized for bothering him again so soon, but something had come up that I needed to check out with him. Did he know of any weird, unsolved hit-and-run deaths?

Without hesitating, he replied: "There are stories floating around that . . . deputies or others may have caused at least one or more fatal accidents. I know there was a bad one within the last two years. . . . The Walker County sheriff has some strong opinions about this. Actually, the people who work in law enforcement in Walker County have a very low opinion of San Jacinto County. You might want to talk with them. You might try to talk with them; I don't know if they'd talk to you."

He didn't seem eager to go into more detail—or perhaps he didn't have any more information. He did, however, give me the name of an FBI agent who had been through San Jacinto County on more than one occasion and suggested that I call him.

I thanked him for his help—again. He said it looked like I was onto something, and he wished me luck.

Next, I placed another call to Lee Mackey, the private investigator, to see if he knew any Walker County deputies or policemen who might help me with my story.

He did. "You might want to try to talk to Charlie Pierce about what's going on. He's a sheriff's deputy here in Huntsville, and he lives over in San Jacinto County. I know he's pretty concerned about all the stuff that's been happening."

Mackey didn't have a number, but I said I'd be able to get it.

By then it was close to 3:00. My next move was to call the Pi Kappa Alpha house on Sixteenth Street in Huntsville to sound out a couple of the fraternity brothers about the arrests in Waterwood.

The young guy who answered the phone call knew about all the arrests, but he hadn't been involved. He said I'd be better off if I called back after 7:00 p.m. that day and talked to Kevin Ashcraft.

Was he one of the ones who got harassed and arrested? I asked, trying to sound like I knew for a fact that they had been harassed.

"Oh, yeah. He was there. He knows all about it."

I finally had my first name. It should have excited me, and except for Martha Charrey's revelation about the dead boys, it probably would have.

I wandered around Livingston and the northern part of San Jacinto County for the next couple of hours, not really looking for anything in particular, and I contacted Ashcraft a little before 7:00 that evening. He was a senior at Sam Houston and would be graduating in about a month. He knew all about the Waterwood incident, and he was still upset about it.

"I'll never forget it as long as I live. It was homecoming, and we had a party out at Waterwood. It was the night of November 24, 1980. It was a formal party and everyone was all dressed up; Delta Tau Delta [another fraternity] was there, and everyone was having a good time. No one got real drunk or anything. Yeah, there was drinking, but you don't get bombed when you've got dates to take back and everyone's all dressed up. . . . Anyway, when it got where it was time to leave, we went out, and, you know, the little sisters had written with shoe polish on the cars. There were a bunch of cars, but only the Pike cars had shoe polish on them.

"They had this roadblock set up down on 190 and they were stopping all the cars, but they were only arresting the guys with shoe polish on their cars. Not any of the other fraternities were arrested. I don't know how, but I went through all the traffic and got on 190 and got all the way to Oakhurst. I was a half-mile from Walker County when they stopped me. I was going fifty-five, I know, because I had my cruise control set. Parker's son was the deputy and he said it looked like I was weaving a little bit. I said I wasn't, and then he said I was going too fast, and I said that wasn't right either. He asked me if he took me to Coldspring if I'd take a breath test, and I said no, because I didn't like what they were doing. But they took me anyway. He handcuffed me and frisked me. And a tow truck was there in fifteen seconds. . . . They impounded my car. I asked him why he was handcuffing me and he said, 'To keep you from hurting yourself.' He drove me to Coldspring at at least ninety-five miles an hour. They were bringing in my fraternity brothers when I got to the jail. And they kept trying to get me to take the breath test, but I wasn't going to. The trusties in the jail said the sheriff's people had been planning the bust all week."

Ashcraft said he called his dad from the jail, and that his father paid $100 to a bondsman to get him out. The bondsman was Jim Browder. He later paid another $260 to the sheriff's department, and $80 for towing.

"It seemed like the whole town was in on it. They had a whole bunch of wrecker trucks, cops, bail bondsmen, and a lot of other people. They all thought it was real funny."

Ashcraft said that although he supposedly was stopped because he was weaving in the roadway, the arrest report said he was stopped because a taillight was out. "I know for a fact that the light was working," he said. The official charge was DWI. In all, eight Pikes were arrested, not ten, not fifteen, not twenty.

"I was scared to death about this, and I got myself a lawyer. He went in there a little while later and went over to the sheriff's department and got all the DWIs reduced to public intoxication. No one ever went before any judge. It was all handled there in the sheriff's office. We paid cash for our fines, got a cash ticket, and got the hell out of there. I bet ten to one that they never sent any of it on to the State of Texas, which is fine with me. But you know, they said they were trying to bust everyone for drugs, and they sure as heck searched all the cars pretty good, and they especially searched one of the vans."

He detailed the frantic searches of cars and the comments of deputies about marijuana. And then he stopped momentarily and added, "You know, when I got out to my car after seeing that report about my taillight being out, my damn light was kicked in. There was still glass and stuff inside the light area. And there were a bunch of others who said their taillights were busted when they picked up their cars. . . . Everyone knew what was going down. They had tow trucks all over the place. And this was a formal party—suits and ties and evening dresses and all that. . . . It was a set-up deal to arrest a bunch of college kids. I guess they needed the money."

He gave me the other seven names and told me how I could get in touch with them. A few had already graduated, and a couple were no longer living in Huntsville. We talked for another fifteen or twenty minutes, long enough for me to realize that he was still angry about the arrest. But he didn't know what to do. He hadn't heard from the county since the arrest. Apparently the entire night's arrests of fraternity boys had been handled out of court—with cash fines, fees, or whatever being paid directly to the sheriff's secretary, who handed the students cash receipts. The same pattern as the other arrests I had checked. The secretary who had signed Ashcraft's receipt was Cindy McCash.

I asked Ashcraft if he had had any further dealings with the sheriff. "Man, I haven't been through San Jacinto County since that night, and I don't intend to, even if I have to drive a hundred miles out of my way. It's a bad experience to go through," he replied.

I told him I'd let him know if I found anything that might help him later, in case he decided to file a lawsuit. It was close to 8:00 p.m., and I had my names of fraternity boys. All I had to do now was track the rest down and get their stories.

And that was how I spent most of Tuesday, April 6. But the first call I made about 8:15 a.m. was to the Department of Public Safety headquarters in Austin; I wanted to update my figures on drug arrests in San Jacinto County. The 1981 figures were supposed to be ready, and all I had were the incredible numbers from 1980: 757 drug arrests. When the latest numbers were recited, I could see what I was up against. The six San Jacinto deputies and twenty reserves had made 1,124 drug arrests in 1981, second only to the 1,172 arrests made by the 706 sheriff's deputies in Harris County. San Jacinto County made more drug arrests than the sheriff's deputies in Dallas County (102 arrests in 1981), Travis County (314), El Paso County (86), and Bexar County (265). How were they making so many drug arrests in such a backwoodsy, isolated county? And what was happening to the drugs that were being confiscated? And why was no one but me looking into those numbers? A quick bit of work on my pocket calculator indicated that San Jacinto County's twenty-six deputies and reserves would each have to make forty-three drug arrests a year to total 1,124; and the grand total of 1,124 broke down to more than three drug arrests a day for the entire calendar year. For a county with less than 11,500 people, those numbers were beyond belief.

Over the next twelve hours, I managed to contact three of the other fraternity boys picked up in the Waterwood arrests, and that meant I had interviewed half of the eight arrestees. Their stories were the same; their indignation, anger, and fear varied only in intensity.

The first one I reached was Glenn Campbell, a close friend of Ashcraft's who was riding with him the night of the bust. He confirmed Ashcraft's story about the stop in Oakhurst by Gary Parker, the sheriff's son, and the diligent search of the car for drugs. "I got lucky," he said. "They couldn't get me for DWI because I was a passenger in the car. They got me for public intoxication, and it only cost me $50. They held a couple of us overnight and said someone would be coming in the next morning to take our pleas.

"It was a woman who took our pleas and took our money, and she is the one who wrote me the receipt."

I asked if he remembered the woman's name, and he said he thought her first name was Cindy.

Cindy McCash?

"Man, I don't remember. But I don't think it was McCash, because there was a woman deputy who had that name, and I don't think it was the same one. But she was the one who told me I'd have to pay a $50 fine. I paid it just to get out of there. It was pretty obvious that they had set us up."

Did the woman who set his fine refer to herself as Judge?

"Yeah, she did."

What did she look like?

"Well, she was an older woman . . . but I don't remember much more about her."

The only female judge in San Jacinto County was Lucille Wolfe, a justice of the peace. Her precinct included part of the area around Lake Livingston. Was that who it was?

He just didn't know. But he thought his receipt was signed by Cindy McCash. He said he'd look around for his receipt and let me know.

Later, I tracked down Glenn Urquhart, another Pike who was picked up that night. He was a little more upset about the arrest, and his memory was a little better, too. The money he had expended to get out of the county was the main thing that troubled him.

"I paid a $250 fine that went straight to the sheriff's secretary. I paid $45 for the wrecker that towed me. And I paid another $50 to a bonds-man. And later on I had another $250 in attorney's fees to get the DWI charge reduced to public intoxication," he said. "I was one of the first taken, and I stayed in there about twelve hours before they let me go. They had a roadblock set up, and when I drove up they asked if we were Pikes or Delts. I said we were Pikes, and they said, 'Let's take 'em in.' They let the Delts go through. From what I've heard, Parker's son used to be a Delt, and that's why they didn't arrest any of them. I don't know that for a fact.

"I remember that they insisted I had to pay everything in cash. They were real strong on that. When they brought me in, they said my bond was $1,000, but I don't know who decided on that. The bondsman was

Jim Browder, and he charged me $50 instead of the usual $100. I don't know why he did that. The judge was an older woman who came in on Sunday morning."

Was the judge Cindy McCash, the sheriff's secretary?

"No, it wasn't her, because she was the one who escorted me to the judge. It was just some older woman. I know I paid my money to Cindy. . . . It's all in my memory, and I won't ever be able to get it out. I was pretty mad during it all. I threatened to bring Racehorse Haynes up here and bust up the whole county, and they moved pretty fast to reduce my DWI to public intoxication."

Did he get receipts for the money he paid to Cindy McCash, to Browder, and to the towing company?

"They told some of us that in a week or so we'd be getting our receipts in the mail, but we never got nothing from them."

Was anything damaged on his vehicle when he picked it up?

"The taillight was busted out—kicked in."

Galen Busse was the third Pike I reached that day. He, too, was only a passenger in one of the cars, and his charge on the front end was public intoxication. His total fine was $53.50.

"This whole thing was strange from the start," he said. "Number one, the place where they arrested us was strange. I used to work at Waterwood, and I never saw a cop car out there. And then, they never said why they were stopping us. They just stopped the cars, asked if we were Pikes, and they arrested us. The girls were not arrested. We got put in the drunk tank with a bunch of other people, and nearly all of them said they'd been stopped because their taillights were out."

He volunteered comments about the thorough searches of the cars, the quick arrival of the tow trucks—"There were a bunch of them sitting there waiting to hitch up and haul us away"—and the next-day appearance before a female judge. He also said that a dozen or more Delts were allowed to pass through the roadblock without a hassle.

Had he heard any more from San Jacinto County since that day?
No.

Did he feel like the Pikes were singled out for arrest?
Yes.

Did he pay his money to Cindy McCash?
Yes.

Busse said a lot of Sam Houston students got hassled by San Jacinto deputies, and that most of them—at least since the arrests at Waterwood—now stayed out of there, away from Lake Livingston. It was not a safe county for a college student, he said.

Was there anything else he recalled that might be of some help to me?
I asked.

He thought a minute and said, "Well, I was never fingerprinted, never
photographed, and never asked to sign anything."

I made a note of that. In most counties, prisoners in the jail had to
sign for their personal belongings when they were released, and defendants in court are routinely asked to sign various documents when they
enter a plea, pay a fine, or post bail. But not in this county.

As I sat on the edge of the bed, thumbing through my notes and
gathering my thoughts, I added up the fines, bail bonds, and towing fees
paid by the four fraternity boys I had interviewed: They came to
$888.50. Not bad for a night's work in the Coldspring jail. If the other
four arrestees paid a similar amount, it was *really* a good haul for the
county. I just wondered how often they pulled roadblocks like that, and
whether the take was the same in each case.

I was convinced that I was close to nailing down this particular incident, which, when coupled with the three others I already had under
my belt, made a pretty interesting tale. But was it the real story of San
Jacinto County? Those dead boys were bothering the hell out of me.

· ELEVEN ·

The drive from Livingston to Austin the next afternoon, April 7, was nauseating. Maybe it was an exhaust leak in the creaky *American-Statesman* car, or maybe it was the buffet breakfast I tore into at the Holiday Inn—scrambled eggs, soggy toast, hash browns, bacon, sausage, sweet rolls, orange juice, and coffee. It was a nice spread, and all for under $4. I ate more than was legally allowable for a news reporter on an out-of-town assignment. At the time I ate—7:30 a.m.—the food was great. I was hungry and had just realized that I had forgotten to eat anything the previous night. I started feeling the effects about two hours later, as I was sitting in my room looking over my notes and making a series of telephone calls. I wanted to double-check a few things from the day before—Tuesday, April 6, a day that marked the turning point in my investigation of San Jacinto County, the day when I first started worrying seriously about what might be going on in that dinky little county north of Houston.

After almost three hours on the telephone, I was able to get some details regarding what Martha Charrey had told me about the mysterious deaths of young boys. From funeral homes, preachers, the Department of Public Safety, and a couple of other seemingly objective sources, I knew, first, that a seventeen-year-old boy named Charles M. Hogue had been killed on May 13, 1979, about 1:50 a.m. by a hit-and-run driver along FM 946 near Oakhurst. And I knew that no arrests had been made in that death. I knew that a twenty-year-old named Joe Lynn Pickering had been killed on October 6, 1979, about 12:15 a.m. on a back road in the southern part of San Jacinto County; again, no arrests were reported. I knew that a sixteen-year-old boy, Jimmy Speer, had been killed near the site of the Pickering death on August 24, 1980, about 3:30 a.m., when he was run over by his mother, who said the boy was apparently lying in the road; the mother, Josephine Speer had been no-billed by a grand jury. I knew that a twenty-four-year-old man, Bill Stone, had been struck but not killed by a hit-and-run driver on U.S. 190. And I knew that there had been two bizarre pedestrian deaths just outside San Jacinto County: Danny Kinder, age twenty-five, was struck and killed by a hit-and-run driver while walking along a back road at 3:15 a.m. in Montgomery County on August 11, 1978, and no arrests were ever made; and another twenty-five-year-old, Raymond Earl Vandver, was struck and killed by a car at 3:30 a.m. on March 1, 1981, on a farm road in Liberty County, and the twenty-one-year-old male driver of the car said Vandver was sitting in the roadway.

There had been two other pedestrian deaths that I could track down during the last five years in San Jacinto County, and both of them had been solved by arrests. One of the victims, a twenty-four-old man named Douglas Liuzzo, was killed while walking along Highway 59 at 4:20 a.m. on October 12, 1979. He was struck by a chicken truck. Liuzzo was reported to have been standing in the roadway. The other, a sixteen-year-old girl named Helen Currie, was killed about 3:00 p.m. on Highway 59 in Shepherd. The seventy-six-year-old woman driver of the car reported that the girl was walking along the roadway.

It was a hectic morning on the telephone. I had come up with names, dates, and sketchy details on seven deaths over a three-and-a-half-year span. All of the victims were pedestrians, and all but one of the deaths occurred late at night or early in the morning. And I had an eighth incident involving a pedestrian and a hit-and-run driver in the accident that critically injured Bill Stone on Highway 190. But what did all this mean? From what I could put together, the only deaths that were still listed as being unsolved were the accidents involving Hogue, Pickering, and Kinder. The others sounded a bit strange, but they were not in the unsolved hit-and-run category.

I thought about all this during the entire trip back to Austin. And so I guess it was a combination of factors that made this drive unusually uncomfortable for me—the buffet breakfast, the deaths, and the creaky economy car. I stopped off at a drugstore in Huntsville thirty minutes after leaving Livingston for a bottle of Maalox and a pack of Rolaids. My stomach was doing little tricks by that time. And as if that weren't enough, it started raining before I reached Conroe, which meant I had to face that winding stretch of Highway 105 between Conroe and Brenham with an upset stomach, a tension headache, a car that jarred me to the bone every time it hit a pothole, and wet streets. The gods were not smiling on me.

Somehow I made it back, and the first thing I did was walk into Ed's office and ask for about fifteen minutes of his time. We had some serious planning to do, and much to his credit, Ed realized it. He told me to wait a minute while he sought out Maggie Balough, the assistant managing editor, because he wanted her to be in on our meeting. I agreed, as long as he didn't bring in too many upper-echelon editors. I knew from experience that productivity of reporters varies inversely in proportion to the number of top-level editors involved in a story; too many chiefs can ruin a good story. And high-level editors have been off the streets so long that they wouldn't know how to find their way out of a nickel-and-dime beer joint fight, much less write about it. But Maggie, in my book, was okay. She listened intently every time I spoke with her, and she seemed to know a news story from a run-of-the-mill puff piece, which put her a notch above most assistant MEs I had dealt with.

The three of us huddled in Maggie's office late that afternoon. The dozen or so reporters in the newsroom could tell something serious was going on because Ed closed Maggie's office door when he walked in. That was always the signal that big stuff was brewing. A crowd of reporters (was it my imagination?) huddled outside—nonchalantly, of course—trying to watch the expressions on all the faces in Maggie's glass-enclosed office. At least, that was what I usually did at my desk. I could always tell when a big story was in the works, or when another team reporting project was in the planning stages, just by watching the faces of people sitting in Maggie's office.

This time I was the one sitting in there with the door closed. And the first thing said in that meeting came from Maggie: she said she had been briefed by Ed about the reports of deaths of young boys in San Jacinto County, and she was a bit concerned. "All I know is that I don't want you going back over there alone," she said. "If there is something like *that* going on, I'd just feel better if you had someone else with you."

The person she had in mind, she said, was Bill Douthat, one of several veteran reporters on the news staff.

Ed nodded in agreement.

And since I really didn't know for sure what I was going to do next on this story, I nodded, too.

I spent most of the next morning and afternoon bringing Douthat up to date on what I had been doing in San Jacinto County over the last three months. I went into pretty good detail about what I suspected was happening on Highway 59, and I related the stories of the victims I had spoken with. The Highway 59 operation, as I was starting to call the highway arrest trap and shakedown racket, seemed to be in a little category all its own, at least in my investigation. And it seemed to be the only part of my investigation that was anywhere close to completion. The marijuana plantation was an area all to itself, as was the disturbing pattern of hit-and-run killings. And everything else—such as rumors I had heard of brutality with prisoners at the jail—seemed to jump back and forth between categories. It took a great deal of talking to explain the paranoia of local residents about law enforcement, and the terrible reputation that San Jacinto County had among lawyers and legal service workers throughout Southeast Texas.

Bill listened intently to what I had to say, taking notes and offering occasional comments. He also persisted in giving the name of the county its Spanish pronunciation—Sahn Yahseento—which I finally said would only antagonize the backwoods folks that he would be dealing with on this story. Reluctantly, he started saying the name the way the rednecks did. Bill, who had been a reporter and assistant city editor for the *Miami News* in Florida before joining the *American-Statesman*, was bilingual, and he prided himself on his ability to cover news that dealt with the sizable Hispanic community in Austin. Just last year he had completed a mammoth project for the newspaper on the plight of Mexican Americans and Mexican nationals living in Austin; that series was one of the four or five that Ed gave to me during my job interview as an example of the type of in-depth reporting that he wanted more of. I read every word of that series and the others, and I was a bit disturbed that a fifteen- or twenty-part series could still come off as being superficial. But that was the impression I got from all the series that Ed gave me. There was just something wrong with the way the *American-Statesman* handled multipart stories. Even if they said something worth saying, you had to dig deep into them to find it.

In a little more than three months on the job, I had gotten to know nearly all the reporters—their areas of specialty, their personalities, their work habits and weak spots. But Douthat was an exception. He seemed to be a bit distant, a bit hard to talk to, a bit preoccupied all the time. These two days after my third trip to San Jacinto County marked the first time I had ever sat down and talked with him for more than thirty or forty-five seconds, and I came away from these meetings impressed with his ability to absorb a lot of information in a short time. We didn't really decide to do anything during our talks, except that Bill wanted to drive over to the Department of Public Safety headquarters on Austin's north side as soon as possible to pick up complete, certified figures on drug arrests by county. I said that sounded like a good idea. He also wanted to take a little time to digest a string of notes that I had been typing into the computer over the last few weeks. That, too, sounded like a good idea.

As soon as Bill felt comfortable with the task at hand, we would plow back over there and see what we could do about (1) the dead boys, (2) the marijuana fields, and (3) the Highway 59 operation. We guessed it would take at least a week before we were ready to plot our strategy. I had a lot of telephone work to do on this story. I wanted to sound out the relatives of the dead boys, to hear their comments and opinions, and I wanted to track down Deputy Charlie Pierce, the Walker County deputy who lived in San Jacinto County who was supposed to know a great deal about wrongdoing in that neck of the woods.

But there was a problem, a recurring problem: Ed had a few other things he wanted Douthat to work on before we got on this story full time. And, almost incredibly, he started to load daily stories on me, too. He even told me I'd need to continue working on Sundays to help out with general news coverage. I was steamed. And I told him so. Didn't he comprehend the gravity of the accusations and reports I'd received about San Jacinto County? Didn't he know where that kind of stuff could lead?

Sure he did. But he was having problems with scheduling, and he was certain I'd be able to get back on the story in a few days. It wouldn't do much damage for me to break loose from the story for a day or two, just to help out.

I'd heard that tune before. Just break away for a few days. A few hours. Just this once. Everyone has to help out occasionally. Sometimes we have to pull together on things like this. You can get back on that investigation next week. Tomorrow. Wednesday. This afternoon. Tomorrow morning. Just as soon as you talk to this mountain climber who's here in my office. Right after the county commissioners' meeting this morning. Just as soon as you help out on this bank robbery story— it's for the p.m. paper.

I decided while stewing over an assignment to cover a work session of the Travis County commissioners that I was going to do everything I could to get some sort of story about San Jacinto County into the newspaper quickly. And it probably would have to be about the Highway 59 operation. If I could overwhelm Ed—and the *American-Statesman*'s 200,000 readers—with horror story after horror story about that stretch of roadway, then the pendulum would start swinging my direction. I needed momentum on this story. And the best way to achieve momentum—as my high school basketball coach used to say— was to go on the offensive. In the daily newspaper business, going on the offensive meant writing story after story on one particular topic. If I could just get that first blockbuster story into print, I could establish that San Jacinto County was the *American-Statesman*'s investigation, and most investigations, of course, lead to more than just one story.

In addition, my first story would certainly attract the attention of the Houston newspapers. San Jacinto County is right in Houston's back yard. Maybe if they learned that some strange reporter from 180 miles away was messing with counties on their turf, they'd jump in and start an investigation of their own. Now, that would grab Ed's attention, and it would establish a sense of urgency that Ed seemed to lack on this project.

As I mulled that over during an interminable session of the county commissioners, I realized that I was back to that old idea about getting another newspaper interested in San Jacinto County. And once again, I realized that that was the last thing I wanted to do. At least for the time being.

· TWELVE ·

Of all the parents of the dead boys, the first I contacted was Hank Kinder, father of twenty-five-year-old Danny Eugene Kinder. Mr. Kinder worked at an automotive shop in Cleveland, and I contacted him by telephone late on the afternoon of Tuesday, April 13. He was a crusty-sounding old man, and he was still upset about the lack of investigation by the local law enforcement agencies into his son's murder.

Not knowing how he would react to questions from a reporter, I first asked him if my information was accurate about the rash of hit-and-run deaths involving young boys in and around San Jacinto County. I explained that I was looking into a wide range of topics concerning the rural law enforcement agencies north of Houston, and that I had been told about a number of unsolved deaths in the area, among them his son's.

He seemed more than willing to talk. He mentioned several auto-pedestrian accidents along the wooded farm roads—all of them already included in my investigation—and he said a number of parents were upset. He mentioned victims Joe Lynn Pickering and Raymond Earl Vandver by name, and he said there were some others that he knew about but just couldn't remember the names. I decided to drop that line of questioning momentarily and ask him about his son's death.

First of all, what had his son been doing walking along the road so late at night?

He took the ball and ran with it. "My son was a nature boy, and he liked to do that. He'd done it all his life. He lived in Conroe at a trailer park, and was just walking around on his way home. I guess you could say he liked to get out and ramble around. He had a car at home, but he just liked to walk. He was living over with a woman, and they had been fussing or something, and he got out and hitchhiked over to New Caney, where he worked at a Gulf station. He stayed there till 2:00 a.m.

"He probably walked about eight and a quarter miles that night. The wreck happened near Grangerland. Actually it was about a mile and a quarter east of Grangerland on Farm Road 3083. He was just walking along the side of the road when he was hit."

I pressed him a little on that point. Eight miles was a long way to walk, I ventured, and it would take most folks a couple of hours to do it. Was he sure that was what Danny was doing out at that hour?

"Oh, yeah. The reason I say that is because he did it all the time. It wasn't nothing for him to get out and walk around."

Had there ever been any leads on who killed him?

"The cops? They don't care about this. They don't care about any of these deaths. I worked with a detective in Conroe, and he just didn't want any of the information I wanted to give him."

What information?

He stopped a minute to answer a question from someone in the shop, then started back at the same rapid-fire pace. He said he had done a little investigative work of his own, talking to people who lived in the area, and had come up with a couple of leads to pass on to the sheriff's department in Montgomery County. He had found out that a couple of young local kids, out partying that night, had been driving around that part of the county in a highly intoxicated state early that morning. He described them as "just some punk kids."

What exactly did he do with that information? I asked.

He said he confronted two of the kids and told them they ought to go to the sheriff's office in Conroe and talk to the detective who was handling the killing.

And what did the kids do when he told them that?

"They got pretty upset at me."

And then what did he do?

"I just told them in no uncertain terms that I suspected they knew something about my son's death. I felt confident with what I found."

What did he do when they got mad?

"I told what I found out to the sheriff's office."

And then?

"I was advised by them to let this thing cool down. They didn't want to hear it. . . . I thought about getting me a private detective to solve this, and maybe I still oughta do it."

I started to ask another question, but he quickly added that he had even offered a reward for information about his son's death but got no takers. He had pretty much given up on the case now, he said.

Mr. Kinder sounded like an interesting old guy, but he was obviously too close to this particular death to have an objective viewpoint. I had talked with other parents like him during my reporting years; they always knew more than the police, and they were always upset with the slowness of the official investigation, the delays in the judicial system, the cool attitude of the investigators, the reluctance of officers to act quickly, or rashly, on thirdhand rumors, and the memory-dulling effects of time. A quick phone call to the Montgomery County sheriff's office told me that the death of Danny Eugene Kinder some three and a half years ago was a closed case. It had been officially closed four months after it happened. That meant, of course, that no one was actively investigating it. No one except me.

But there didn't seem to be a lot I could do. There were only two eye-witnesses to the murder—Danny and the person who ran over him. I filed away my notes and sat in front of my typewriter for the better part of thirty minutes. The unsolved killing of Danny Eugene Kinder was not going to be solved from 180 or so miles away, and it wasn't going to be solved anytime soon. Maybe never. Mr. Kinder, though, had told me quite plainly that no drugs were involved, and that, at least, con-tradicted some of my earlier information. Yet all my efforts to track down the years-old information on this death were not going to get my story on San Jacinto County into print anytime soon. And the longer I took to write a story, the easier it was going to be for Ed and his assis-tant city editors to pull me off the story on a regular basis—just for an afternoon, of course. No, I needed something that wasn't so open-ended on the time element.

I got back on the phone and started making my daily checks, hoping that I'd be left alone long enough to finish my calls. Fat chance. Even as I was dialing the phone, Ed was walking in my direction with a piece of paper in his hand. Another crisis.

By Thursday, April 15, I had disposed of the latest of my steady string of daily stories for the city desk, and I was finally able to do some more work on the hit-and-run deaths. I was completely preoccupied with the idea that I had to get some sort of story into the newspaper as quickly as possible. It had gotten to be something of a joke around the news-paper how the assistant city editors regularly pulled people off "specially requested stories" and put them on other "even more important special-ly requested stories." But I had too much to do to worry about it.

As I studied the Department of Public Safety accident reports on the seven deaths (which I had managed to obtain between daily stories), I was perturbed by the notation that Charles Hogue was "lying in the roadway" when hit by the car; by the notation that Raymond Earl Vandver was "sitting in the road" when hit; and by the notation that

Jimmy Speer was "lying down" in the roadway when hit. Of the seven deaths, I concentrated on the three that were still listed as unsolved— Hogue, Kinder, and Pickering—and on two others, Vandver and Speer, because of the "sitting" and "lying" remarks. In all, I wanted to find out as much as I could—in a short amount of time—on five of the seven pedestrian deaths that occurred either in or just outside San Jacinto County from August 1978 to March 1981. A two-and-a-half-year period.

One of the first things I did that afternoon was plot the deaths on a large Highway Department map of San Jacinto County. Four of the five deaths I was investigating occurred within a fairly narrow portion of southern San Jacinto County and northern Montgomery and Liberty counties, an area roughly five miles long by four miles wide. The fifth death that intrigued me—Hogue's—occurred in the opposite part of the county. After plotting the deaths on the map, I made myself a chronological chart at the bottom of the map, listing the deaths I was looking at and what little information I had on them:

1. August 11, 1978—Danny Kinder, 25, struck and killed by a hit-and-run driver at 3:15 a.m. No arrests. Body found in Montgomery County on FM 3083, south of SJ County border. No physical evidence at scene.

2. May 13, 1979—Charles Hogue, 17, struck and killed by a hit-and-run driver on FM 946 in north part of SJ County. No arrests. No physical evidence. Head crushed. 1:50 a.m. "Lying in the roadway."

3. October 6, 1979—Joe Lynn Pickering, 20, struck and killed. 12:15 a.m. South part of SJ County near Montgomery and Liberty counties. No arrests. Little evidence.

4. August 24, 1980—Jimmy Speer, 16, struck and killed by his mother near site of Pickering death. Mother never saw him, told DPS the boy was lying in road. 3:30 a.m. Mother arrested.

5. March 1, 1981—Raymond Earl Vandver, 25, struck and killed by 21-year-old man, who told DPS Vandver was "sitting down" in the road, thought Vandver was "a log." 3:30 a.m. Ruled accidental.

About 3:30 p.m., I reached a man who had served on the county grand jury that investigated the death of Jimmy Speer. I asked him what the grand jury did when Mrs. Josephine Speer was brought in on charges relating to her son's death . . . if, of course, he didn't mind telling me. He said there wasn't a whole lot he could say, because nothing much ever happened. He didn't seem to mind talking, however.

"It happened a year or so ago, down on Hill-Story Road, that's in the south end of the county. This lady, the mother, claimed she ran over the boy. She said she had let him off earlier that night in Cleveland, and he was hitching a ride home. He was supposedly passed out in the road. . . . She said she was coming home from a date, which meant she had been out partying. And she ran over him pretty early in the morning."

What did the grand jury do?

"Well, we couldn't do a thing with it. I mean, it was his own mother who was there, and she admitted that she did it. She just said she never saw him. She said she felt a bump, turned her car back around to see what she hit, and then she found him. . . . She took full responsibility for it. Now, there was an autopsy done, and they claimed that he died instantly. When the boy's own mother said she killed him, there wasn't much we could do. We no-billed her on it."

He seemed to hint at the possibility that there might have been more to the Speer death than what was reported to the grand jury. But he stated clearly that the jurors could only make their determination based on the evidence presented to them. I took a chance and asked him about the other deaths I was looking at, about the mysterious sitting and lying in the roadway.

He muttered a half-laugh, paused briefly, and said slowly, almost parentally, "I've been traveling on these roads many a time, and I have never, ever seen anyone lying down or sitting down in the road. Does that answer your question?"

It did. There was really nothing more he could say. No amount of suspicion, intuition, or fleeting bursts of conscience could make up for a lack of physical evidence. He knew that, and so did I. He wished me luck in my pursuit. I told him I was going to need some luck, because so far there didn't seem to be *any* evidence to tie those deaths to anyone.

I spent most of the next day trying to track down the autopsy report that Brumley said was prepared on Speer's death and presented to the San Jacinto County grand jury. While I was at it, I decided to snoop around for the autopsies or coroner's reports on the other four deaths. That presented a few problems. I didn't particularly want to arouse suspicion at the sheriff's department by inquiring loudly and openly about the deaths of young boys. And I knew from experience that various governmental agencies can have widely differing policies regarding the release of information about a death. Medical reports, as a rule, are harder to get than anything else. I didn't even know for sure that an autopsy had been performed in every case.

I spent the next hour on the phone to the Harris County Medical Examiner's Office in Houston, the office that handles large numbers of

autopsies resulting from violent deaths in the rural areas north of
Houston. I spent at least half the time on hold. A secretary looked up
the names I gave her and confirmed, after ten minutes, that an autopsy
had been conducted on Charles Hogue, but blood samples only had
been tested from Joe Lynn Pickering and Jimmy Speer. She could find
nothing on Danny Kinder or Raymond Earl Vandver. When I asked
if I could verify the causes of death, she forwarded me to the toxicology
department.

I was a bit startled that I had gotten so much information without
lying, groveling, or threatening. The people who work in medical
examiner's offices – or county morgues, or coroner's offices – can be most
uncooperative. They don't like dealing with people who are still alive.

A man who identified himself as the chief toxicologist brought a halt
to my inquiry by stating explicitly that his office could give out no information on private autopsies, or PAs, as he called them. He said I'd have
to call the judge who ordered them.

So I backed off. "Oh, okay. Do you have the judge's name there? I'll
just make a trip by his office."

"Judge Neuman in San Jacinto County. It says here he's a JP."

I hung up and called Martha Charrey to find out about Judge
Neuman, to see if he would talk to me without reporting every word of
my questions to Sheriff Parker.

Martha said the judge no longer lived in San Jacinto County.
Another judge had taken his place. And anyway, Neuman and the
sheriff were close friends and it probably wouldn't have been worth my
trouble to talk to him.

What about the new judge?

She said his name was Mike Jeffrey, and he ran a boot and saddle
shop across the street from the courthouse. And, she added, he was
pretty unhappy about the way the sheriff's department operated. He
might talk to me if I approached him in the right manner. What exactly
was I looking for?

I explained my interest in the autopsy report and blood tests from the
Harris County medical examiner on three of the auto-pedestrian
deaths.

"Oh," she said, a bit startled. "Those reports are all kept in the sheriff's
office, so you'd have to go through him if you wanted to see them."

Highway 59 near Urbana, just north of Shepherd. The favorite stopping point of the San Jacinto Sheriff's Department.

The old San Jacinto County Jail, constructed shortly after the Civil War, closed in the late seventies. Now a public landmark.

Downtown Coldspring on a busy Saturday morning.

The San Jacinto County Courthouse.

J. C. "Humpy" Parker and his wife, Melba, leaving the courthouse in Houston after his conviction. © 1983 The Houston Post. Reprinted with permission.

· THIRTEEN ·

I was back to square one. All investigations in San Jacinto County seemed to begin and end at the sheriff's department. Everything from accident reports to autopsies seemed to gravitate into the sheriff's files. It had been done that way for years, and no one had seen fit to change it. There was no way, apparently, that I was going to get much information on the medical causes of death without going through Sheriff Parker. I didn't feel ready to do that just yet.

So I got back on the phone. There was a great deal I needed to find out and not much time to do it. Ed and his assistants on the city desk were finding it easier and easier to pull me off this story to work on other pressing matters. The amount of time I was being permitted to spend on this story was decreasing daily in direct proportion to the length of time I was taking on it; if I didn't write something within a few weeks—a month at the most—I would soon find myself spending only one day a week, or less, working on my investigation. It was a hell of a way to run a newspaper—and a hell of a way to try to conduct an investigation.

On Wednesday, April 21, I finally contacted the young man who struck and killed Raymond Earl Vandver on March 1, 1981. Vandver was the one who was supposedly sitting down in the street when he was hit. The driver of the car, Ricky Johnson, who was twenty-one at the time of the accident, was a difficult person to track down. He had moved a couple of times over the two-year period since the accident, and he was now living in Cleveland. But even though I finally located him, I almost didn't get to talk to him.

I called about 1:30 p.m. and apparently woke up another young man who was staying with Johnson. I asked to speak to Ricky Johnson, and the young man set down the phone for a full fifteen minutes. He finally got back on the line and said Johnson would be with me in a minute.

After another fifteen minutes, Johnson finally picked up the phone.

I identified myself as a reporter from Austin and asked if he was the person who was involved in a bad car accident in Liberty County two years before.

He said he was.

I told him I was double-checking the reports from the DPS and just wanted to ask him a few questions about the wreck.

"Sure," he said.

Well, the report said that Vandver was sitting in the road. Was that accurate?

"The cops said he had been drinking, or was bombed or something," Johnson said laconically. He talked even slower than some West Texas ranchers I had met, so slowly, in fact, that I got the impression that he must be working nights, and that my call had disrupted his sleep, too. "But I haven't heard anything in a while from the cops."

Did he know Vandver?

"No, not really."

Well, was the man really sitting down in the road?

"I don't know if he was sitting down or lying down. . . . I went along and didn't see nothing. Just felt a bump. [The police] said they found a bottle of something pretty close by."

A bottle of what?

"They didn't tell me what it was. They didn't know if it was booze, Coke, or what."

So he really didn't see Vandver in the road?

"Naw. I just felt a bump."

It appeared that he didn't really want to talk to me. But I decided to ask him if he knew of any other similar deaths in that area.

"I haven't been keeping up with much of anything the last few years," he said.

I thanked him, hung up, and began scratching a few notes to myself. These deaths were going to be next to impossible to do anything about from Austin. Even if I spent three months in San Jacinto County, I still might never be able to put together anything plausible in the way of a story on them. But I had to hustle. I called Martha Charrey again and asked if anything new had happened since I last talked to her.

"I've been trying to call you," she said. "The FBI showed up this morning at the sheriff's department."

Within five seconds—or less—I took back everything I had ever thought about wanting someone else to investigate San Jacinto County. FBI agents snooping around Sheriff Parker's office were not doing me any good right then. I was sitting in an ultramodern newsroom 180 miles away, trying to scrape up enough time to make telephone calls, and there, eight counties away from me, were FBI agents going over records that I desperately wanted to see. I suddenly had visions of young G-men wearing three-piece suits and dark glasses (why do federal agents always wear dark glasses?) tearing into medical reports, accident reports, jail records, fine collection receipts, and all sorts of other records pertinent to *my* investigation. And I felt sick to my stomach.

I probably sounded like a ruptured water main, sputtering and spewing as I tried to think of something to say to Martha. Eventually I managed to spurt out some sort of line like "What do you think the FBI is looking at?"

Martha didn't know. I got the impression that hangers-on around the county courthouse in Coldspring were gossiping at that moment at an incredible rate. The word was out that the FBI was in town, and everyone was starting to compare notes about that Austin newspaper reporter who had been hanging around for the better part of three months. Some people were even saying that I was really an FBI agent masquerading as a reporter. Their logic was impeccable: What would an Austin reporter be doing way over here? He must be a fed working undercover.

Martha said that the word on the street was that the FBI men were interested in arrests that were made and never recorded on the docket. They were especially interested in those cases where money was taken from defendants who were then never notified about court hearings.

They were playing my song. I was convinced that some of the defendants I had talked with (the fraternity brothers, perhaps?) had contacted the feds with their complaint. Several of them had threatened to call the FBI, and a couple had indicated an interest in hiring lawyers to sue San Jacinto County. I spluttered a few more seconds before asking another question: "Do you think they're finding out anything?"

Again, Martha didn't know for sure. But, she added quickly, there were reports floating around town that the sheriff's department had known for several weeks that the FBI agents were on their way. And she herself had noticed over the last few days that the sheriff and his deputies had seemed unusually busy filling out reports. "I feel like they've been working on their books for a good two weeks," Martha said.

"What in the world could they be doing? Doctoring reports?" I asked, a bit confused.

"I don't really know; that's what everyone's saying," she replied. "I think the sheriff suspects that Mike Jeffrey called the feds. And one of the constables here has been saying that none of the people who made bonds and forfeited ever got contacted, that none of that money was ever collected. . . . I don't know. People are saying some strange things around here."

She suddenly stopped talking because a couple of people were walking up to her office. Then: "You know I told you about Mike Jeffrey, the new JP? Well, he just walked into my office. You want to talk to him?"

Indeed I did.

Martha handed him the phone. I introduced myself and said I'd been talking to Martha for a while about the things going on in the sheriff's department. And then I made a comment about my surprise at learning about the FBI.

He took it from there. "I'm getting all the heat for that, too. I don't know for sure what they're looking at, because they don't say a whole lot. But they came in and asked for the jail book and all the arrest reports. I have a feeling they're going to compare what they find with the court dockets. I know they have a few names they're looking for, and they've got dates of arrest and specific charges. I'd heard they had fourteen names."

Jeffrey seemed excited and perturbed, yet his voice was low-key, and at times he spoke in a monotone. He said he was tired of sitting in his court and watching defendants paraded before him on trumped-up charges. He said he'd turned a couple of names over to the FBI himself.

I asked him how he got involved with the FBI, how he decided to help them. After all, a lot of people seemed to be scared to death of the sheriff.

"The reason I got involved in the first place was just that I won't go along with them on some of these things. They think of me as an out-sider over at the sheriff's department. . . . And they arrested a friend of mine from Baytown—a young man who doesn't drink, smoke, or any-thing else. He wasn't speeding, or anything, but they stopped him out on 59, pulled him out of his truck, and found some sort of little stick. They charged him with carrying a prohibited weapon. He paid a bond but never went to trial. . . . There's a bunch of that stuff going on."

I related a few details about Jeffrey Foley's arrest on 59 and mentioned that his father had never heard from the county or the bondsman, even though he paid $410 for the bond and something called escrow.

Jeffrey laughed. "Anytime that word 'escrow' is written on the arrest paperwork, I can guarantee you that case will never come up on the docket," he said. "They're just trying to get more money. Now, who gets that escrow, I don't know."

I mentioned my interest in the pedestrian deaths, and especially in locating the autopsy report for Charles Hogue and the blood test results for Jimmy Speer and Joe Lynn Pickering. I said I had been told by the medical examiner's office in Houston that the reports had been sent back to Judge Neuman, Jeffrey's predecessor as Precinct 1 justice of the peace. Did he know of any medical reports like that in his office?

"When Judge Neuman was here, all the autopsies came back to the sheriff's office. The sheriff got all of that. But I've changed it since I got here. I feel like if I order an autopsy, I ought to be the one who gets the report, not the sheriff."

In his opinion, did I have a chance of locating those reports at the sheriff's office?

He just laughed. "Not hardly."

I changed the subject and asked whether he was afraid of what might happen if the word got around that he was helping the FBI.

"I know sometimes they follow me around at night. I deliver the *Houston Chronicle* early in the morning, and I've been followed a couple of times. I don't know what kind of little games they're playing, but I'm not going to go along with them."

I decided to bounce a few more things off him. Had the sheriff been having trouble with his secretaries? Parker had told me that most of his problems dealt with bookkeeping mistakes and his inability to keep a secretary on the job.

"Is that what he told you? I wouldn't believe everything I heard over there, if I were you."

What about those pedestrian deaths? Hogue? Pickering? Speer? Did he know anything about them?

"I remember when they happened. There was a lot of talk about them at the time, about how they just didn't seem quite right."

What specifically wasn't right about them?

"How many people have you ever seen lying down in the middle of a road waiting for a car to come along and hit 'em?"

Was the FBI looking at them?

"I don't think so. All I know is they're interested in charges that never got on the docket. I can point them out to you every time they come before me. When I see that word 'escrow' on there, I know that case is never going anywhere. . . . I've got a pretty good idea that's what the FBI is looking at."

What about that friend of his who was arrested? The man from Baytown?

"Kippy Carr. His family runs a tire store down in Baytown. I can get you their phone number if you want it."

What was the stick doing in his truck? Why would the deputies think it was a prohibited weapon?

"They just wanted his money. That arrest happened last November, and it ain't ever appeared on any docket around here. . . . That stick was propping up a CB microphone."

Would Carr talk to me?

"You bet."

I started to ask another question, but Jeffrey said he had to get back to his office. I almost refused to let him off the line. He had helped me more in twenty minutes than most people had in two weeks, and I was afraid to let loose of him. And then it dawned on me: I had a San Jacinto County justice of the peace talking to me, not a lawyer in another county, not a preacher who didn't want to come forward, not another defendant. This man was a county official, and he was upset with what was going on in the San Jacinto County Sheriff's Department. He appeared willing to answer every question I had. He appeared to be candid. And he wanted to do something about the way the sheriff operated. In short, I had a legitimate reason to get back to Coldspring as soon as I could. A reason even Ed couldn't argue with. I mean, the FBI was snooping around on my story at that very moment, and a judge in that county wanted to help me find out what was going on. I didn't have only one reason to make another trip. I had two reasons.

Before I let Jeffrey off the line, I asked, "If I get myself over there tomorrow morning, would you sit down and talk with me some more about all this?"

"Just come on. But don't go to my office at the sheriff's department. Come by the shop across from the courthouse. I'm usually in here after 10:00."

I hustled over to Douthat's desk and told him not to plan anything for the next few days. I filled him in on the FBI and Mike Jeffrey, and the fact that we had better step up our pace to get something into print. Bill agreed. We both descended on Ed and *told* him that we had to go out of town—that we were onto something that wasn't going to wait. I explained the activity of the FBI and my contact with the JP. Ed's eyes brightened; he seemed seriously interested, listening to every word I said.

After I had talked for four or five minutes, he leaned forward in his chair and said, "You probably ought to get an early start tomorrow, don't you think?"

· FOURTEEN ·

Douthat and I left Austin a few minutes before 8:00 on the morning of Friday, April 23. It was Bill's first trip to San Jacinto County since joining me on the story two weeks before; it was my fourth trip in the fourteen weeks I'd been on the story. I spent as much time as I could describing that beautiful and sparsely populated section of the state, its people and their attitudes about law enforcement. The Free State of San Jacinto, as some called it, contained thousands of acres of spectacular, towering pine trees, a little-known national forest covering sixty percent of the county, and 11,500 residents who didn't particularly care to be bothered by city dwellers, including reporters from Austin. The six full-time deputies last year had made 1,124 drug arrests and pulled in a reported $300,000 in fine collections, which was exactly enough to fund the department's operations that year. But there seemed to be more compelling topics: arrests that were made and never recorded on the court dockets, fine money that was paid and not recorded, people who were arrested and never given a court date, frantic searches of motorists on Highway 59, and—not the least of these—the perplexing deaths of young men on the dark, winding back roads. And we had something else to check on: the activity of the FBI. All in all, we had enough to keep us busy for a while.

By the time we reached our destination for this journey—the Holiday Inn in Huntsville (I wanted to vary our base of operations)—we had decided to divide up the work at the courthouse in Coldspring. Bill wanted to visit county auditor Jo Landrum to study the official county budgets for the last two or three years and to find out how the small county bureaucracy operated, and I wanted to track down as many more victims of the Highway 59 operation as I could. Then we would pay a visit to justice of the peace Mike Jeffrey. This was our first plan of attack, one we figured would quickly fall apart as soon as we got to the courthouse.

I had learned by this point that trips to this part of the state were never predictable; something completely unexpected always seemed to occur. At any rate, we decided to give this plan a shot.

We got to the courthouse about 1:15 that afternoon—perfect timing, since the doors had just reopened after lunch—and Bill headed off to the auditor's office. I returned to the caverns of the county clerk's office to consult again the docket books and lists of criminal charges that were filed. It was becoming a regular task of mine, jotting down names and docket numbers and looking up the official charges. And once again, I was intrigued by the lack of information—no addresses, telephone numbers, cities, states. And no narrative about the arrests—only terse statements that so-and-so on such-and-such date was in possession of such-and-such amount of dope. No location was given for any of the arrests, no probable cause listed for the search or stoppage of the car—indeed, no mention made of searches or cars. From what little information was given, it could easily have been that everyone had been arrested while walking along some road in the county. And of course the names of the arresting deputies were omitted, along with the time of the arrests. All of the charges were sworn to by the sheriff's secretary, who, I had discovered, was not currently a commissioned peace officer in the state of Texas. There could only be two reasons for this startling lack of detail on the official records: either the county was terribly inefficient and inept or the county was trying to hide something. My guess was a combination of both.

After forty-five minutes of jotting down names and checking the file folders for the charges, I was again shocked to see the large numbers of marijuana possession arrests. That was about the only type of arrest that was ever made in this county. Judge Bryant and Sheriff Parker, I deduced, had been trying to mislead me with their remarks that an equal number of weapons charges and DWIs were made. Sure, there were a few UCWs (unlawfully carrying a weapon) and DWIs, but the overwhelming number had the notation "possession of marijuana" in the margin. In the two weeks before this trip to Coldspring, the sheriff's department had filed forty-three possession charges and only five DWIs. I recorded all the names, docket numbers, and dates of arrest; next came the fun part—trying to find the people, who could have been from Houston or from out of state, or from Dallas, or from Longview, or from Austin. All I had to do was match the names with a city. Any city. And then I had to contact the names to see if they were the ones who were arrested in San Jacinto County. And then I had to persuade them to talk to me. And if all of them said, "Yeah, I was guilty and the deputies did a good job," then I wouldn't have anything to write.

About 2:00 p.m., Douthat wandered into the clerk's office and found me with my nose in the files. He said he hadn't had much luck, but he had gotten copies of the last two county budgets. The county auditor wasn't too cooperative. As a matter of fact, he said, she was a little belligerent.

Welcome to San Jacinto County, I said.

Douthat and I had been in the courthouse close to an hour, and Bill was beginning to believe one of the things I had told him during our journey: that two strange men in a strange car with out-of-county license plates can attract a lot of attention in downtown Coldspring. A few people wandered into the clerk's office while we were there, looked us over quickly, and then left. Bill, with his neatly trimmed black hair and clean-shaven chin, probably looked like an FBI agent. Remembering the rumor floating around that I was an undercover agent, and not wanting to disappoint anyone, I put on my sunglasses and tried to look as undercover as I could.

With that, we hustled out of the courthouse and across the street. The boot and saddle shop was right next door to the Coldspring Resale Shop, which bail bondsman Herb Atwood ran. Both were located in an old-timey storefront mall, the type that every small town used to have, with wooden walkways and wooden beams holding up wooden awnings. I was a little shocked to find the name ABC Bonding Company on the same window as Jeffrey's Boot Shop. That was going to be one of the first things I asked about.

Mike Jeffrey looked like anything but a judge. He was a slender man who looked very much the part of a boot and saddle shop owner. He wore fairly thick glasses, which seemed to swallow up his narrow face and brow; his brownish hair was very closely cropped, and his sideburns were—in a word—nonexistent. He had the type of countenance that made him appear deep in thought at all times. His eyes were the kind that quickly sized up a situation, or a person, and his words always came slowly, as though they were given the greatest possible consideration. He seemed right at home in a white sport shirt, blue jeans, boots, and a wide brown belt. Although he had sounded over the telephone to be fifty or older, he appeared to be in fact a good ten or twelve years younger.

Douthat and I walked into Jeffrey's shop about 2:30 p.m., and we seemed to startle an elderly man behind the counter who was meditating over a disassembled rifle. A small sign on the front door indicated that a gunsmith worked in the boot shop, and I figured this must be the gunsmith.

"Is Judge Jeffrey in?" I asked.

"Mike? Yes, he's around in back. You wait a minute and he'll be right back."

We took a seat on an old vinyl couch propped against a wall across from the counter. From where I sat, I could look to my right out the front window of the shop and see the full length and breadth of the courthouse. The shop counter stretched almost the entire length of the opposite wall. There were boots and shoes and assorted odds and ends on a table and counter to my left, and various machines and more odds and ends on countertops directly behind the service counter. A back corner of the shop was partitioned off into a tiny office with a door that was shut, and there was a double door leading into another work area at the far back.

Less than two minutes after we sat down, the judge walked through the double door. I stood and introduced myself and my partner, and I told him we'd just gotten into town a little more than an hour earlier.

"I know," the judge replied. "Everyone in town knew you were here five minutes after you drove up and went into the courthouse." I must have appeared perplexed, because Jeffrey explained that "word travels pretty fast" around the courthouse when strangers pull up . . . especially when the strangers have note pads. He pointed out that a lot of the little stores on the courthouse square are situated so that everyone can see who goes in and out of the ancient edifice in the center of town. And, he explained, some people make a habit of watching for outsiders. Now that the FBI was nosing around, it seemed like that was all anybody did.

The first thing I asked about was the incident involving the friend of his from Baytown, Kippy Carr, the young man who supposedly had been stopped on Highway 59 and arrested for carrying a stick. Hadn't he told me that Carr was never charged with the offense, even though he had to pay a bail bondsman?

"They never charged him. They brought him in and he bonded out and that was the end of that. He didn't pay a fine or nothing. He was pretty smart. He knew he was being railroaded. . . . He took down the names of everyone in the jail with him, and he went to the FBI."

I asked if he had been able to locate Carr's telephone number, and he had. I jotted it down. Since he had mentioned bonds, I asked him about the sign in his window for ABC Bonding.

"I lease the building from them. They just have that little office," he said, motioning to the partitioned space at the back left corner. "All they've got in there is a desk and a telephone. The phone is on an answering machine. . . . I don't have nothing to do with them."

I asked about the huge numbers of marijuana arrests, and specifically about what happened to the dope that was confiscated.

"There's been a lot of talk around here about dope disappearing from the property room," he responded. He said there had been a large dope raid last year in the northern end of the county, and all of the evidence had mysteriously disappeared.

Was that unusual? I inquired.

He laughed. "Not for around here," he said.

Before I could ask another question, he said that the previous summer the sheriff's department had harvested a forty-seven-acre marijuana field between Coldspring and Pointblank, using prisoners from the jail and county dump trucks. "There was no telling how many loads of dope they hauled out of that field," he added, shaking his head.

Forty-seven acres? That was hard to believe. "Did the local paper shoot any pictures, or were any newspaper stories ever published about that incident?"

The judge laughed again, but it was more a laugh of disgust than of humor. "Nothing got written up, and there was nothing on TV about it."

"Where exactly was the field?"

"It was way out in the middle of the national forest, on timber company land, off 946, between here and Pointblank."

"Where did they burn the dope? It must have made quite a blaze."

"They didn't burn it. They haven't had a burning in at least a couple of years. They were supposed to have buried it."

"Buried it? That's not too professional a way to dispose of illegal drugs, is it?"

"All I know is what they did," Jeffrey sighed.

We talked for about five minutes about the FBI, and about how none of the deputies wanted to be seen around Jeffrey or his shoe shop. He said he was taking the blame for the FBI being in town, and that the word was out that "the sheriff doesn't want his officers to be seen with me." He also said he believed the FBI was looking at cases in which bail bonds were paid and no charges were filed. And then he said the agents ought to be looking into a drugstore break-in that occurred in January.

Why?

"Because none of it made any sense." He said the sheriff's son and another deputy had been the first on the scene, and that they had said they were shot at by the burglars. Half a dozen officials—including Jeffrey—arrived at the drugstore within minutes and could see no trace of any burglars, except that a large quantity of drugs had been stolen. And after a thorough search, a garbage bag full of drugs was located by Gary Parker and the other deputy, Ronnie Greer, in an alley behind the store.

"What's so unusual about that?" I asked.

"I had just driven down that alley and didn't find no bag of drugs where they said they found it," Jeffrey said.

We talked another few minutes about the sheriff's son, and Jeffrey said that Gary Parker made most of the arrests on Highway 59. But, he added quickly, Gary had not been very active since the night of the drugstore break-in.

Then Gary was no longer working as a deputy?

"He still works, but he changes his voice on the radio, and uses other [patrol] numbers. But I can recognize his voice when I hear it." He pointed to a scanner radio on a table in the shop work area.

Douthat asked about the large numbers of arrests and said things must get pretty hectic around the jail.

"It's nothing for them to make about fifty arrests a night," Jeffrey replied. "And they're bonding them out as fast as they bring 'em in. Since Gary quit, or stopped working, it's slowed way down. . . . They work 59 way up by the bridge, way up in the north. There's not a whole lot up that way.

"Just within the last three weeks they started writing probable-cause tickets, and eighty percent of them say there were no license plate lights. At least eighty percent. And then the people they bring in have to pay their towing fee—they've got to pay that before they can get out of jail. That's what I call guaranteed money."

Wasn't it a bit strange that all those cars had faulty license plate lights?

"It's not strange. It's just not true. I won't accept any of those tickets if they come into my court. I won't accept that as probable cause for a stop."

How many arrests did the reserve deputies make, on an average? I asked.

He didn't know exactly, but he said the only compensation the reserves got from the county was $100 a year for uniforms. He said they had to pay their own gas money, had to buy their own weapons, and had to be bonded.

And how many reserves did the sheriff have?

"They have twenty-two listed, but there are probably more than that. If you counted up the reserve badges that have been passed out in the last twelve years, they could fill up this building, easy. And some of them don't even work at all."

He also mentioned some things he'd heard about bookkeeping foul-ups at the sheriff's office, and about how a lot of fine money was not being turned in to the district clerk on a timely basis.

The mention of fine money triggered a question in my mind about the potential for incredibly large bond forfeitures in that county, what with all the bonds that were being written. So I asked him about that.

"As far as I know, there's never been a bond forfeiture in San Jacinto County, and that goes as far back as bonds were kept," he said.

Wouldn't that be a dead giveaway when the state found out about the lack of forfeitures?

"They don't report anything to the state," the judge said.

What about the Texas Criminal Information Computer (a computer linkup of law enforcement agencies in the state, run by the Department of Public Safety)?

"It doesn't cause them any trouble here, 'cause they never enter anything into the TCIC."

Then how in the world could they justify making all those arrests on 59?

"I really don't know," Jeffrey said, sighing.

Douthat and I were staggered by the judge's information. Jeffrey had a close observation point for the operations of the sheriff's department, and he quite obviously was disgusted with what he saw. He felt that the bonding business in the county was bordering on criminality and was about to become a serious problem, and he believed that there was a sizable amount of money being raked in from bonds. The other topics— drugs disappearing from the property room, the forty-seven-acre dope field, the drugstore burglary, the large numbers of arrests by Gary Parker— were intriguing as hell. Some of them would be difficult to trace, especially the numbers of arrests by the sheriff's son. Since all the charges on file in the county clerk's office were sworn to by the sheriff's secretary, and not the arresting officer, it would be next to impossible to get an accurate count of arrests by deputy. The forty-seven-acre dope field was a possibility; so was the drugstore break-in. Douthat and I got Jeffrey to go into considerable detail about the night of the drugstore heist, particularly about the people who arrived at the scene within minutes of the radio report by Gary Parker of shots being fired. I wasn't sure what we'd be able to do about the disappearing drugs, unless we could track down a deputy or two to confirm Jeffrey's report.

As we hashed over these topics with Judge Jeffrey, several other points came to light: that, in his opinion, Jim Browder wrote the majority of the bail bonds in San Jacinto County; that he was the only judge who had ever approved a personal recognizance bond in that county (everyone but Jeffrey required cash); that several people close to the sheriff's office were of questionable character; and that at least two of the dead boys knew each other. I could see by the look in Douthat's eyes that he was stunned by this incredible burst of information from a justice of the peace. If an official of similar standing in Austin made such remarks, the front pages of the *American-Statesman* would be filled for days. I know Douthat was stunned; hell, I'd been working on this story for fourteen weeks, and I was stunned.

After we left Jeffrey's shop, I hustled over to a pay phone on the corner of the courthouse square and called Lee Mackey, the Huntsville private investigator. He had managed to get in touch with Deputy Charlie Pierce of the Walker County Sheriff's Department. I got Mackey on the line about 4:00 p.m., and he said that Pierce would meet us about 9:00 that night at the Hungry Hobo on Interstate 45 in Huntsville. "He knows a lot, but he's scared," Mackey said.

· FIFTEEN ·

Deputy Charlie Pierce was the perfect example of an East Texas good ol' boy. In fact, he fit that description better than any law officer I had ever met. He was of medium build, though slightly rotund, and he had a classic moon-shaped face – sort of like Charlie Brown wearing a deputy's uniform. Douthat and I drove into the Hungry Hobo about ten minutes before 9:00 p.m. on Friday, April 23. The all-night restaurant was one of those that specialize in everything, which some people say means they specialize in nothing; I prefer the former characterization. Anyway, it was a typical all-night establishment. The smell of hot coffee was everywhere. So pervasive was the odor, in fact, that I knew immediately what I wanted to order – iced tea and a piece of pie. It was too hot outside for coffee.

We waited approximately fifteen minutes for the Walker County deputy and his partner to drive up in their squad car. They were on patrol that night, which in a small county means there is a lot of time to kill. They were going to kill an hour or so with us. Douthat and I walked over and introduced ourselves, and we were immediately floored by Pierce's Texas drawl. He sounded almost like someone imitating a Texas law officer, right down to the quick-talking, breathy, trailing-off-at-the-end-of-a-sentence style. But he said he sincerely wanted to "get to the bottom" of the brand of justice being administered in next-door San Jacinto County. The only problem was that he didn't want us to print anything he said in the newspaper. He explained quickly that he lived in the northern part of San Jacinto County, and that he had been contacted by "some folks over there" about running for sheriff in 1984. He said he had to protect himself.

We agreed to keep his name out of our stories . . . for the moment. We wanted to see what he had to say. With that extremely unclear agreement, Douthat and I began to question him.

For the next three hours, we sipped coffee (the smell finally overwhelmed me) and talked about the San Jacinto County Sheriff's Department. About an hour into our conversation, we were joined by two other Walker County deputies. The Hungry Hobo, it seemed, served as a sort of late-night precinct house for the deputies, much in the way those disgusting all-night doughnut shops served in Fort Worth, Dallas, Memphis, and several other cities I had seen. Everyone knew everything there was to know about San Jacinto County. Believe me. And all of it was second-hand information—hearsay, in other words. About all we found out positively was that Walker County officers didn't like what seemed to be going on in San Jacinto County. They tried to have as little to do with that county as they could.

But the talk was interesting, nonetheless, and I felt secure that we were on the right track. According to the Walker County officers, there was a great deal of drug trafficking in San Jacinto County, primarily mari-juana, and—they contended—most of it was in the northern part of the county, at the opposite extreme from Highway 59. The deputies felt that the Highway 59 operation was being used to draw attention from the other parts of the county; they called it busywork. Of course, they had no evidence.

A few minutes after 11:00, however, one of the deputies mentioned a marijuana bust north of Oakhurst in San Jacinto County that was coor-dinated by the Department of Public Safety and their department. Humpy Parker and his department, they said, were not informed of the raid until five minutes before it occurred.

"We weren't about to let them mess it up," Pierce remarked. "There was too much at stake."

What was at stake, he said, was a raid targeted at a major marijuana supplier who allegedly was operating inside San Jacinto County.

I pressed him for details.

He couldn't remember the date, but he said the raid uncovered a few bales of weed and an assortment of machine guns. Pictures were taken by the Walker County contingent, he said.

And then what happened?

"San Jacinto got involved and the evidence disappeared," he said.

What?

"Disappeared. . . . They never went to trial. They didn't have any evidence."

We thanked Pierce for his help—although, as it turned out, we could never confirm his story—and said we'd get back in touch with him within a few days. And we zipped back to the Holiday Inn to plan tomorrow's itinerary. A big political rally was planned in Coldspring the next day, and we decided that was where we ought to be.

Saturday morning was a dull, drizzling, humid experience. I was awake and making telephone calls a few minutes before 8:00, and it was steamy and dreary outside the Holiday Inn room. I wanted to try to catch a few people on the phone before the big rally on the courthouse lawn. Saturday mornings are a wonderful time to catch people at home; many folks sleep later than usual, and others sit around sipping coffee and reading the newspaper. Of course, most of these people do not like to be bothered with questions from a reporter, but at least you can get them on the line. Sometimes they'll talk; sometimes they won't. I figured I didn't have a lot to lose.

I reached Kent Morrison, the San Jacinto County treasurer, at his home about 8:15. Morrison, who reportedly was upset with the law enforcement methods being used in the county, was running a fairly heated race against county judge K. P. Bryant, who was campaigning just as hard. Signs bearing those two names were scattered darn near everywhere in the county. Mike Jeffrey had suggested talking to Morrison, and I wanted to see how dependable Jeffrey's tips were.

Morrison did not seem taken aback by my telephone call. As a matter of fact, he agreed to meet with Douthat and me later that day, but not at the political rally. He hemmed and hawed for several seconds, then said he didn't think it would be a good idea for him to be seen talking to out-of-town reporters at the rally.

My second phone call was to C. D. Hogue, the father of Charles Hogue, the seventeen-year-old youth who was killed on FM 946 between Oakhurst and Coldspring. I had been trying to get Mr. Hogue for several weeks, but he apparently was a woodsman type and was not always surrounded by telephones. His wife, Joyce Hogue, was a deputy clerk in the county clerk's office, and I really wanted to talk to her about the procedures in that office. For the time being, however, I figured it would be better to approach them simply by saying I had been looking over some DPS accident reports for the past few years and found a rather unusual one involving their son. That should get them talking . . . I hoped.

Mr. Hogue answered the phone on the seventh or eighth ring. I explained who I was and what I was doing, and then I asked if there had been anything out of the ordinary in his son's death.

"I guess so," he said quickly. "They killed one of my boys over here."

"They?" Who were "they?"

He said he didn't know exactly but added, "The sheriff's never solved it. They hushed it up. There is something awful rotten about it."

I asked him if he could go into more detail.

And he did:

He said the wreck occurred on May 13, 1979, at about 1:50 a.m. He and his brother were out in a pasture about 1:00 that morning hunting

wolves, and when they got back to the house about 2:00, they found
that Charles was not home. So they went out looking. It was not unusual
for Charles to be out late at night, but 2:00 a.m. was a good bit later
than usual. Mr. Hogue's brother started south on 946 toward Coldspring
and ran across a car with its headlights on that was stopped on the side
of the road. A reserve sheriff's deputy was in the car. "He told my brother
that there was something back up the road and that he was fixing to
turn around to see what it was. He was acting real scared and said he
thought it might be a body or something.

"Well, it was my boy lying back there, dead."

What was unusual about it, other than the fact that it was a very upset-
ting scene?

"We all know, and everyone knows, that something was awfully funny
about it. We don't know what to do about it. They first said my boy
was hit in the head by a hard instrument, and that's what they said the
autopsy showed. Then the sheriff's department said there was a car or
something that hit him. And then the sheriff said he was laying down
in the road, then that he was standing up, and then that he was bending over. They never could make up their mind what was going on. . . .
It was just real strange."

Anything else unusual?

"Well, my boy had told us that he was going to get killed, that someone
was going to kill him. I asked him who, but he never would say. You
know, he worked for me out in the woods, and he must've told me that
two or three times. His brother was in the Marines, and he told his brother
that he was going to get killed before he turned eighteen."

Had Mr. Hogue related this to anyone?

"Hell, yes. I've been to the sheriff, the Texas Rangers, the district attorney. Nobody has done nothing about it."

Did the accident have anything to do with drugs or dope?

"Well, all I know is that he knew something that he shouldn't have
known. I think he saw something out in the woods that he wasn't supposed to see."

Did his son use drugs or dope?

"He answered without hesitating. "He didn't take no more than any
other children. I can't say that he never smoked a marijuana cigarette,
but he wasn't hooked on it. I just believe he knew something that someone didn't want him to know."

He then handed the telephone to his wife, who wanted to talk to me.

"He told me that someone was going to kill him before he turned
eighteen," she said. "He was to turn eighteen on August 18. He never
said who it was. We just figured that he knew something."

I asked her what her son had being doing the night he was killed.

"That night, he'd been up to a nightclub at Pointblank, and they were asked to leave. . . ."

So he had not been alone?

"He was supposed to be with another boy, that's what the sheriff said, and they were too young to be at the club. We never heard anything from the boy who was supposed to have been there with him. . . . I really doubt that story."

Why?

"Well, usually on a Saturday night, they'd have this thing called a trail ride dance. They don't have it anymore. But it was this open building where the kids would have dances. It usually ended up about 1:00 a.m. That's where we think he went. And then he hitchhiked with someone and they stopped off in Coldspring. Some colored girls said they saw him get out of an old yellow car. And then some other kids that we know saw him walking further up the road. They said he looked all right and everything.

"A little while later, some relatives of ours saw him still walking up the road. They hollered at him and he said he was okay."

What road was that?

"Nine forty-six."

What time was all that taking place?

"It was after 1:00."

And what time did the accident happen?

"They said it was 1:50."

And what about the reserve deputy who first came upon the body?

"The sheriff said they questioned him, and that he had just run past the body there on the road. Said it was no big deal. He was just scared . . . not being used to seeing bodies and all. He was scared."

Was it unusual for her son to be out walking along 946 at that hour?

"Sort of, but not really. He usually was in one of our cars, but sometimes he'd be out walking."

We talked for another twenty minutes, going back over the night of the accident and the confusing reports that came from the sheriff's office in the days and weeks thereafter. Mr. Hogue and his wife kept handing the phone back and forth, as each one would remember some piece of information and want to relay it to me quickly. They were still terribly upset, and still perturbed at the investigation. But they weren't pointing fingers the way Mr. Kinder did about the hit-and-run murder of his son, Danny, on August 11, 1978 — nine months before Hogue's killing. I asked the two parents if they ever got a copy of the autopsy report.

Both said they never did.

Did they ever get a copy of the official accident report filed with the DPS?

No.

Did they ever receive copies of the death scene photographs that they said were taken by the San Jacinto County deputies?

No.

Had they requested copies of those documents?

Yes. Numerous times.

I decided to test them with one last question. Both parents had said that no one—sheriff, DPS, district attorney, or Texas Rangers—seemed interested in interviewing them. No one wanted to hear about their son's fears of being murdered before his eighteenth birthday. No one wanted to pursue the killing beyond the initial accident-scene investigation. Were the Hogues going to cross the line between merely wanting the probe reopened and accusing someone of the death without cause? I had to find out. So I asked, "Who do you think killed your son?"

"That's what the investigators are supposed to tell us," Mrs. Hogue said. "And all I know is, they haven't told us nothing."

Douthat was sitting almost transfixed on the edge of a chair, listening to my half of the interview. It was almost 9:15. The political rally was going to start pretty soon, and that's where we were headed. But my mind was still on FM 946 in the early morning hours of May 13, 1979. What in the hell had happened there?

Our trip from the Holiday Inn in Huntsville to the political rally in Coldspring would take us straight down 946, right across the scene of the homicide.

· SIXTEEN ·

The pavilion in the northwest corner of the courthouse square was all decked out in soggy red, white, and blue banners, and the ground around it was beginning to resemble a moat. Between seventy-five and one hundred people huddled impatiently beneath the wooden awnings of the tiny stores across the street to the north. A dozen or so candidates hustled through the crowd and passed out buttons and pamphlets. Half a dozen other people fumbled with microphones and amplifiers inside the pavilion. My guess was that it was awfully dangerous to be monkeying around with electrical equipment during a rainstorm. But the good people of Coldspring seemed determined to hold their big political rally, come hell or high water. It looked like high water might win.

I eased our *American-Statesman* car around the courthouse and turned onto a side street immediately south of the brick edifice. I parked head-in on the gravel lot, right under one of the many swooping trees and right next to a brand-spanking-new Chevrolet pickup with a huge K. P. Bryant bumper sticker and banner on the side. We hustled into the court-house, primarily to get out of the rain but secondarily because the smell of barbecue seemed to be oozing out of the courthouse's cracks and crevices. Not a bad place to cook a barbecue feast — right inside the foyer of the courthouse. Especially since it was pouring outside.

A dozen or so people shuffled around inside the building, checking out the paper plates and napkins, the beans, cole slaw, potato salad, and other assorted goodies. And a few people seemed to be having a good time watching the others work. Although it was barely 10:00, I felt a tremendous craving for a plate or two of that smoky delicacy. But we had other things to do right then. We eased our way out the west door of the building and across the street to mingle with the crowd. A middle-aged woman was explaining over the crackling PA system that the political speakers would begin talking just as soon as they all made their way over to the pavilion. I immediately noticed a tall, red-haired woman with a camera and recognized her from her self-description as Martha Charrey, the editor of the weekly newspaper.

I exchanged small talk with her for a few minutes while Douthat went to find a telephone. He wanted to call highway patrolman Red Blanchette, the primary DPS trooper assigned to the area around San Jacinto County and the person who had investigated most of the fatal accidents in that county over the last five or six years. Blanchette, who lived in Shepherd, had been highly recommended by Mike Jeffrey and Martha Charrey, among others, and we were told that he had some firsthand insight into the problems inside the San Jacinto County Sheriff's Department.

Several state legislative candidates muttered a few words about how proud they were to be natives of that area, and then a couple of unopposed officeholders trudged to the stand and thanked everyone for their support. And then the attention began shifting to the more hotly contested races. I thought of the clichés that could be used to hype this Saturday morning event: how "the excitement mounted" as everyone waited for Judge K. P. Bryant and his opponent, treasurer Kent Morrison, to take the stand and address the crowd. But then, suddenly, one of the women running against Imogene Trapp, the elderly county clerk, hurried to the microphone for her short talk and promised that if elected, she would keep the courthouse open during the lunch hour. Stop the presses! Now, here was an issue to top all issues. I could really identify with this type of campaign promise. And judging from the response of the crowd, I believed that they could as well. Was Mrs. Trapp destined for defeat? Stay tuned.

Douthat came back and said that we were on for a meeting with Blanchette at 12:30 that afternoon.

The drive from Coldspring to Shepherd took us right past a used-car lot on Highway 150 that had a sign proclaiming Morrison's Used Cars. Since the lot was perched on a hill off the highway right next to a house fitting the description Kent Morrison had given me for his house, I figured that the lot must be Morrison's. Brilliant deductive reasoning. The rain had stopped, and I was able to concentrate on the plateful of brisket, potato salad, and cole slaw that I had devoured a few minutes earlier. It was, without question, some of the best barbecue I had ever eaten, even though it cost $5 a plate.

We entered Shepherd about 12:20 — right on time — and headed straight for U.S. 59. Blanchette had told Douthat he lived on a dirt road right off the highway, south of Highway 150. We found the road without problems. And it didn't take the mind of Sherlock Holmes to find the house; a DPS patrol car was parked in the driveway of a stylish, neat one-story brick house. We knocked on the door at exactly 12:25, neither of us knowing for sure what this lawman would say when we told him we were looking into the deaths of young boys in his territory. We had decided to approach Blanchette point-blank with our questions, which we figured would give the impression that we knew a lot about what was going on. Or possibly that we didn't know what in the hell we were talking about. It was a calculated risk, but one we elected to take.

The highway patrolman was much younger than I had anticipated. He appeared to be in his early thirties and—true to his name—had closely cropped red hair. Medium built and rugged-looking, he was wearing the uniform of Southeast Texas—a white patterned shirt, jeans, and boots. He greeted us warmly and asked us to have a seat in his den. The house was impeccably furnished and remarkably neat. Most law officers I had known kept houses that looked like substandard jails.

After a minute or so of introductions, Douthat passed the ball to me. I got right to the point and said we were looking at a lot of things involving the San Jacinto County Sheriff's Department, and that we were particularly interested in the rash of auto-pedestrian deaths involving young men over the last three or four years. What disturbed us, I said, was the fact that so many of them were unsolved.

Blanchette shuffled uneasily in his chair and said he only knew of one that hadn't been solved—the Hogue death in May 1979.

What about the death of Joe Lynn Pickering on October 6, 1979? I asked.

"A man stopped on that," the trooper said. "He swerved to miss the boy, but as I recall he failed to say that he hit the body. He was no-billed by a grand jury on it."

Why didn't the accident reports filed with the state indicate that?

He said he didn't know. But he said that Pickering was supposedly on his hands and knees when he was struck by the car.

Wasn't it unusual for all those young boys and men to be out walking along those farm roads in the middle of the night, miles from anywhere?

"Not really. I see a lot of kids out walking along the road at night."

What about the Hogue death? The sheriff told the local newspaper that drugs were involved.

"The boy had a bag of grass in his shorts when he was hit. . . . And I believe he also was on his hands and knees."

Why wasn't the drug reported on the accident form?

He said he didn't know.

With all the similarities, were those deaths connected in any way, in his opinion?

"I don't think they were connected. . . ." He thought a minute, then said that neither Hogue nor Pickering had any broken bones from the collisions, and that both seemed to have died from blows to the head.

I got the impression that he wanted to help us but really didn't have a great deal of information to pass along, at least in this area. I asked a dozen or so questions about the procedures used in the San Jacinto County sheriff's office, and he explained that he tried to mind his own business and let them do their own jobs. He said he had enough to do without worrying about what other officers were doing.

Douthat asked a few questions about evidence that Blanchette obtained when he searched cars on U.S. 59, and the trooper said all his evidence was sent to DPS labs.

I asked if he did many searches on 59.

Not really, he said. He wrote a lot of tickets, but he tried to stay out of the way of the sheriff's department and never worked the same area that the local deputies did. He explained that he often had to cover for local departments in Liberty County, Polk County, and Montgomery County, in addition to San Jacinto County, and that he seldom paid a lot of attention to what everyone else was doing. He said his DPS partner, Trooper Van Loggins, lived next door to him and accompanied him on a lot of his duties. They believed it was the best policy to stay out of local matters whenever possible, but they were always available to help out if a local department needed assistance.

I could tell where this interview was heading, so I began to wind it down. Douthat had a few other things to ask, most of them dealing with the types of people Blanchette stopped on 59, and the types of people arrested for various other crimes in that part of the state. None of this was going to see its way into print, but it was good background, at least for Douthat. He needed to hear someone else tell him the things I had been telling him.

We left inside of forty-five minutes, after spending a good ten minutes on idle chitchat. Blanchette was a nice man who would probably help us if he could. But he obviously was not going to get involved in a name-calling contest with local law enforcement agencies. And he wasn't going to say anything that might jeopardize his tenured position as a trooper . . . especially since he had a nice house and secure place in that part of the state.

The drive back from Shepherd to Coldspring seemed to take forever.

It was raining again in Coldspring by midafternoon, and the political rally had finally broken up. By all accounts, it had been a roaring success. About a hundred people got to listen to two dozen candidates talk about what a good job they'd do if elected the following Saturday, May 1, and how everything would be much nicer if only the good folks would cast their ballots in the proper Christian, Democratic, and American manner. Everyone got to hear a fairly scathing five-minute talk by Kent Morrison, who lambasted Judge Bryant for running a negative campaign that, according to Morrison, included lies, name-calling, and other horrible things that just flat were not true. And then Bryant got to moan for another five minutes about how everyone was ganging up on him, when all he was trying to do was, simply, the best job he could. Bryant reminded everyone that he had never really wanted to run for a second term, but a large number of people had persuaded him to . . . to save the county from the evils of creeping bureaucracy, or worse. Suffice it to say that a glorious time was had by all, and the weather be damned.

We had almost two hours to kill before our 4:00 meeting with Morrison, so we spent some time cruising around Coldspring. We stopped at a couple of coffee-shop-type places, went in and ordered a couple of cups, and generally tried to see if anyone would show up and say anything that we could overhear. Both of us were sorting through Blanchette's comments in our minds, and we were confused about how we could pursue the hit-and-run deaths. We were faced with a perplexing situation: no real documents, no evidence, no medical reports, no suspects, nothing except the fears and concerns of the parents of the youngsters. Always the parents. It seems that the parents are always the ones who say the most intriguing things, who put the pieces together better (or worse) than anyone else, who complain the most about conspiracies and stalled investigations. Unfortunately, they are also the ones who are closest to the cases, and their statements are the most biased and nearsighted. Damn. What were we to make of Blanchette's claim that none of the deaths bore any connection to the others? What were we to do about his statement that only the Hogue case, to his knowledge, was unsolved? Obviously, he had either forgotten or never known about the August 11, 1978, killing of Danny Kinder down in Montgomery County, and about Hank Kinder's concerns about a tie-in between the death and the others. Was I the only person who listened to the parents? Was I wrong in doing that? And how would the words of the parents help me to get a story into print before my city editor pulled the plug on the whole thing? Douthat and I hashed over these questions for most of that two-hour period. We didn't come up with any answers, but we felt we might do better to downplay the homicides for the time being while we pulled out all the stops on the Highway 59 operation. Maybe something would surface later.

We drove up the steep gravel driveway just to the left of Morrison's large brick house about 4:05 p.m. It was still raining. Another car was pulling up behind us, and a large, heavyset man with a thick brown beard got out after we did and followed us to the side door. The county treasurer greeted us at the door and explained quickly that the person behind us was "just a friend" who was dropping by. At the time, I didn't think anything of it. Morrison led us into his dining room and offered us a cup of coffee, which we readily accepted. It would be at least my tenth cup that day.

As we settled into our chairs, Morrison — who looked for all the world like a country musician with his jet-black hair combed straight back on top of his head Elvis style — brought in the coffee and asked what he could do for us.

I explained, again, who we were and said we were looking into a number of things related to law enforcement in San Jacinto County, in particular the activities along Highway 59. And I said we had come up with some unsettling information about the hit-and-run deaths of young boys. We were in the process of talking to a number of county officials to see if they could help us shed some light on all this. I tried my best to sound official, yet at the same time a little searching. I wanted to give Morrison every opportunity to say . . . well, anything he wanted to say. And we weren't necessarily interested in quoting him by name in our newspaper, I said; all we wanted to know was what was going on.

Morrison remained standing. His bearded friend took a seat nearby. The treasurer laughed a little and then apologetically asked to see *our* identification. "You've got to understand that I'm in the middle of a pretty important political campaign, and I can't take any chances." He wanted to see our identification! Rather than risk our tenuous places in his house, we quickly pulled out our press cards and passed them over. He gave them a full twenty-second look and then passed them to his friend, whose presence suddenly become more noticeable. Finally Morrison said he was satisfied that we were who we said we were. He apologized again.

No problem, I said. We understood how things can get in a heated political campaign. Now, what could he tell us about the drug arrests on 59?

Not a whole lot, he said. He tried to stay out of all that.

Well, what about the deaths of the young boys? Did he recall anything that might be of use to us?

He thought for a few seconds, then whispered quickly with his friend. He said he would be candid with us: he really didn't have any firsthand information, *but* . . . the whole county was pretty upset by those deaths. Something wasn't quite right about them.

"You mean the Hogue death?" I asked.

Not just that one, he said. He didn't recall the names or the dates, and the circumstances of each were a little fuzzy in his mind, but he did know for a fact that those deaths were bizarre.

And the investigations by the sheriff?

Even more bizarre, he said.

Could he be more specific?

"I only wish I could," he said.

We spent more than two hours with Kent Morrison, his wife, and the bearded friend. (We never did find out who he was.) Our conversation covered a wide range of topics, from the hit-and-runs to procedural matters in the courthouse. As treasurer, Morrison was primarily a check writer for the county, and he only rarely became involved in anything else. Well, he did raise horses and sell some cars, and he played in a country-and-western band, but he really didn't have anything to say about or do with the administration of justice in San Jacinto County. He was merely an onlooker. But, he said pointedly on several occasions, he was not happy with what was going on, and he would be making some real changes if he was elected county judge.

Oh, what kind of changes did he plan?

He hedged a bit but said he would make sure that people who appeared in his court understood what they were charged with and that everything that came before him was documented and written up in the court dockets. He said it was awful how cases were handled by Judge Bryant. Again, he said he wished he could be more specific, but. . . .

We left his house about 6:15 and decided we needed to get back to our motel in Huntsville to work the phones. It was starting to get dark—or was it just heavy clouds?—when we drove onto Highway 150 for the pass through Coldspring. I felt a little queasy driving up FM 946 again, wondering where exactly the death of Charles Hogue took place. That fifteen-mile trek along 946 from Coldspring to Oakhurst was one of the most desolate stretches of road I had ever seen, and the fact that it was smack in the middle of the Sam Houston National Forest made it seem even more isolated. We didn't pass one car in either direction during this trip, and I wondered if anyone ever used this road on a regular basis, other than the few people who lived back in the woods . . . like the Hogues.

According to Mike Jeffrey, there was as good bit of marijuana up in that area off 946; at least, there had been one forty-seven-acre haul in the recent past. Was there more? Were there marijuana plantations out in that dense forest? Did young Charles Hogue know about them? Did he find one at the wrong time? I had to stop thinking about it; that boy's death was driving me crazy. And what was messing me up the most was the fear I had that I wouldn't be able to do anything about it.

This Saturday night was going to be our last night in the forests for this trip. We needed to get back to Austin to report to Ed, to check on a few things, and to clear our minds. We figured that the best way to appease our boss was to nail down the apparent widespread harassment on Highway 59. If we could write the definitive story on Highway 59, we might be able to buy time to work on other aspects of this ever-growing, ever-aggravating story.

About 7:30, I reached Lee Mackey, the Huntsville private investigator, and thanked him for getting us in touch with Walker County deputy Charlie Pierce. Mackey, however, had someone with him whom he wanted me to talk to, a young man by the name of John Patrick who had been arrested within the last two years by the San Jacinto County sheriff. The arrest, according to Mackey, was ridiculous, and it involved gunshots fired by the officers. It sounded promising.

Patrick got on the line, and he said he treated the incident now as a big joke. I asked him to explain, and he did: He and a friend were partying in Huntsville on Sunday night, August 31, 1980. The friend was pretty drunk, but Patrick didn't drink, so he agreed to drive his friend back to his residence in Waterwood, located in the far north section of San Jacinto County. "I stopped by a convenience store in Huntsville to get some chocolate milk and a granola bar. I was driving a new Lincoln, and we were on 190. I wasn't speeding or anything. I guess we were fifteen or twenty miles from Huntsville when we passed an old Ford going real slow. We passed in a passing zone. I figured nothing was wrong. . . . But then I saw these lights flashing on bright and dim real fast, you know, the headlights. I wondered just what in the hell this guy was doing.

"I sped up to sixty-five or seventy miles an hour trying to get away. I didn't know who it was. We went two or three miles, when he pulled up beside me and motioned for me to pull over. There were two colored guys in the old car. I didn't know who they were, so I just kept on going. That's when they peeled off a couple of rounds at me, pulled up again, and flashed a badge. I nodded and pulled over in a driveway."

He said he didn't know what the trouble was, or why he'd been shot at. "But they came up to the car like a couple of madmen and kept saying, 'Why didn't you pull over? Why didn't you pull over?' Man, I was driving a $15,000 Mark V and I wasn't about to put it into a ditch!"

Patrick said he and his friend were arrested, the car was impounded, and they were taken to jail in Coldspring. They were told they were being charged with speeding, passing in a no-passing zone, and resisting arrest. According to Patrick, they never went before a judge, but a bondsman said it would cost each of them $150 to get out; they paid the money after staying in jail about three hours.

"Everyone was treating it as sort of comical. The bondsman and everyone said it was just a couple of nigger cops out to bust some guys in a nice car. . . . I'll bet you this: I bet we don't have any kind of record over there. They just dreamed up a number to charge us. It was Labor Day weekend, and they figured how much money we could pay and they just took it. We were out $150 each, and we paid the money straight to the bondsman. I've still got my check to him."

Did anyone mention the shots being fired?

"Nope . . . and we didn't bring it up."

Did he plan to take any sort of action?

"No, not really. . . . Compared to some of the things going on over there that I've heard about, this is pretty minor."

Patrick certainly seemed to be taking his arrest in stride. Still, he was another victim, another name to add to my list, another person processed through the criminal justice system in San Jacinto County. Only he'd been shot at—by two officers driving an old unmarked Ford.

I was keyed up again. I spent a good two hours comparing names from the court dockets with the names in the Houston telephone directory, and I made at least three dozen calls to the directory assistance operator in Houston. It was tedious work. None of the names seemed to match exactly. But I was prepared to contact as many victims of the sheriff's department as I could. And the only way to do that was to stick my ear against the telephone and start punching out numbers.

· SEVENTEEN ·

I tracked down Kip Carr by phone at 4:00 p.m. on Tuesday, April 27, two days after we returned from Huntsville and fourteen weeks after I started working on this story. Justice of the peace Mike Jeffrey had said that Carr's arrest on Highway 59 for carrying a stick was one that I ought to check on. I had checked all the docket books and criminal files in the county clerk's office in Coldspring for 1979, 1980, 1981, and the first three and a half months of 1982, and I had found no name similar to Kip Carr's. But that was about what Judge Jeffrey had said I'd find. Now I had to hear what Carr had to say:

"It happened the day before deer season opened last November, on a Friday night [November 13, 1981]. I had gotten off work. My family owns this tire store here in Baytown [thirty miles east of Houston], and I live in Dayton in Liberty County. I was going up 59 to meet my brother in Livingston to go deer hunting. . . ."

"Had you heard about San Jacinto County's reputation for patrolling Highway 59 on weekend nights?"

"Oh, yeah. Deputies and constables always patrol it. I'd driven up that way a lot and seen them."

"What happened to you that night?"

"Well, I was driving fifty in a fifty-five and this deputy pulled out and got behind me just north of Shepherd, and he pulled me over. I asked him why, but he just told me to shut up and give him my license. I had sacks of deer clothes with me, and he got in the car and went through all them. He looked in the ashtray; heck, I don't even smoke, but I keep some loose change in there. He looked all under the seats and everything. I had this piece of broom handle that my six-year-old girl plays with; it was in there propping up my radio, to keep it from rattling. . . . I asked him what he was looking for, but he told me again to shut up. Well, he found that broom handle and smiled real big and said, 'Son, you fixing to go to jail for having an illegal weapon.' I thought he was joking."

"What time did this happen?"

"It was between 7:00 and 7:30 p.m."

"Then what happened?"

"He arrested me, handcuffed me. They had this tow truck there real fast, too. He took me to jail like a wild man, like he was in a big hurry."

"What was going on at the jail when you got there?"

"They had eight people in jail when I got there. All of them had been picked up on 59 . . . mostly for stupid things. They arrested three guys in one car for having one diet pill. I had to call my parents in Baytown to come up and get me. They said my bond was $1,000."

"Who set the bond?"

"I have no idea."

"Did you go before a judge?"

"No, they just told me that my bond was $1,000, and that it would cost $50 for the towing fee. You know, before that deputy got me back to his car, the tow truck was already there. He couldn't have radioed for it, because he never went to his car to use the radio."

"Did you know who the deputy was?"

"Not at first. But I found out at the jail that it was the sheriff's son."

"Gary Parker?"

"Yeah, that was his name."

"What else occurred?"

"Well, the bondsman said it was all ridiculous, that he was bonding me out on a charge that didn't really exist. I was pretty mad, and I was going to get a lawyer, but I decided to go to the FBI first."

"When was that?"

"A couple of months ago. I gave them a six- or seven-page statement. . . . You know, I'm not a long-haired hippie or anything. They were just out on the highway looking for someone driving alone."

"Do you remember who the bondsman was?"

"Yeah, it was Herb Atwood. It turns out he knows my parents."

"How long were you in jail?"

"I got out at 1:30 a.m. I had to pay $100 and $50 for towing to get out."

"Who got the money?"

"Some secretary there in the jail. She gave me a receipt."

"Where is the receipt?"

"I've still got it. I showed it to the FBI."

"Was there a lot going on in the jail while you were there?"

"Oh, yeah. They were so busy they had to call in another bondsman to handle all the people. It was really ridiculous. Atwood said it was ridiculous. . . . A lot of the people were pulled over for nothing, then they said they found beer or marijuana in the car."

"What can you tell me about the broom handle?"

"It's about one and a half feet long and one inch thick. It was pretty flimsy. There was nothing on it, no lead, nothing. It was just a plain old broom handle. My daughter liked to keep it in the car. Heck, if I even tried to hit someone with it, it would probably break."

"What else do you remember about the people in the jail?"

"There was one man in the jail who said his girlfriend was searched pretty good in a ditch on the side of the road. . . ."

"Do you have his name?"

"No."

"Anything else?"

"All I know is they got $150 of my hard-earned money. If I was speeding or doing something wrong, then I'd 've deserved it. But it was all totally out of the ordinary. I mean, the way he handcuffed me and threw me in his car. And he put those cuffs on real tight."

"Did Gary Parker drive you to jail?"

"No, that was what was strange. He called for another officer to drive me."

"Any reason why?"

"They never said. . . . I thought it was weird."

"If Parker didn't take you to jail, who wrote up the arrest report and the jail paperwork?"

"You won't believe this, but it'll give you a big idea what kind of racket they have going. I wasn't ever read my rights by any officer. There were two jail trusties who were writing up all the arrest forms and reading the rights to the prisoners. One of them read me my rights. He was some wino-looking guy wearing white jail clothes. I couldn't believe it was really happening, but it was going on all night. The trusties said the officers were too busy on 59 to stop and write up reports. And I can believe it."

"Did you tell all this to the FBI?"

"Every bit of it."

"Have you heard any more from them?"

"Not one word. Nothing."

"Would you be willing to testify to all this in court?"

"What do you think? I stayed mad about it for three weeks. Now all I want is to get them to stop what they're doing up there."

"So you would testify?"

"You bet."

"And you don't have any problems with my using your name in my story."

"Nope. . . . I just hope you can get something done. I've been waiting around for something to happen, but nobody seems very interested in all this."

My victims of justice in San Jacinto County were starting to add up. From a slow beginning that included primarily the word of J. E. Foley of Jamestown, Kentucky, I had progressed in a little more than three months to the point where I could establish a definite pattern of activity on 59 and 190. I had the stories of Mr. Foley, Jeffrey Foley, and Patsy DeBorde, the Kentucky travelers who wound up in the Coldspring jail; of Darrell Johnson, the Livingston oil field worker who found his way to the jail; of the three teenagers from Longview, who suffered the humiliation of a court hearing in which Judge Bryant sentenced them to be tested for VD; of the eight fraternity brothers from Sam Houston State University who found themselves victimized by a stop-and-search roadblock; of John Patrick, the Huntsville man who wound up on the receiving end of gunshots during a weird stop in the northern part of the county; and, finally, of Kip Carr, a Baytown businessman who had apparently done nothing wrong. Seventeen people in all. Thousands of dollars in bail bonds. Hundreds of dollars in towing fees. Hours of humiliation and degradation. Of these seventeen, no charges or fee reports could be found for six; indeed, even for the eleven for whom charges were recorded on the court dockets, the record did not include such substantive information as the name of the arresting officer, the exact location of the arrest, the exact time of the arrest, the arrestee's address, the probable cause for the search and seizure, a narrative description of events that led to the arrest, a detailed account of what occurred after the arrest. If my random searching for names had come up with this many victims with this many incredible stories, how many more were there out there? I kept plugging.

The day after I talked to Kip Carr I added three more names to my list, bringing the total to twenty.

Richard Morris Ponder was a Houston resident whose name appeared on one of the misdemeanor dockets in the county clerk's office; he had been charged with possession of marijuana. I located him on Wednesday morning, April 28, at his home in Houston.

Ponder, his wife, Deborah, and his friend Kenneth Wayne Oliver were driving up Highway 59 from Houston on Friday night, March 19, 1982, about 9:30, on their way to Lake Livingston to fish. They were stopped in a typical spot—just north of Shepherd—by San Jacinto County deputies.

"We were driving about fifty miles an hour, and none of us were drinking or anything," Ponder recalled. "This cop pulled us over and said he couldn't see our license plate light from 150 yards back. It was really crazy, because I had two new bulbs in it, and it was a new car. And then he said he saw some marijuana on the floor of the car and made us get out."

Was there dope on the floor? I asked.

"No, but there were some marijuana seeds in the glove compartment. I told this cop when he found the seeds that I would take full responsibility for it. He just said, 'That's tough,' and arrested all three of us. What was weird was that he handcuffed my wife, but not me or my friend."

"What kind of car did you have?"

"A brand-new Toyota Celica."

"Was the license plate light out?"

"No. The bulbs were brand-new. *Everything* was new on the car."

"Who read you your rights?"

"No one did. The only person we talked to was the bondsman. He's the one who took our money and wrote us a receipt."

"Did you get searched along with the car?"

"They frisked us pretty good. And they strip-searched my wife at the jail."

"Did you go to court?"

"Not that night. We never saw a judge. But our trial was supposed to be today in Coldspring. But I called the judge and got it delayed until May."

"What are you going to do about it now?"

"I guess I'll go up there and see what happens. I just wish there was something I could do."

More and more victims. The arrest trap on 59 was unbelievable; it seemed to be operating in gross violation of constitutional rights. I mean, there are supposed to be guarantees against unreasonable search and seizure, stipulations about probable-cause, and strong demands for due process of law in the Bill of Rights, aren't there? I had sat in enough criminal courtrooms over the last ten years to know that every defense lawyer worth his salt will first challenge the probable-cause angle for an arrest, a search warrant, or a vehicle stop. In most of the cases I had seen, the state, represented by district attorneys and police officers, was able to produce written documentation stating the reasons that probable cause existed. But in San Jacinto County there were no written documents with that kind of information! What judge would uphold an arrest or search in which this detail was lacking? None that I knew of, but then I had never before investigated a county like this one. It was truly the Free State of San Jacinto, complete with its own rules and regulations and its own interpretation of probable cause and due process. And of course, it had no full-time district attorney, no resident state district judge, nobody but Sheriff Humpy Parker and county judge K. P. Bryant. As

long as they never filed any felony cases, they could hear everything in
Judge Bryant's court; and as long as no one raised a stink, they could
run their little game as long as they wanted. I determined right then that
it was my job to raise a stink. A barrage of stories should do it. All I
had to do was convince Ed.

Sure, Ed was interested in the story, and he wanted to see it in print
as soon as possible. But his expressions of interest seemed to be con-
tradicted by his scheduling arrangements for his reporters. This week was
no exception. Here I was, back in the office, which in the minds of Ed
and his assistants on the city desk meant that I was free to handle emergencies. At the *Austin American-Statesman*, there were emergencies every day.
I spent most of the last week in April wasting my time on daily news.
Douthat, too, was being bombarded from several different directions, and
he was unable to do much work in the office. I wound up spending most
of my nights at home on the telephone talking to "my victims" and "my
sources," trying to find out first of all if anything new had occurred, and
second of all what the FBI was doing. From what I could tell, the federal
boys were not doing a great deal. And, thank heavens, no other reporters
were nosing around.

On Sunday, May 2, I called Martha Charrey to find out how the election had gone the previous day. Martha was beside herself with
excitement — the voters of San Jacinto County had struck a blow for . . .
what? Justice? Well, the outcome at least was quite unexpected: Imogene
Trapp, the seventy-nine-year-old county clerk, had been defeated by Lois
Cooksey, the woman who promised to keep the courthouse open during
the lunch hour; Gary Parker, the sheriff's own flesh and blood, had been
trounced in his race for Democratic party chairman; Frank Winfrey, a
commissioner appointed by Judge Bryant to fill an unexpired term, had
gotten knocked off; and, amazingly, Kent Morrison had defeated Bryant
in the race for county judge.

I quickly called Morrison to offer my congratulations; I decided not
to call Bryant. From a half-dozen calls, I ascertained that the populace
of San Jacinto County was in shock; people almost couldn't believe what
had happened on Saturday, May 1, the day the incumbents were bounced
out of office. The only problem was that the newly elected officials, according to state law, would not take office for another seven months, not
until January 1, 1983. And several residents were wondering if there would
be any retaliation by the incumbents during those months. It sounded
almost too medieval to believe; but in that county, anything was possible.

The next two days were spent on the telephone. Charlie Pierce, the
Walker County deputy, called several times to pass on bits and pieces
of street gossip about the San Jacinto County department, and Lee

Mackey, the Huntsville investigator, called twice to say that Pierce was scared and didn't ever want to be quoted by name.

And then, suddenly, on Tuesday, May 4, Pierce called a third time. He said a San Jacinto County deputy wanted to talk to me. The deputy was fed up with Sheriff Parker and his department, according to Pierce, and he was sick and tired of breaking the law on Highway 59 and elsewhere. The deputy wanted to tell us everything he knew. But there was a condition. Pierce said the deputy had been getting death threats and was a little uneasy about his situation, and he wanted to meet us somewhere outside San Jacinto County.

I quickly mentioned Huntsville, and Pierce said that was fine.

Where in Huntsville? I asked.

At the Hungry Hobo restaurant on the I-45 access road.

What day? What time?

Pierce said in a low voice, "The sooner the better."

I glanced down at my calendar and replied, "How about tomorrow? We can get over there any time you want."

Pierce said the San Jacinto County deputy could meet us at 9:30 tomorrow night, at the Hungry Hobo, if we could make it.

"We'll make it," I assured him. "And can you tell me who this deputy is?"

"Greg Magee."

· EIGHTEEN ·

I spent at least nine hours on the telephone on Tuesday, May 4, the day before we were to leave for Coldspring. Most of the calls were what I would consider productive. I learned that Deputy Greg Magee was openly upset about the procedures used on Highway 59 and had refused to make any more arrests out there. And Magee also was troubled by the apparently routine habit of doctoring up arrest reports right before court dates and — according to justice of the peace Mike Jeffrey — right before the FBI boys arrived to look them over. I couldn't ascertain what was meant by "doctoring," whether it meant falsifying information or merely belated recording of already documented facts. No one seemed to know. But I bet Magee did.

Judge Jeffrey and Lee Mackey also were concerned about veiled threats of violence directed at persons who appeared willing to help us or the FBI. The judge even said that Deputy Magee had been ordered not to be seen around him. Mackey said that Magee's life had been threatened. But no one would tell me who was making all these threats, if in fact they ever occurred. My gut feeling was that everyone was starting to get paranoid, for real or imagined reasons. Other names of deputies and reserve deputies started coming in, persons who *might* talk to me if I approached them inconspicuously. I took down every scrap of information I could get.

But then, about 11:00 p.m., Lee Mackey called and said some people in Governor Bill Clements' office were starting to get interested in San Jacinto County, especially about the death threats. Mackey said he knew a few people in Austin who did not want anything embarrassing to come out in the newspaper before they had a chance to see what was going on.

What was that supposed to mean?

He said he wasn't real sure. But the potential for a big scandal was looming on the horizon — at least in the minds of some state officials — and the governor's people might want me to hold up on my story, at least until a task force could be appointed to look into it.

Hold up on a story? I couldn't agree to do that. I questioned Mackey extensively about his talks with "people" in Clements' office, and it appeared that most of the furor had been generated by the unspecified rumors of death threats and vaguely described unsolved murders. Paranoia was spreading, and that was a terrible omen for me. As wild stories spread, the chances increased that the Houston newspapers would find out that something was going on seventy miles north of them. And if they found that out, they could short-circuit my work by flooding the area with reporters who would be out to disprove rumors rather than to find out the truth. I got pretty panicky, and I called Douthat a few minutes after midnight. We decided to make an early start—as early as possible. We had our backs to the wall. There was no way to fight a spreading rumor. We had to start planning to write a story, and soon.

I could just imagine Governor Clements calling a press conference to announce that a task force was being named to look into problems in San Jacinto County. Every damn newspaper in the state would be sending people to Coldspring to find out what, indeed, was going on. The story would be gone. My victims would be gone. Greg Magee would be gone. The Hogue family would be left behind, with no real hope of any solution to their son's homicide.

There was no time to lose. And Douthat agreed. It was 12:15 a.m. on Wednesday, May 5, and our interview with Deputy Greg Magee was more than twenty-one hours away. We figured that after this trip, we would have to write a story within two weeks, at the most. The story would have to be the best, the strongest, the most revealing we could put together. And it would have to be something we could back up with names, dates, facts. We were a long way from writing anything about the unsolved homicides, the marijuana plantations, the disappearing evidence, the weird drug raids, or any of that. But we were very close to writing about the marijuana arrest trap on Highway 59—and we could back it up with several stories from victims. If Greg Magee confirmed our stories, and if we could double-confirm them with some other deputy or reserve, then we could write. Those were two big ifs.

Magee introduced himself to us at exactly 9:35 p.m. at a small table near the fireplace at the Hungry Hobo. He was much younger than I had expected, only twenty-five. It took me a few minutes to recall that old proverb about appearances being misleading. Not knowing what Magee would say, or how he would react to questions, Douthat and I kept our notebooks concealed in our pockets. We had a tape recorder but decided to leave it in the car. We were walking on eggshells. This, without question, was the most apprehensive and cautious I had ever been at the beginning of an interview. I mean, here was a San Jacinto deputy who, according to several people, was willing to talk. But there were some anonymous death threats lurking in the background. Would he talk to us?

I doubted it. At least not there. Three or four Walker County deputies were sitting at an adjoining table sipping coffee. I was almost certain that Magee was feeling uncomfortable when he sat down, although he was the type of person who masked his feelings well. After five minutes of forgettable chitchat, I mentioned that we were staying right up the road at the Holiday Inn, less than a half-mile away, and I asked whether "we" wouldn't all feel more comfortable there.

Douthat nodded quickly (we didn't have that part planned).

And so did Magee.

We made a quick exit from the restaurant to the parking lot, where Magee got into his dark-colored coupé and said he would follow us to the hotel.

The drive took, by the clock, less than three minutes, but it seemed more like three hours. We got into our first-floor room (with the obligatory pool view) at a few minutes before 10:00.

The next time I looked at my watch it was 1:30 a.m.

In a three-and-a-half-hour interview, Magee confirmed most of the information I had obtained during the preceding four months. His memory was a bit hazy in places, and he really didn't know a great deal about the hit-and-run deaths, and he had a tendency to engage in gossip and speculation to cover gaps in his firsthand knowledge, but he did indeed have a great deal of firsthand knowledge.

He said he had started to work for Humpy Parker in February 1975 as a dispatcher, and except for a couple of brief intervals when he had quit and been rehired, he had been around and involved in the San Jacinto County Sheriff's Department ever since. He said he decided to talk to us because the arrests on Highway 59 and elsewhere had gotten "out of hand." The deputies were instructed by Sheriff Parker, he said, to break the law, to ignore due process, probable cause, and other constitutional rights. And frankly, he said, he was tired of it.

"We started a few years ago making all these marijuana arrests, and I found that a lot of them were not right. They weren't good arrests."

In what way?

"There was no probable cause. K-101 [a Houston rock radio station] bumper stickers were probable cause to stop a car. Any old cars were

probable cause. No hubcaps. A driver wearing a headband. Any of that.
The sheriff said that any Louisiana license plate with a G in the middle
was probable cause, because he said that came from a county that was
controlled by the Dixie Mafia."

Over the seven-year period since he first went to work as a dispatcher,
Magee said, he had quit three times. The first resignation revolved around
a knife fight at a black night spot, in which a load of weapons was seized.
He said Sheriff Parker didn't handle the arrests the way they should have
been handled and then ordered him not to go before the grand jury that
was investigating the case. The second resignation, he said, stemmed from
a disagreement about time off; and the third one occurred when he refused
to obey an order from the sheriff's secretary. He said there was a great
deal of tension in the department as a result of the work of Gary Parker,
the sheriff's son, and Cindy McCash, the sheriff's secretary. Both of them,
according to Magee, tried to run the sheriff's department.

We asked him to describe a typical night on Highway 59.

"We'd sit at the crossovers way up north, near the Trinity River bridge,
near the liquor store there, and look for likely suspects."

"Who were likely suspects?"

"Like I said, young kids, people with headbands, blacks, old cars, K-101
bumper stickers, out-of-state license plates, all that."

"And that was sufficient cause to stop a car?"

"Yep."

"Why did you do it? Why does everyone do it? Who told you to do
all this?"

"The sheriff is the one that taught us all this. He's the best at it."

"What did you tell someone who asked why he was stopped?"

"Oh, you'd just make something up. You'd say that the car was weaving, or that the lights were blinking on and off, that there must have
been a short or something."

"And then you'd search the cars?"

"That's right."

"Are you doing any of this now?"

"No, when I came back the last time I refused to search cars out on
59. I'm transporting now."

"Transporting?"

"From 59 to the jail."

I asked about the stories I'd heard about jail trusties reading rights to
people and filling out arrest reports.

Magee said that happened all the time, mostly to free the deputies to
get back onto 59 — to make more arrests.

"What is the most arrests you've seen in one night?"

"Sixty-nine . . . just a couple of months ago."

I related a few details from the victims I had talked with—the Foleys, the fraternity kids, Kip Carr, John Patrick, Richard Ponder—and asked if those types of arrests were possible in that county.

"Oh, yeah. All the time."

"And the complaints these people are raising about probable cause and illegal arrests . . . ?"

"They're good complaints. . . . Not many of the arrests out there are good ones."

I asked about tow trucks and bondsmen, specifically about how they always seemed to show up at the right time.

His answer was simple. "They know all about what's going on," he said.

"And the activities of Gary Parker?"

"He's the most active out there."

"But the sheriff told me Gary wasn't working anymore."

"Not anymore . . . that's what they say. But he still gets out there."

"Using other radio call numbers?"

"A lot of times, yes."

"With all those marijuana arrests, there must be a lot of dope in the property room."

"That's what you'd think."

"Then there isn't a lot?" I told him I had heard stories about evidence disappearing from the property room.

"Happens all the time."

"What about complaints of deputies planting dope in cars they stop?"

"I've heard a few of those myself."

"Does it happen?"

"I feel pretty sure it does."

We spent several minutes discussing the heavy drug usage of several local residents, and the discovery of several large dope fields in the county, but Magee said that very little was ever done to "the locals."

"The sheriff wanted us to concentrate on people who don't live here," he said.

We also retraced the bizarre burglary of Johnston's Pharmacy in the early part of the year—the incident in which Gary Parker and a friend of his, Ronnie Greer, said they were shot at by the burglars, but none of the investigators ever found a trace of the assailants. Magee said he was one of those investigators, along with Judge Jeffrey and several others.

Greer, according to Magee, was someone we ought to check on. He said Greer was working as a deputy but was not a commissioned peace officer. And he could never be commissioned, Magee added, because of his criminal record.

A criminal was working as a deputy?

"That's right."

How was that possible?

"He's Gary's friend."

I asked again about disappearing evidence. What types of things could get taken out of the property room?

"Drugs, guns, whiskey, almost anything."

Who had access to the property room?

"Before the FBI came to town a while back, anybody could go in there."

Wasn't there a log, a check-out sheet, or something of that nature to show what was brought in and what was taken out?

"No, sir. Nothing."

What about the evidence he personally took from the scene of a crime? What did he do with it?

"I take all my evidence home with me. I know it's going to stay there when I take it there."

We spent a good half-hour talking about the hit-and-run deaths. Magee, though, had little concrete information. But he did say that he had taken it upon himself to investigate the killing of Charles Hogue.

I asked him why he did that.

"Me and my partner worked it without the knowledge of the sheriff. The sheriff said it was a Highway Patrol deal."

"But why did you do it?"

"It just didn't seem right."

"In what way?"

"Just about every way."

I asked him about the other deaths, but he knew even less than I did. But he said all of them were more than strange coincidences. He said there was a lot going on in that county that would be very hard to prove.

We asked for more information about the rumors we'd heard about doctored reports.

"If you mean falsifying information, I'd say that that's not uncommon."

I asked if he'd personally seen any information being falsified.

"Not personally. But I haven't been up there [Coldspring] since the FBI came in here. . . . I try to stay away from there as much as I can."

Douthat asked again for details about the arrest trap on 59, and Magee seemed eager to provide them.

"They park out there in the crossover lanes with the headlights on bright—just to see what the cars going by look like. They're almost always up there near FM 1127, because that's where the crossovers are closer to each other. And if the cars don't turn off 59 onto 1127, then that means they're out of county. The general consensus is 'Don't jack with the local folks.' "

I asked about the concealment of names of arresting officers on the paperwork filed in court. Was there any reason for that?

He said he didn't really know.

Digressing a minute, I asked if it was possible that much of the marijuana seized in the Highway 59 arrests wound up getting burned.

Magee laughed. "There hasn't been a dope burning around here at least in three years."

And what about that forty-seven-acre dope field up near Oakhurst? Did that actually happen the way we'd been told?

"It really happened. Me and a game warden, Bobby Bartlett, were working that deal, but the next thing we knew, Rathell Denson and Carl Lee took a bunch of prisoners up there to get it."

Denson the constable and Lee the deputy?

"Yes, sir. It took them weeks to get all that stuff out of there. They supposedly took it all to the county dump and buried it."

Why wasn't any of that reported? It would have been the biggest dope seizure in state history.

"I have no idea what went on. All I know is that I was working the case and all of a sudden it got taken away from me."

Did any of this ever get reported, if not to the newspapers, then at least to the state?

"No. Nothing we convict around here ever goes to the state, except DWIs, and that's only because it's required by law."

What about fingerprints? Did they get turned in to the state or the feds?

"They don't. Because no one is ever fingerprinted around here. Not for anything."

Any reason for that?

"Your guess is as good as mine."

Douthat asked about a report that the tow truck drivers had county radios in their vehicles.

"That's true. They . . . have county radios, and they talk back and forth on the same frequency. The sheriff's department dispatches for all of them."

We started going back over a few points, clarifying some things. For the most part, Magee was unable to come up with specific dates or names. But he gave us the names of several other deputies and former deputies who he said could confirm everything he had told us. We carefully wrote down the names. And then he handed me a handwritten statement he said he had found in one of the files in the sheriff's office. It was a three-page document that was dated "10-15-80." And it was from a man who claimed he had been subjected to water torture while in the custody of the San Jacinto County Sheriff's Department.

I told Magee I would make a copy of it and return the original to him.

It was 1:30 a.m. by my watch. I asked the deputy, as we were winding down our interview, if he had been threatened.

He gave one of those half-laughs that were so common to that area—a sort of half-sigh, half-chuckle, a guttural sound that seemed to indicate a sense of fear and uncertainty. It certainly wasn't a true laugh. But he never answered my question. He merely said he would appreciate it if we could leave his name out of the newspaper for the time being.

We explained that sooner or later his name was going to surface, and he nodded in agreement. That was the extent of our deal for attribution. However, I thought we ought to be very careful at first not to ruin Magee as a source or to endanger him in any way.

After Magee drove off, and after Douthat and I walked back into the room, I tried to find something appropriate to say to sum up the previous three and a half hours. I could tell that Douthat was looking to do the same. Instead, we just sat there leafing through our notes. Both of us were pretty close to being speechless.

· NINETEEN ·

Thursday morning, May 6, was court day in Coldspring, and county judge K. P. Bryant — now lame-duck county judge K. P. Bryant — was all decked out in a nice three-piece suit. I bumped into him in the main hall of the courthouse a few minutes after 9:30 as he was heading into the county probation office. Bryant gave me a condescending frown and a quick nod of the head, as he always did, and as usual he asked what I was doing back in that part of the state. And I answered him the same way I always did: I was "just passing through." Shoot, two hundred miles is nothing these days, not when you have occasion to meet people as friendly as he was. I figured Bryant was a little upset about the election, and about the FBI, and about me and Douthat, so I let him go on about his business. I had other things to worry about.

Like the criminal dockets in the county clerk's office — or, rather, the office of lame-duck clerk Imogene Trapp. I had spent an hour that morning looking through those books, and I had found a most interesting bit of information: exactly one hundred marijuana possession cases listed as open on the dockets for all of 1981 and January of 1982 were beyond the ninety-day limit for prosecution set out in the Texas Speedy Trial Act; in other words, the cases were no good and were subject to immediate dismissal if the defendants raised the Speedy Trial Act as a defense. The act was Texas' contribution to the Sixth Amendment, the famous constitutional guarantee of a speedy and public trial. I was willing to bet my next paycheck that San Jacinto County was not, er, prepared to follow the Speedy Trial Act.

Douthat and I spent an hour or so watching the proceedings in Bryant's court, and my colleague was a little underwhelmed by the lack of attention to normal courtroom detail. On more than one occasion, a defendant had to point out to Bryant a fact that the judge omitted in some of his rambling orders. And one defense lawyer corrected Bryant when he tried to impose a twelve-month probation on a young man who pleaded guilty to possession; the lawyer said that state law specifically allowed a maximum of six months of probation for that particular offense. Bryant guffawed and spluttered when that was pointed out. Defense lawyers were a rarity in his court, at least from what I could tell.

After court adjourned shortly after 11:00, we strolled over to Judge Jeffrey's boot and saddle shop and wound up spending close to an hour going over some of the things that Greg Magee had told us the night before. We never mentioned Magee's name, but the judge seemed to know we had talked to him. The judge's firsthand information, again, was limited; he did not routinely patrol Highway 59 and did not see exactly what was going on out there. But he saw the results, and he said everything we had found out about that arrest trap was true. He said several deputies had come to him and wanted to know what they could do to break out of the revolving-door type of justice used by the sheriff's department. Jeffrey said he had encouraged a few deputies to talk to us. He didn't know whether they would, however.

I decided to ask the judge about a reserve deputy whom I had called a few days before, a deputy whom Douthat and I were scheduled to meet at 2:30 that afternoon—Ernie Bostic, a part-time officer who worked full time as administrator of the county's only health clinic. Bostic, from what I had been told, was very upset with the Highway 59 operation and wanted to do something about it. Judge Jeffrey nodded quickly when I mentioned Bostic's name.

"He oughta talk. He's been heard to say that he'd talk to anybody who came to him."

"So you think he'd help us out?"

"I *think* he will."

We chatted for a couple more minutes, and Jeffrey gave us the name of Constable Charles Clark. He suggested that we give him a call. And as we were leaving the small boot shop, he added, "I guess you got a lot of stuff from Greg."

So he did know that we had met with Magee. I nodded and said we had had a long talk, and the judge said Greg was a good deputy, a person who could be trusted.

We ambled back through the courthouse, which, by that time, was closed down for lunch. I couldn't picture what this place would be like under a new administration. I mean, the courthouse remaining open during the lunch hour? It was too incredible to imagine.

The health clinic that Ernie Bostic ran was situated right in the middle of the town's most modern shopping center—make that the town's

only shopping center—a storefront mall across Highway 150 from the
Bank of San Jacinto. There was a little grocery store at one end, and
the clinic was at the other. In between were a restaurant, a drugstore
(Johnston's Pharmacy, the one that had been burglarized four months
before), and a couple of other retail shops. It was a fairly nice complex
that appeared to be less than five years old.

Bostic walked into the waiting room, introduced himself and ushered
us into his office. He was sweating heavily by the time we sat down in
two straight-back chairs opposite his desk. That wasn't a good sign.

After the preliminaries, I asked him how long he'd been associated with
the sheriff's department as a reserve deputy.

About two years, he said in a quick, nervous voice, but he hadn't really done much work over the last two and half months. He'd been working part time as a security guard in Camilla, a small community a couple
of miles east of Coldspring, instead of doing patrol work for the sheriff.

I decided to get to the point: We knew for a fact that deputies broke
the law on Highway 59—because they had told us. And we had some
strong stories from victims who said their rights had been violated. Now,
we weren't interested in quoting him by name in our newspaper; we just
wanted to talk to as many deputies and reserves as we could, to give them
a chance to tell us anything they wanted.

Bostic almost choked. His face was dotted with sweat beads, and he
was shifting nervously in his chair. Finally he said, "I've always followed
strictly by the rules. . . . To me, if you're going to do something, then
you should do it right."

Fine, I said. No one had ever accused him of anything. As a matter
of fact, I explained, several people had given us his name as an example
of a good cop who was a little upset by what was going on out there.

"Have you ever seen other deputies break the law?" I asked.

"Well, what other officers do is pretty well their own business," he said.
"I personally have never seen any of that happen. . . . My main concern
is, I'm just not wild about people driving real fast in this county."

"What about the complaints about lack of probable cause?"

He shifted uneasily again. "I don't know of any car being stopped, by
myself or anybody else, that didn't have probable cause."

"Never?"

"That's right."

"And what about the complaints about illegal searches?"

"I don't search cars."

"Well, then, as an officer, can you tell us what you think would be
probable cause to search a car for marijuana?"

"Well, if you go up to a car and see a bag of marijuana on the seat,
then that's against the law, in my opinion."

This interview was getting nowhere fast. Bostic appeared to be on the verge of a heart attack. His collar was drenched in sweat, and yet he was trying his best to appear cooperative and friendly. He just wasn't going to tattle on anyone. We asked a few more questions about jail procedures, and Bostic continued to deny any hint of irregularities. As we were standing to leave, I decided to leave him with something to think about: "Have you been contacted yet by the FBI?" I asked, emphasizing the word "yet."

He sat upright quickly and said he hadn't.

I thanked him profusely for his help and wished him a good day.

That night, we hit the phones. Judge Jeffrey had given us a complete roster of all the deputies, reserves, constables, county officials, dispatchers, and tow truck drivers, and the roster was complete with home telephone numbers. We decided to check out a few names that had been given to us by Magee, Jeffrey, and others.

Douthat called reserve deputy Steve Rutledge and, shortly after identifying himself as a reporter for the *Austin American-Statesman*, was hung up on.

I called reserve deputy Robert Hoot and got the same treatment, except that Hoot said he would tell the sheriff that I had called him. Before he could slam down the phone, I got in one sentence: "I'm sure the sheriff will be glad to hear it."

The word was out. Sheriff Parker had instructed his loyal troops in the proper manner to handle telephone calls from us. Judge Jeffrey had told us that; so had Magee. But we had to see who would talk. Any confirmation of Magee's remarks would suffice, as long as it came from a deputy.

At a few minutes after 7:00, I reached former deputy Doug Yarbrough at his home. Yarbrough had worked as Magee's partner for several years, until he had been injured on the job. At present he was working at the Bank of San Jacinto. I asked him if he would be willing to meet with us sometime the next day, Friday, May 7.

He said he'd be glad to. The sooner the better.

I explained that I'd talked to Magee, and he said he already knew that. He and Greg were close friends.

We set up an appointment for 9:00 a.m. at the bank.

Douthat, meanwhile, had reached San Jacinto County commissioner Donald Cox on the phone, and Cox agreed to meet with him that night. Bill took the *American-Statesman* car and headed back into San Jacinto County. I stayed to work the phones, switching to my list of names from the county court dockets. I wanted to add as many more victims as I could.

And I struck pay dirt on my first phone call.

A twenty-two-old Houston man, David McIlvaine, said he and his twenty-five-year-old brother, Charles, and a twenty-one-year-old friend, Tommy Ezernack, had run into problems on Highway 59 about midnight on August 29, 1981. He said a deputy stopped them because they supposedly had a loud muffler. The deputy proceeded to search the car.

"He pulled us out of the car and made us pull down our pants right down there on the side of the highway. There wasn't a lot of traffic, but there was a little."

Did he know who the deputy was?

"Yeah, he said he was Gary Parker."

What happened?

"He told this other guy to hold a gun on us, and he said if you had long hair you was going to get searched in that county. We had this hamburger bag on the floor of the car, and Parker said, 'Aha, I found your dope now.' And I said, 'Aha, open it up and see what it is.' And I guess that made him mad, 'cause he made us pull our pants down."

Did he give you a reason for doing that?

"He said he was looking for weed."

Did he find any?

"Yeah, on my friend Tommy. In his pocket."

Then what happened?

"He arrested all of us for possession, and then some other deputy took us to jail. They got these inmates to book us in jail. They said they always did that."

The three paid bondsman Jim Browder $100 each and the tow truck driver $50. They did not see a judge. I asked whether they had ever heard from the county again.

"We went to court about two months ago, and the judge told us if Tommy would plead guilty they'd let the other two of us go. Tommy pleaded guilty."

"Did he go to jail?"

"No, they fined him $300 plus $71 for court costs."

"Did you get your bond money back?"

"No."

"What exactly happened when the deputy made you pull down your pants?"

"Man, he made us pull down our pants, our shorts and everything. He was mad as hell. And he shined that flashlight over us for a good five minutes."

"Were you out of sight of the road?"

"Hell, no. We were right there on the shoulder."

As I was starting to ask another question, McIlvaine said that I ought to call his brother-in-law and ask about his arrest in that county. He said I wouldn't believe it.

Why was that?

"Because they searched his baby's diaper when they arrested him."

I got his brother-in-law's name and phone number. The name was J. W. Moore. I had copied down every name and docket number from the criminal dockets for the previous eighteen months, and I could find no name to match Moore's. McIlvaine's name, his brother's, and Ezernack's were all on the docket, but the charges against all three were listed as having been dismissed. Ezernack was listed as having paid $371, however. But there was no mention in the dockets of the bond payments.

About 9:30 that night, I reached J. W. Moore in Tyler. He seemed very eager to talk. I asked him to start at the beginning:

He said he and his wife (now his ex-wife), their six-year-old daughter, and their six-month-old son had been driving up 59 about 7:30 p.m. on Friday, June 5, 1981. They were driving a van. "This deputy—his name was Gary Parker—pulled me over and said the license plate light was too dim. Then he told me to get out and walk back to his car.

"My wife had the baby in her lap, and this guy climbed right into the van and began to throw stuff around. He was cursing like crazy. He cursed my wife and pulled the blanket off the baby and pulled open the baby's diaper and looked in there. We didn't know what in the hell was going on. He emptied my wife's purse, and they were all in the van crying. The kids were crying. This guy was acting like a crazy man."

"Did he find anything?"

"My wife had two [roaches clips] in a medicine bottle in her purse. There was nothing on them, no dope or nothing. But they busted me for marijuana possession. They were going to take her, but I told them it was mine."

"What happened next?"

"They took me to jail."

"Did you see a judge?"

"Shit, no. I paid $100 to a bondsman and got out about 3:00 in the morning."

"Have you heard anything more from them? Any court hearings?"

"I never went to court. To this day I have not heard one word from them. Hell, I want to go to court. I want to look them in the eye and see what they have to say about all this. I talked to a lawyer and he said it was best just to let the whole thing drop. It'd be more trouble than it's worth."

I checked four times through my list of docket names and could not find the name J. W. Moore. The next day I went over and over the docket books in the county clerk's office and still couldn't find his name. The fine receipt reports also turned up nothing. But what else was new in that county?

Douthat got back to the Holiday Inn about 12:30 a.m. I was still on the phone to the long-distance operator, trying to match names from the court dockets with telephone numbers in Houston and other cities in that area of the state. But I felt I was getting close to having enough victims for our story. Counting the four new names I had come up with that night, I had twenty-four real people who had real stories to tell about some incredible, inexplicable incidents.

And if we could get Doug Yarbrough, Magee's former partner, to confirm a few things, then we just might be able to write a few stories about this crazy county.

The Bank of San Jacinto opened its doors at 9:00 that morning, Friday, May 7. It was a small but very modern office building that was situated—as nearly everything in Coldspring was—just down Highway 150 from the courthouse. And it was located in the same block as the new Public Safety Building, home of the sheriff's department. The brick-and-glass facility appeared to be pretty new, and there were a half-dozen people waiting to enter a few minutes before 9:00. Douthat and I were two of them.

A receptionist directed us to a small glass-enclosed office just to the right of the front door. That was where we'd find Doug Yarbrough, she said. She was right. Yarbrough was working as a bank officer, and he appeared to be about the same age as Magee, twenty-fivish. He was tall and had close-cropped dark hair. While Magee didn't necessarily look the part of a lawman, Yarbrough did. At least he looked more like an outdoor person.

After we introduced ourselves, Yarbrough led us into his office and closed the door. I could imagine what the other employees in the bank were saying at that moment. Everyone in Coldspring knew who I was—or who I said I was—but a few people had expressed reservations to me about Douthat. Judge Jeffrey, for one, said several people thought Douthat looked like an FBI agent. I got a kick out of that.

With Yarbrough, it was hard to tell if he was nervous or if he just normally talked in a quiet voice. I started out by telling him for the second time that Greg Magee had suggested that we talk to him, and I told him what we were doing and some of the strange things we had learned about the Highway 59 arrest trap. Then, not knowing how candid he would be with us, I asked if those weird things—deputies breaking the law, conducting illegal searches, stopping cars without probable cause, falsifying report information—sounded about right to him.

"Yeah, that sounds about right," he said. "That's the stuff I'm familiar with."

We had struck pay dirt again. Yarbrough was just as sick about the illegalities in that department as Magee was. He wasn't as talkative as his former partner, but perhaps that could be explained by the fact that he was talking to us less than a block from the sheriff's office, and Magee had met us in another county. Nevertheless, Yarbrough said he had started to work for the San Jacinto County Sheriff's Department on October 10, 1977, and had worked there until late the previous year. He spoke in a firm but soft voice.

"I saw some pretty kinky deals out on 59. We'd just stop a car for any old reason. . . ."

Such as?

"Oh, three blacks in a hiked-up car, any car with Louisiana plates, long hair, K-101 bumper stickers. Ha, the sheriff said that if we saw anything with a K-101 sticker on it, to shut it down. Stuff like that was probable cause."

When did the sheriff tell this to his men?

"In little meetings he'd hold. Once every couple of months. He wanted us to do some ass-kicking. He'd say, 'I'm committed to $250,000 and we've got to go for it.' He was a hell of a motivator. You can't really blame the deputies and the reserves; the sheriff is the one that motivates them."

But why did they do it?

"I don't know. Heck, it's a kick. They get a high out of it. The main deal is to search the car—'stop 'em and toss 'em.' "

And the large numbers of dope arrests?

"The numbers are no big thing. They're no sweat. It's real easy. It's out there. You just develop a cocky attitude and go after it."

Did he and Greg do it, too?

"Greg and I pushed probable cause to the limit. It's just a gray area. . . . Looking back on it, anybody who'd do all that is a dummy. . . . They're a bunch of dummies. Busting your butt for fourteen hours a night like that. And the reserves, doing it for free. They even have to buy their own badges."

But what happened to the victims? And the criminal charges? I'd found several cases that just seemed to disappear.

"The charges themselves? I don't know what happens to them."

"Aren't there any bond forfeitures?" I asked.

"K.P. [Bryant] has a list of forfeitures, but I don't know what happens to them. Nothing, I guess."

"What about the 'escrow' amounts charged by the bondsmen in addition to the regular bond fees?"

"That escrow is just an added incentive to get them to come back to court. The bondsman collects it and holds it."

"And if there is never any court hearing?"

"There you go."

"But where does all this money go, the money collected from the victims in the jail?"

"I don't really know. . . . I do know that the sheriff does have a separate [bank] account, outside the county."

"A personal account?"

"No."

"What kind of account?"

"It's listed as the San Jacinto County Sheriff's Department."

"At this bank?"

"Yeah, we've got it."

"Can you tell us anything about it, or would it be violating your position at the bank?"

"I don't have anything to do with that account. I don't even okay checks for him [Parker] when he sends them over here, because I know the way he is. I let Browder do it."

He indicated he really couldn't go into more detail about the separate bank account, or about other bank-related matters. So we asked for more information on the Highway 59 arrest trap.

"Well, you can't just sit out there and pick out cars to stop until you learn the sheriff's deal. He's the best at it."

"You mean, you just stop cars that you think will have dope?"

"That's about right."

"And how extensive are the searches?"

"A few times we took out the seats, we took the breather out, the carpet out, the hubcaps off. It wasn't unusual for trunks and suitcases to be opened and scattered out on the side of the road."

"What if the driver asks why all that is happening?"

"You just pull something out of the air—trump up a reason for stopping them."

"And if it was a family that looked respectable?"

"Then you'd just apologize for the inconvenience and let them go on their way."

"Can you tell us more about the types of cars you'd look for?"

"Sometimes we'd just look for 'heads,' hippies, blacks, old cars, vans, cars with a bunch of kids, teenagers."

"And you'd stop them and not anyone else?"

"That's right."

"Why did you quit? You and Greg?"

"We got sick of it. They were doing crazy things out there. It was way out of hand. . . . We'd had enough of it."

"And you say that the sheriff was the motivator behind it?"

"Just like a snake charmer. He had those guys thinking they could do anything."

"You obviously regret you ever did it. . . ."

"It's taken a hell of a lot of years, and a lot of hard work, to wipe the stench off me from that place."

"We've heard also that a lot of items regularly disappear from the property room in the jail."

"That's something I'm well aware of. I made one arrest on 59 and took in ten ounces of coke. And it just disappeared. Another case I made I confiscated an old coin collection and gold certificates, and they came up missing, too. A bunch of things that I personally placed in there disappeared. There's no way to keep the chain of evidence in a place like that."

We talked a few more minutes. Yarbrough confirmed everything we had learned from Magee about Highway 59. He, like Magee, did not have any firsthand information about the hit-and-run deaths, but he was well aware of the rumors going around the county about them. And he, too, felt something terrible was happening in the county's drug business. But he couldn't put his finger on it, at least not with assurance of being right. It was almost 10:00, and he said he had better get some work done. Douthat and I thanked him for his candor and left. We got back to the courthouse a few minutes later. There were still a few things left to do on this trip, but we were getting very, very close to writing a series of stories that would burst San Jacinto County's bubble once and for all.

· TWENTY ·

Kent Morrison was in his high-ceilinged cubbyhole of an office in the county courthouse at 10:30 that Friday morning, thirty minutes after our interview with former deputy Doug Yarbrough. The current county treasurer and soon-to-be county judge was wearing a pure-D Texas ten-gallon hat, blue jeans, a Western-style snap-button shirt, and boots—an outfit he swore was his business suit. He said he didn't feel comfortable wearing anything else. As a matter of fact, he said, he'd ridden a horse to work a time or two, not only because it was less hassle than driving a car but also because he just flat liked horses. He said he usually left his horse tied up in front of the courthouse. Talk about your stereotypical Texas scene. . . .

But on this morning Morrison seemed a bit perturbed, a bit upset. I told him he didn't look particularly happy on this sunshiny Friday morning six days after his upset win over county judge K. P. Bryant. What was up?

"Well, you know you were asking me about those hit-and-run deaths. . . . Well, they found another one last night. About a nineteen-year-old black woman. Killed either late Thursday or early today, on Big Creek Road down south."

"Another hit-and-run accident?"

"Appears to be. I heard she looked to be dead before she was run over."

"Who was she?"

"She supposedly didn't have any ID on her. . . . They took the body to the medical examiner in Houston."

"Do you know any more about it?"

"Red Blanchette is working it."

Morrison said he'd make a call to the DPS trooper right then to see if anything more had been determined. And he did. But apparently Blanchette didn't know a whole lot more. There was some reason to believe, though, that the woman was not a local resident, that she might have been from Houston.

I made a few notes, but it was hard to get fired up again about the hit-and-run homicides, not with the dramatic progress we'd made on the Highway 59 arrest trap—progress that included dramatic interviews with a deputy and a former deputy. Still, we would have to run the traps on this young woman's killing later.

I asked Morrison if he envisioned any changes he might make as county judge, particularly in reference to the sheriff's department and the handling of misdemeanor criminal cases.

He said he really hadn't thought a lot about it, but he would make sure that all fines, bonds, and charges were logged on his dockets the minute they were paid. "If someone is brought in the door, I'll see that they're logged up right," he said.

Did he know that the sheriff operated a non-county-controlled business checking account for his department?

He said he knew about it, and could confirm that it existed.

What money went into the account?

"That, I can't say. I just don't know."

And then he stopped quickly and said: "Did you know that the sheriff had his stepdaughter on his payroll over there?"

"Isn't that nepotism?"

"Appears to be."

"Who is she again?"

"His stepdaughter. Sheila Cronin. She's been on the payroll about ninety days."

"Doing what?"

"I think she's a dispatcher."

"Making how much?"

"Seven hundred dollars a month."

Could he confirm this from his records as treasurer, or was this another rumor?

"I've got the checks and all right here. I can confirm it."

It wasn't an earth-shattering bit of news, but it was interesting. I jotted it down and decided it would be a question to bring up with my favorite county official, the ever-talkative county attorney Robert Atkins. It sounded like a legal question, and anyway, I wanted to have another chance to talk to him. But at that very moment, it wasn't a high-priority item with me.

I made another pass through the county clerk's office to look over the dockets and criminal charges, and I jotted down a bunch more names, dates, and docket numbers. And then I met Douthat about 11:30 across the street in Judge Jeffrey's boot and saddle shop. We compared notes with the judge and learned that the latest hit-and-run death appeared to be a "dumping" from Houston—a killing in Houston that resulted in a body being dumped in a quiet, rural county.

As we were talking, Jeffrey said that our interview with Ernie Bostic must have been a real doozy.

"Why is that?" I asked.

"Well, Bostic went right over to the sheriff's department after that and turned in his resignation."

I met again with Greg Magee at 1:30 that afternoon outside a small convenience store and gas station in Pointblank, in the far north part of San Jacinto County near the western edge of the Highway 190 bridge over Lake Livingston. Douthat remained behind to talk with Judge Jeffrey. Magee was excited. He had called our hotel room in Huntsville several times that morning without catching us, and he finally left word with Judge Jeffrey that he wanted to meet again. Pointblank is roughly fifteen miles north of Coldspring, and to get there from Coldspring you have to traverse another winding, tree-lined road, Highway 156. But this road seemed much more populated than its twin five miles west, FM 946; at least I could see a few houses back off from the roadway.

First off, Magee said, he wanted to pass on something to me from Doug Yarbrough, something Doug didn't want to tell me face to face: the sheriff's department's special checking account had been overdrawn for five months. "Doug just wanted you to know, and he didn't want to tell you directly."

I appreciated the information, though it really had little bearing on anything I was doing right then. But Magee also wanted to tell me about Ernie Bostic's resignation, and that he, too, was going to quit the department.

"I can't go on with this. I've decided to get out while I still can. I may go down there and quit today. As I told you, this thing is just out of control. There's too much going on that has no place in law enforcement."

"And what will you do when you quit?"

"I may go to work for Waterwood in security. I don't know."

"And that's what you wanted to tell me?"

"One other thing. I want you to talk to Bart Holifield, a wrecker driver. He lives pretty close to here."

I got back in the *American-Statesman* car and followed Magee over some unpaved back roads that meandered through the forest. About ten minutes later, we arrived at a nice little cul-de-sac that had a half-dozen neatly trimmed brick houses. One of the first houses had a wrecker truck parked in an L-shaped driveway.

Bart Holifield was an elderly man who appeared to be in much better physical shape than most twenty-year-olds I've known. He was semiretired from business in Houston and ran the small wrecker company with his son on a part-time basis. He came right out and said he was sick of what went on on Highway 59.

"The way they do people is just awful," he said. "I've seen them jerk people out of their cars and open their suitcases and trunks and spill everything all over the road. All for no reason. Nothing."

And what role did the wrecker drivers play in this?

"We just sit out there and pick up the business. Sometimes we sit out there like a bunch of vultures. It's nothing to tow forty-five to fifty cars in one night. . . . Several times, I felt like hauling up my wrecker and leaving it. But the way I look at it, somebody's going to get the business, and maybe the next guy won't care as much as I do."

He said the Highway 59 arrests were the worst he had ever seen, but the roadblocks set up by the sheriff around Our Place in Oakhurst were pretty bad, too.

I told him I'd heard that that roadblock was usually set up at the Y intersection of FM 946 and Highway 156.

"That's the place. Man, I've seen them pull boys out of their cars and make them unzip their pants and stand right there buck naked from the waist down. . . . But if they knew you, they'd let you go right on through the roadblock."

I said I'd heard stories about marijuana being planted in cars. Had he seen evidence of that?

"It happens. I know that. And I've seen a few things that look like it."

Why was all this being done? The arrests? Bonds? Towing fees?

"There's money out there, that's why."

Well, were there any kickbacks that he knew of, say, from wrecker drivers to the sheriff's people?

"I believe there are. There's got to be."

Was he paying any money back to the sheriff's department?

"Nope. And I ain't about to, either."

Then he said that the sheriff's department bought and paid for the two-way radios that were installed in the wreckers around the county. "I know because I paid $1,000 of my own money to have my radio put in my truck, and the sheriff offered to reimburse me, or he said he'd just have the work billed to the sheriff's department. He just told me, 'We'll take care of it.'"

Had he taken the sheriff up on that offer?

"I wasn't about to take nothing from that guy."

Why?

"Because I didn't want to get obligated to him."

Was he now working 59, or had he quit?

"I've stopped. No way I'm going back out there. No way."

The following Monday, May 10, while working the phones back in the office, I gathered some interesting news from Judge Jeffrey: the FBI was back in town, and they were gung ho about seeing all the arrest reports that Gary Parker filled out.

For what reason?

"There's no way to tell. They ain't talking a whole lot . . . but it looks like they're concentrating on some marijuana arrests from 59."

The judge also said that Greg Magee had appeared before the county commissioners that morning and turned in his resignation and asked for— and been granted—two weeks of vacation time before the resignation would take effect. And there was supposedly a special task force appointed by Governor Clements that was starting to look into the operations of the sheriff's department.

Of all this, I was most interested in the task force, and I asked the judge whether he knew any more.

He said only that Greg Magee wanted to talk to them, and that they wanted to talk to Greg.

So I decided to call Greg. But first I called Lee Mackey, the Huntsville private investigator who said he had contacts in the governor's office. I figured that Mackey would know a great deal about this task force, since it was my talks with him that got him stirred up about the hit-and-run deaths in the first place.

Mackey said that the task force had in fact been assembled, and that it consisted of a couple of Texas Rangers and a couple of DPS intelligence and narcotics officers. He called them handpicked boys.

"What will they be looking at?" I asked.

"The same things you've been looking at," he said. "They're going to be in Huntsville tomorrow to talk to Magee."

That meant I needed to get to Magee first, to see what our star witness planned to say. I finally tracked down the elusive deputy a little after 5:00 p.m. He said he would answer any questions the task force had for him, and that he might volunteer some information of his own if it looked like the handpicked investigators could be trusted. But then he dropped some even more interesting information on me: a reserve deputy by the name of Bob Steele was ready to talk to me.

I'd heard that word "ready" before. "Have you talked to Steele?" I asked. "And did he *say* he would talk?"

"I did talk to him. He's been out for a couple of weeks, and he may not know a whole lot, but he'll tell you everything he knows."

That was good enough for me. I took down Steele's number.

I implored Magee to stay near a telephone at all hours, because I might need to get in touch with him quickly after our first stories ran, and they would be running very soon, probably within a week. Douthat and I had already started writing.

I reached reserve deputy Bob Steele at 7:00 p.m. on Wednesday, May 12, at his home in Evergreen, a small community west of Coldspring on State Highway 150. Steele, who Magee said was an older deputy who was well respected by everyone in the county, started talking slowly, but he soon picked up speed:

"I know what goes on out there, as far as what I've done and what I've seen. I can say that what they were doing out there just isn't police work. When I was working out there, we had a good, legitimate reason to stop them. . . ."

Such as?

"A headlight out, or taillight out, or something like that. But all I did was talk to them and sometimes I'd write them a ticket."

But he didn't search them?

"Not for a reason like that."

What about the other deputies and reserves?

"They were making a lot of arrests on the weekends when I worked. Now, I prefer to work north. I'd rather not have any part of what they're doing on 59."

I asked him to explain that.

"The reason I joined the reserves was I thought it was practically impossible to patrol the county with only four or five deputies. I wanted to be of help. Plus I always wanted to be a deputy, but I'll tell you this: my idea of police work is not sitting out on 59 making up reasons to stop cars."

Did he make any arrests on 59?

"The few arrests I was in on out there, there was definitely a reason. But to me, it wasn't true police work to be sitting out there trying to arrest people from out of town."

What did the other deputies say to him about all that?

"I've heard 'em laughing and kidding about it. I've heard 'em say they can find any old reason to stop a car and search 'em."

Why? Why was it going on?

"I assume it's a money-making deal. . . . I know they keep score. They'll say, 'How many arrests did you get? I got so-and-so.' All I know is that unless I get a direct order I'm not going back out there. To me, it's just not legitimate."

We talked another five or six minutes, going over the types of work done by various deputies and the fact that the sheriff didn't want anyone to talk to us reporters from Austin. But Steele seemed to feel that he could talk to anyone he wanted, that he didn't have anything to hide. During our thirty-minute conversation, it became very clear that we had our third bombshell testimony from a lawman—all of which backed up the complaints raised by my twenty-four victims. Immediately after hanging up, I called Douthat, and we agreed to finish our Highway 59 story the next day. But there was one thing we were going to need to complete our story: an interview with Sheriff Parker. I decided to do it immediately. At 8:30 p.m., I called him at his home in Shepherd.

Parker sounded glad to hear from me, but my first comment turned his tone in the opposite direction. I said I had talked to at least two dozen people who said their rights were violated by his deputies, that they were stopped without probable cause and were denied their constitutional rights to due process of law.

The sheriff paused for half a second, then proceeded to respond at a rapid-fire rate: "It seems they would have made a complaint to me. I can't imagine them not doing that. . . . We've only had three cars running the last month or so, way off what we usually run."

And then I told him that several of his deputies said they were instructed by him to go out on 59 and make arrests, even if it meant bending some laws.

"I don't ever remember telling anybody that," he snapped back.

But that's what the deputies and reserves told me they'd been told.

"It wasn't me. Carl Lee would be the one who told them if anyone told them. And I don't see how he could have. Hell, we just completed our last reserve school, what, three, four weeks ago? We don't put any emphasis on putting cars out there and making arrests."

I asked him if he was denying that he ever told any of his officers to break the law, and he said he was. "And what about the reserves?" I asked.

"I don't even work with the reserves," he answered testily. "Hell, it's been four or five years since I've worked any street."

"Well, who told these men to break the law?"

"I'll certainly check with the chief over patrol to see what he's telling them. But I just figure if that's what they're saying, then maybe they figure it's a way to make sergeant or something. . . . I don't know where they'd be getting that information."

I then told him I wanted to give him some names of people who had complained to me about their rights being violated. I said I would like for him to consult his records and respond.

He said he'd be glad to do that. "That's the kind of stuff I need to know," he remarked. But he asked me to call him back about 11:30 the next morning, so that he could look over his records right then and give me a response over the phone.

I agreed. I gave him the names and dates of arrest the next morning, Thursday, May 13, and I told him the complaints were of a very serious nature.

Parker said he would check his files on each one. He asked me to call him Friday afternoon.

I did. But he said he had been too busy to pull his files.

I called him again the next morning, Saturday, May 15, and said we were going to run a story about these complaints. He again said he was too busy to pull the arrest folders. And then he said he was "not going to take time to do this."

It was time to print our first stories.

· TWENTY-ONE ·

It took a full twelve hours on Wednesday, May 12, to put our first two stories into final form. Since I had done most of the investigative work, I did most of the writing. Douthat and I decided to write two stories initially—one detailing the Highway 59 operation with extensive comments and admissions from deputies, the other listing the twenty-four horror stories from the victims of justice in San Jacinto County. Both stories were extremely long, much longer than any the *American-Statesman* had run during the four months I'd worked there. But it was devastating material, the type of investigative work that was certain to spark comments all over the state from other victims, other law enforcement officials, other newspapers, and civil rights laywers.

When I typed the last paragraph into the computer at 7:45 p.m. and made three printouts (one for me, one for Douthat, and one for Ed, our city editor), I felt good. Douthat said he felt good. Several other reporters who were hovering around us that afternoon and early evening said they, too, felt good, although their euphoria could have been caused by other things. I left the third printout with Ed a little before 8:00 and went home—not to relax, but to call Greg Magee, Judge Jeffrey, and a half-dozen other people to let them know that the first stories were in the works for the upcoming weekend. I dropped off to sleep after midnight but awoke at 2:00 a.m. to spend another hour going over the stories paragraph by paragraph. I tried not to pat myself on the back, but I couldn't help feeling that I'd seen criminal cases prepared by assistant U.S. attorneys that weren't as thorough as those two stories. We'd absolutely gotten to the bottom of the Highway 59 racket—from confessions from officers and tow truck drivers to the tiny details supplied by the arrestees.

The next morning, Thursday, May 13, I decided to start working on our third story—this one detailing the activity of the state-appointed task force and looking back briefly at the first FBI investigation and the ACLU lawsuit in 1978. But before I'd gotten three paragraphs into that story, I got a phone call from a Texas Ranger named Wes Styles, one of the the members of the task force. I had been expecting it.

Styles said he had just started his investigation of San Jacinto County and was hearing some rather bizarre things. And since I had done a good bit of work over there, he said, he would like to sit down and talk with me. Of course, he had no way of knowing that our first stories were getting ready to run, and I wasn't about to tell him. I hedged. I never have liked dealing with law enforcement investigators, and I have never agreed to help any investigator on any probe. That, to me, was not my job. But beyond that, I had some ethical problems about reporters "cooperating" with the authorities. My role was to report the news, not to prosecute criminals; the latter was their job. I told Styles I'd be glad to meet with him, but there might not be very much I could tell him. He wanted to talk anyway, and we set up a meeting for 10:00 a.m. on Monday, May 24, at DPS headquarters in North Austin. I felt that Styles would be wasting his time talking to me, because I wasn't going to tell him anything that wasn't in our first stories, which would be in print by the time of the meeting.

The first two stories ran as scheduled on Sunday, May 16. The story setting out the arrest trap started on page one, underneath a one-and-a-half column picture of Sheriff Parker. Out beside the picture were two boldfaced, graphic-style quotations, one from a former deputy and the other from Parker. The first said: "You just trump up a reason for stopping them." Parker's quote was "I don't ever remember telling anybody that." The story went on to describe the admittedly illegal stops and searches, complete with quotes from deputies and reserves. Douthat had also contacted San Jacinto County constable Charles Clark the week before and was able to quote Clark as saying that most of the arrests on 59 were illegal. The huge numbers of marijuana possession arrests were included, along with a three-column chart showing San Jacinto County's 1981 arrests in bar-graph form compared to Houston, Dallas, Austin, Galveston, and San Antonio. The systematic operation of the arrest trap was analyzed: the illegal searches, the quick arrests, the sudden arrival of tow trucks, the speeding trips to Coldspring, the waiting bail bondsmen, the reading of the rights by jail trusties, the mysteriously set bail bonds, the absence of judges, the handover of money for bonds and towing, the receipts signed by the sheriff's secretary, the disappearance of charges at a later date. JP Mike Jeffrey was quoted as saying he no longer accepted faulty taillights as probable cause in his court for the search of a car. County judge K. P. Bryant was quoted as saying he had nothing to do with anything in the sheriff's department. The lack of description on arrest reports and charges was included, as was the activity of the twenty-one unpaid reserves. Story number one was devastating.

Story number two ran on a half-page inside the first section of the newspaper, opposite the concluding portion of the page one story. It dealt solely with the victims of the arrest trap, and it began with J. W. Moore's description of his arrest and the searching of his infant son's diaper. I went into great detail about Moore's arrest and booking, and the fact that his marijuana possession charge just seemed to disappear. No record of his arrest and charging, or of his payment of bond or towing fees, could be found in the county clerk's office. A paragraph at the end of Moore's section of the story said that Sheriff Parker had been given a list of victims and arrest dates and asked to respond, but he had declined to do so.

The second victim in the story was Kip Carr, the Baytown tire store dealer who was arrested for having a piece of broomstick in his car. His arrest and booking were detailed, along with the apparent disappearance of his charge. The third case cited was that of the Foleys from Jamestown, Kentucky, whose charges had also disappeared. The fourth group of victims were David and Charles McIlvaine and their friend Tommy Ezernack, all of whom were strip-searched on the side of the road. The fifth horror story came from Richard and Deborah Ponder and their friend Kenneth Wayne Oliver, who were searched strenuously on 59 and arrested. The last group of victims included two young men that Douthat had tracked down a week before, Mark Stonestreet and Ricky Aycock. They had been stopped on 59 for having a muddy license plate, and a search of their car turned up a pair of martial arts sticks inside a zippered bag in the locked trunk of their car. They were charged with carrying a club. A further search turned up a marijuana cigarette and resulted in a marijuana possession charge against both. The effect of all these stories—most of them involving people who had never before been in any trouble with the law—was overwhelming.

The stories saw their way into print shortly after midnight on Sunday morning, May 16. And I was there to pick up several of the first copies to come off the press. I was keyed up when I got home about 12:30 a.m. Sunday, and I slept only a few hours. My telephone began ringing a little after 10:00 that morning, and I spent most of the rest of the day on the phone. Our stories had struck a nerve. Lawyers called to ask how to get in touch with the victims; the victims who were able to get a copy of the paper called to express thanks and ask what I thought would happen next; San Jacinto County officials who had helped me called to report on the stories' "Hiroshima effect"; legal services workers called to express their outrage at the Highway 59 operation; and a couple of reporters and assistant city editors at the *American-Statesman* called to praise the two stories. But I didn't hear a word from Ed.

· TWENTY-TWO ·

My reward for the first two stories came quickly from my higher-ups at the *American-Statesman* — and it came in a form that I had almost gotten used to, in the form of a contradiction. First off, on the Monday following the publication of the stories, the newspaper's publisher, Jim Fain, sent a note through the city desk saying that the stories were tremendous, and that they were the type of investigation he wanted the newspaper to do more often. That was the front end of my reward. The back end came from Ed, who walked over to my desk shortly before noon and handed me two new stories to work on. "It's time to tackle something light," he said, adding that he would need me to start working on Sundays again, to help out with general-assignment coverage. That meant more festivals in the park, more Sunday afternoon civic seminars, more convenience store armed robberies, more vacant-house fires. It was the only thing Ed said to me that day.

I made a quick call to Mike Jeffrey to tell him that I'd be away from my investigation for a few days, but I tentatively planned to have another story in the newspaper the very next weekend. Everyone in Coldspring had read the stories, the judge said, and an FBI agent who was in the courthouse that day also had a copy of them.

So the FBI was back on the trail? What were they doing?

"They got every scrap of paper they could get from the sheriff's office for the day when Kip Carr was arrested," he said. "And I think they've got two or three other days they're looking at."

Maybe they were the dates mentioned in the victims' story on Sunday?

"Could be."

I also called Martha Charrey to see if she had talked to the sheriff about our stories as she had said she was going to do. She had indeed, and she said that he wasn't looking too well, that he had told her most of the information we had printed had come from deputies who wanted to take over his job. Martha quoted the sheriff as saying our stories were "all political." She kept telling me how out of sorts the sheriff looked.

About 2:30 p.m., Judge Jeffrey called me back to relay one specific piece of information: state district judge Joe Ned Dean wanted to talk to me about what was going on in San Jacinto County.

Joe Ned Dean was a rotund, round-faced man who looked and sounded like a judge. I had seen him only once: at the political rally on April 24 at the courthouse square in Coldspring, that rainy, windy day on which every politician who showed up got to say a few words to the drenched crowd. Dean had been one of them, even though he was running unopposed for his state district court seat. I don't know exactly why I remembered him, but I did. Perhaps it was his firm, judgelike voice that came through loud and clear over the crackling public address system. Or then again, maybe it was the fact that he spoke for only about thirty seconds.

I reached the Honorable Judge Joe Ned Dean at 9:15 a.m. on Tuesday, May 18, at his office in Groveton, in Trinity County. Dean, it turned out, was one of those circuit-riding judges that you read about in history books. He was based in Trinity County, but he had jurisdiction over cases arising in several other counties, including San Jacinto County. And he spent a few days each month in all of those counties. Officially, there were no state district judges based in San Jacinto County, just like there was no district attorney assigned to that county on a full-time basis. But three district judges, according to state law, had authority to hear cases of a serious nature in Coldspring.

Dean sounded just as judgelike over the telephone as he had at the rally. I introduced myself and said I was one of the reporters who had written the stories in the Austin newspaper, and Dean immediately said he had read the stories and was interested in what they had to say. But, he quickly added, he was a judge and not a prosecutor, so he couldn't be quoted in the newspaper about any substantive issue involving a county within his jurisdiction.

I told him I knew that already, and that the reason for my call was to ask him if he'd heard any cases from San Jacinto County in which a legitimate question about probable cause or illegal search had been raised.

He jumped right in. "I haven't heard of any cases from that county. I've been going over there since September of '77 . . . and maybe there were one or two cases several years ago. But none in the last two or three years. You do know that they handle most of their cases right there in county court. Not many ever get to me."

I knew that. I told him I had checked the criminal dockets for the last three years and had found less than half a dozen felony criminal cases, which, of course, would fall outside the authority of the county judge.

Dean was aware of that, too. He said it was very unusual for the authorities in San Jacinto County to file a felony case.

Rather than go over things that both of us already knew, I asked him — since he had read our first two stories — whether he had any information that might help me in my investigation. I told him that I was interested in several other things aside from the marijuana arrest trap on Highway 59.

He paused, and then explained again that he did not want to jeopardize his impartial stance as a judge. But he went on to say that though he did not have any "concrete evidence" about any official wrongdoing, he did "have some concerns about what is going on in that county."

Such as?

"Off the record, I've inquired about the sheriff's son working there as a deputy, and his activities as deputy. I can't figure out how the son of a sheriff could work like that." And then he said that he couldn't really say any more, but he wanted to sit down and talk to me face to face. He asked when I would be in Coldspring again.

I couldn't tell. And I couldn't really explain, either. Ed had loaded me down with cruddy little stories that were going to take most of the week, and he had indicated that he had some other "long-range" stories he wanted to give me later. The guy was doing his best, whether he realized it or not, to kill the San Jacinto County investigation. Why else would he pull me off a story that was starting to percolate across the state? Newspapers in Port Arthur, Lufkin, Longview, and a couple of other cities had picked up our two stories off the Cox News Service wire and run them on the front page, and the *Houston Post* and the *Dallas Times Herald* had made telephone calls to a couple of county officials within twenty-four hours of publication of our two stories. (I had met enough people and gotten them to trust me in four months to know when other reporters started nosing about, just like I always knew what the FBI was doing and when the FBI men were in Coldspring. Sources, you know.)

Anyway, I told Judge Dean that I probably wouldn't be back over there for at least two weeks, but that I would call him several days ahead of time to arrange a meeting.

He agreed. And then he asked me if I planned to write any more stories in the near future.

I hedged. I don't like to tell people what I'm going to do before I do it. The newspaper business can be tricky — especially when there are competing newspapers, which Austin, of course, does not have. But for all I knew, Judge Dean might call the *Houston Post* and tell them everything

I asked, and—even though Ed Crowell and the *American-Statesman* might not realize it—the Houston newspapers were very serious competitors on this story. They could have yanked this story away from me at almost any moment. They could outgun and outspend the Austin newspaper, especially when you consider that the *American-Statesman* was not used to competing with anybody for anything. I fully expected that when the Houston papers picked up on this story, Ed would pull me off it and let them have it.

But it wasn't just Ed. The *American-Statesman* liked to decide things by committee, by holding time-consuming meetings with reporters to plan strategy, outline an investigation, talk about what questions to ask, decide on a catchy marketing gimmick. All of it was a gross waste of time. And even when these god-awful team assignments were completed, it was not uncommon to hold the stories for a few more weeks to let the newspaper's marketing and promotion department come up with cutesy cards for the newsstand racks. I could just imagine what Mary Crutcher, my crusty old city editor in Fort Worth, would have done if she'd been asked to hold a story until rack cards could be produced. She'd have gone absolutely bananas—and she'd have run the story in the very next edition. "We're not putting out a damn paper for the damn circulation department!" Mary used to scream about three times a week. Those were the words of a true newsperson. Of course, true newspeople are a vanishing breed; they are being replaced by corporate moneymen.

So I told Judge Dean that I was still plugging away on a few other stories on San Jacinto County, but I had absolutely no idea when they'd be finished.

That afternoon I finished story number three and turned it in for publication the next weekend.

Our third story ran on Monday, May 24, on the second page of the second section in the newspaper. In one week's time, the *American-Statesman* had relegated the San Jacinto County story from the front page to the junk page. Another omen from corporate headquarters, I assumed. This story, though, announced that the state task force had been assembled and had jumped into San Jacinto County, all because of what I had done in four months. The story also said that the FBI had begun looking into that county, for the same reason. Now, the story did not mention Douthat or me by name, but it could have. Both investigations were started because I was turning over some pretty slimy stones and taking a hard look beneath them. The story said the task force had interviewed a couple of deputies, a state district judge, and several other San Jacinto County officials. The focus of the probe, the story continued, was—at least preliminarily—to find people who had been arrested on 59, had paid their bond and towing fees, and had never been given a chance to appear in court. In other words, the task force was looking for people like Jeffrey Foley and Patsy DeBorde of Kentucky; Kip Carr of Baytown; J. W. Moore of Tyler; and John Patrick of Huntsville. People I had already talked to. People who would be glad to help out any investigation of the San Jacinto County Sheriff's Department.

Another part of this story noted that one San Jacinto County deputy had given a lengthy statement to the task force a mere two days after he was interviewed at length by "reporters for the *American-Statesman*." The remainder of the story traced the curious history of the 1978 ACLU lawsuit and the resulting FBI investigation—including the strange fact that the FBI agents set up headquarters in the bank building across the street from the courthouse after announcing their arrival on the front page of the county's weekly newspaper. And there was a quote from a Coldspring businessman who said that no one wanted to help the FBI on that first probe because the bank building was right across the street from the courthouse, and around the corner from the sheriff's office. My best guess was that the FBI would not be very happy to read that. But whatever had happened, or failed to happen, during that first investigation was their own fault. I wanted to mention it in this story primarily to see if the agents who were in Coldspring in 1978 would call me to gripe about my mentioning it. (They didn't.)

The day before this story ran, Sunday, May 23, found me sitting by myself inside the newsroom as the day's "early general-assignments reporter." I was really busy, too. I got to call all the rural sheriff's departments and police departments around Austin to see if anything big had happened the night before, and I got to answer the city desk telephones for a couple of hours to hear people complain about their missing newspapers that morning and how they couldn't get an answer from the newspaper's circulation department. It was a lot of fun. I could hardly wait until 2:00 p.m. when the night assistant city editor got to work to see what busywork he had in store for me. Maybe, just maybe, if I was lucky, I'd get to go down to the Austin police station to read arrest reports from the night before! Or maybe I'd get to go to Zilker Park to ask people what they were doing! Or maybe a water main would burst somewhere in the city and I'd get to go look at it and ask people what they thought about it! The excitement was killing me. I almost couldn't believe that almost five months before I had left a job in which I literally ran the city desk at a much larger newspaper, overseeing investigations, political and governmental news coverage, and the four police reporters who worked under me. If they could see me now.

My euphoria was interrupted at exactly 5:15 p.m., when I got a telephone call from the publisher of a small chain of newspapers in the suburbs east of Houston. Jim Giles asked me if I was the reporter who had written the two long stories about San Jacinto County the week before.

I said I was.

He said he had just talked with a young woman who was interested in getting in touch with me. This nineteen-year-old woman, he said, had read my first two stories and had some things that she could add to them. But she wanted to find out indirectly if I would agree to keep her name out of my stories, at least for the time being.

I told Giles I couldn't make any agreements without knowing who this mysterious young woman was. And even then I might not be able to commit to anything. Who was she?

"Her name is Cassie Parker. And she's just been divorced from Gary Parker, the sheriff's son."

· TWENTY-THREE ·

My disillusion with the *American-Statesman* was growing daily, in direct proportion to the number of extraneous daily stories I was assigned to cover. There seemed to be a never-ending deluge of daily crises on the city desk. It was quite clear to me, at 5:15 p.m. that Sunday, May 23, that I was going to have to claw and scratch to get any more San Jacinto County stories into the *American-Statesman*. But between 5:20 p.m. and 7:30 p.m., I was able to forget the minutiae of the day, the burst water mains, the two-car accidents on rain-slick streets. During that period, I interviewed the divorced wife of Gary Parker, the son of San Jacinto County sheriff J. C. "Humpy" Parker.

Cassie Parker answered every question I put to her. She was, however, terrified—not only of talking to a strange reporter but of the idea that she might be pulled into the FBI or task force investigation. The main reason, she said, was that she had a two-year-old daughter, Courtney, who had been born during the very brief period Cassie had been married to Gary. Courtney was her entire life, and she didn't want to say or do anything that might jeopardize her daughter. She was currently living with her parents, Mr. and Mrs. Jack Kluck, in Crosby, Texas, a tiny bedroom community twenty miles northeast of Houston. They had all lived there since February.

One of my first questions was "Why did you move?"

Her answer was complicated, but basically, she said, they were scared—scared of what was going on on Highway 59, scared of the unsolved hit-and-run deaths, scared of the large numbers of marijuana arrests, scared of the large amounts of drugs that seemed to float in and out of the sheriff's department, scared of everything associated with San Jacinto County. Too many people were making too much money, she said, and the money was making them do weird things.

Cassie was familiar with every type of misdeed that was covered in my first two stories. She said she had ridden patrol with Gary and with the sheriff and was aware of the things that were going on. She said she even took part in some of the frisks of women who were searched alongside the roadway. On several occasions, she said, drugs were confiscated from motorists, but no arrests were made. And a great deal of money was exchanged between the deputies, tow truck drivers, bondsmen, and businessmen in the area of Highway 59. All of it scared her.

I went down my list of deputies and reserves and asked her for her opinion of them, and she answered candidly. Some of them, she maintained, appeared to have drug problems. Others just liked to harass people. She also confirmed that the department had a lack of controls over the property room, and that it wasn't unusual for evidence—drugs, pills, guns—to "get up and walk out." Everything, she said, was a joke.

I pressed her for details, and she supplied them. She had seen an unbelievably sordid side of the law enforcement business for someone only nineteen years old. I was impressed with her apparent sincerity. She had virtually lived at the sheriff's department and had seen what was going on, and she wanted to see something done about it . . . if—and this was a big if—she could be assured that her daughter would not be harmed or taken away from her.

After listening to her for almost two hours, I told her that some of the things she had seen could send a lot of people to jail.

She said she was aware of that.

I told her that the FBI and state investigators probably, before too much longer, would be asking me for the names of people who I thought might help them. Would she be willing, at a later date, to talk to them?

The young woman hesitated before answering. "If it would get something done . . ." she began, pausing again, "then I might."

What if I called her first, before giving her name to the investigators?

She said that sounded a lot better.

I explained that I really didn't like to cooperate in that manner with the official investigating agencies, but I, too, wanted to see something done. And if a few names from me would help the official investigations, then I would probably give them some names. Probably. I was having some problems about my role in all of this, too, I explained.

Cassie seemed very understanding, and she said she felt she could trust me, even though she had never met me. She pointed out again her concern for her daughter, and mentioned that Gary at one point had violated their custody agreement by keeping Courtney longer than he should have. And she had gone into district court in Conroe and gotten a judge to issue a writ of attachment, an order directing the local law enforcement agency to pick up the infant and return her to the rightful guardian.

"The local law enforcement agency? Wouldn't that be the San Jacinto County Sheriff's Department?"

"Yeah. I couldn't get any of the deputies to serve the papers on Gary. I almost went crazy."

"So what finally happened?"

"I finally got Charles Clark to serve the papers. I got my daughter back and left the county that night."

"Charles Clark the constable?"

"Yes."

She said the whole incident had frightened her, and her family, and driven them out of the county.

We talked a great deal more—mostly about her impressions and observations about Gary, about the sheriff, and about the fear she felt toward them now. She said she was going to nursing school at a Houston hospital and would be graduating in December. She hoped to be able to make a living for herself after that.

I asked her about the death of Charles Hogue, as well as the other young boys who were killed on the farm roads late at night, and she said there had been "a lot of talk about all that, but no one ever did anything."

And then she said several deputies used to joke about taking prisoners out of the jail into the forests, tying them up, and beating them. Although she never saw any of that happen, she said, she believed it. "They all thought it was so funny," she said.

Names and more names. She knew some people in the county who made their living by selling drugs. They did it openly and notoriously, without fear of being stopped by the sheriff's office. Any of those people, in her opinion, were capable of killing. She gave me several names of people—some of them deputies and reserves—who had boasted about beating prisoners.

Did she truly believe, I asked her, that everything she had told me was actually going on? Was it really happening the way she said?

"It is. . . . That's why I moved out of there, and that's why I'll never go back."

On Monday, May 24, several San Jacinto County people called to tell me that Sheriff Parker was filing an incredible number of criminal charges in the county clerk's office—and that many of them were older cases. Deputy Greg Magee said many of the charges were more than 180 days old, which made them "no good at all" because of the 90-day limitation of the state's Speedy Trial Act. Magee also said several reserve deputies had approached him about the validity of the old charges; they were concerned about their involvement in those cases, and whether they could be linked to any possible charge of conspiracy. "I don't know what to tell 'em," Magee said. "All I know is that I got off that sinking ship. . . . What they do is their own business."

At 2:30 p.m., John Duncan, executive director of the Texas Civil Liberties Union, called to ask me a few questions. He wanted to know what was happening with my investigation and the criminal investigations by the FBI and the state task force, and whether I felt that a new investigation by his agency would speed things up. Duncan wanted something done about the problems in that county as outlined in our first three stories. And if a lawsuit by the ACLU would help, that was what he'd do. He asked if I knew anyone who would agree to be a plaintiff in a class-action lawsuit.

I did, and I gave him the names of Kip Carr and the Foleys. I also pointed out that Foley's original complaint—the letter to Governor Clements—had been ash-canned by his agency in January.

He said he was aware of that. "But if we could wind up with some plaintiffs again, then we might consider trying to bring some action out of our Houston office," he said.

Things were starting to happen. Justice of the peace Mike Jeffrey called toward the end of the afternoon to tell me of the late charges being filed by the sheriff—"He's just grabbing at straws now," Jeffrey said—and to inform me that he was meeting at 10:00 a.m. the next day with the FBI. "I'm gonna tell them everything they want to know," he said.

And then the judge told me about a strange case involving two brothers from Little Rock, Arkansas, who were arrested on Highway 59 while carrying a carful of stereo equipment. The brothers, according to Jeffrey, were arrested on January 19, and the stereo equipment, which belonged to the boys and had not been stolen, was impounded.

"So?"

"Now all that stereo stuff is gone. The sheriff says he doesn't have it."

"But is this going to be a case of the sheriff's word against the two brothers?"

"I don't see how it can be. We inventoried all that stuff before it was locked in the sally port [at the sheriff's department]."

"Who is 'we'?"

"It was me, [probation officer] Bill Burnett, [juvenile probation officer] Jean O'Dell, and [teacher] Richard Currie. We made up our own inventory list right here. We saw there was some expensive equipment there, and we knew that it had a good chance of—what do you say?—getting up and walking out of there."

"And is the stereo equipment really missing?"

"Well, none of us has seen it in there. And it ain't where they put it when we did that inventory . . . and now those people have gotten a lawyer from Little Rock to write some letters about it. There's a lot of missing stuff."

I began to think that this could be an effective fourth story. If that equipment actually did vanish from the sheriff's custody, it would be a good example of the revolving-door property room procedures that Greg Magee, Doug Yarbrough, Judge Jeffrey, and several others had told us about. And it would graphically illustrate another serious problem at the sheriff's department, a problem not mentioned in great detail in the first three stories.

I went to work immediately. That afternoon I interviewed by phone Jean O'Dell, the juvenile probation officer, who confirmed Judge Jeffrey's account of the arrest and the subsequent inventory of the equipment. But O'Dell was scared. She said the sheriff had been a bit curt with her because of her involvement in this particular matter. And she didn't want to antagonize him further. Still, she said, she had contacted her state district judge to tell him about this case.

Bill Burnett, the adult probation officer, also confirmed the story. It definitely appeared that I was onto something, something extremely interesting.

The next day, Tuesday, May 25, I reached the attorney who had sent the letters from Little Rock inquiring about the stereo equipment. Ginger Atkinson was representing the two young men who owned the equipment, Bruce Michalek, seventeen, and Brian Michalek, twenty. Atkinson was very helpful, but she was in the dark about one key fact—what had happened to the stereo equipment, which she said was worth close to $7,000. We talked for almost an hour, going over the facts of that case as she understood them to be. But she wasn't my best possible source. I still needed to talk to the boys.

Brian Michalek, it turned out, was an escapee from the county jail in Little Rock, where he had been convicted on an arson charge, and the car they were driving had been reported stolen from a parking lot in Little Rock. The car was stopped on Highway 59 for a familiar reason: an allegedly faulty taillight. The two brothers were searched, and a marijuana cigarette was found in the older boy's pocket. Both were arrested for possession.

Atkinson said Sheriff Parker released the younger brother into his mother's custody, dropping the possession charge, but the stereo equipment was not turned over then. Instead, according to Atkinson, the sheriff said he would return the equipment when the older brother was returned to Arkansas in the custody of Little Rock authorities. That had not happened. And now they were confused about what was going on in that two-bit little county on U.S. 59 north of Houston.

I told Atkinson about my investigation, and the three stories that had appeared already in my newspaper. She asked for my help in trying to track down the equipment. I agreed to do what I could, which meant keeping her informed of what I found out.

About 6:30 p.m. the next day, I reached the Michalek house in Little Rock, but it took a little reportorial ingenuity to do it. The Michaleks had recently gotten an unlisted telephone number, and Atkinson didn't have the new number. Luckily, I had run across this type of problem before, so I knew how to proceed. I had the Michaleks' address, so I called the Pulaski County Library in Little Rock and had someone look up the address in the city directory, sometimes called the crisscross directory. Those directories are invaluable; they list residents street by street and house by house, making it quite simple to find out who lives next door, or across the street, or two houses down. I had the library attendant give me the names of four people who lived within a house or two of the Michaleks and then find their numbers in the telephone directory. In short, I reached a next-door neighbor of the Michaleks' and asked him to run next door and tell them to call me collect in Austin. Mrs. Gladys Michalek called me within three minutes.

She related the story of her son Brian's escape from the Pulaski County Jail, and his theft of a car from a parking lot. Bruce, though, was not an escapee or a criminal; he had just "gotten mad at me and upped and left with Brian," she said. "He took all his possessions with him, all that stereo and recording equipment that he had bought himself. He worked part time at a K-Mart, and that's what he spent all his money on."

She confirmed the account given to me by her lawyer, but she added a few interesting details about her trip down to Coldspring on January 26 to pick up the younger boy:

"First off, they refused to return any of the stuff to me because they said it was stolen. When I told them it wasn't and that I could prove it, then they said they didn't have a key to the room where everything was kept. I said I'd wait while they found the key, and they said the woman who had the key was off sick and they couldn't get to her. Then they said she was in St. Louis on vacation. . . . Of course, I didn't believe a word of it."

Did she see Sheriff Parker?

"Yeah, I saw him. But he just gave me a runaround and kept passing the buck to somebody else. I stayed there from 8:00 a.m. until 3:00 p.m. waiting on them. Finally, Bruce and I went into that little parking area [the sally port] and Bruce found a bunch of his stuff missing. A few things were there: a tool chest, a spare tire, things like that. Then they said the rest was locked up in the property room and they couldn't get it. One deputy got downright ugly with me when I asked about the rest of the things. It was the weirdest experience I ever had in my life."

Another unusual fact was brought out: Bruce Michalek was only sixteen at the time of the arrest, and Texas law requires juveniles to be kept in separate detention facilities from adults—which obviously did not occur.

I asked her if they had ever gotten any of the equipment back, and she said they hadn't. "Ginger, my lawyer, has written them twice asking them to send the stuff back to us collect by UPS, but we haven't heard even one word from them. I tell you, I think they were just out to make some money on this."

But why did she wait so long to go down there? The arrests were made on January 19, and she didn't drive down until January 26.

"I just couldn't afford the trip. I work two jobs, one from 5:00 to 8:00 at night, and another from 11:00 p.m. to 7:00 a.m. at the hospital here. We don't have a whole lot of money—I raised four boys by myself—and I just couldn't afford to take off."

And what were the boys doing on Highway 59 in the southern part of Texas?

"They had driven to Houston and were on their way back here. The day Bruce left I had a juvenile pickup order put out on him."

And what would she do now?

"I'd really like to know what I can do. I'm thinking about driving back down there to try to get some of the keepsake things back, at least *some* of the things. But I have my doubts about whether any of the stuff was there when I was. The whole thing made me think it was all gone. I mean, when Bruce started raising a fuss about it, they got real nasty and told him he might never get any of it back. What's so sad is that all of the equipment was brand-new. Bruce bought it at a discount while working at K-Mart. It really hurts to see a kid like that put out all his money and then have it taken away from him like that. . . . It was everything he owned in the world, and they kept it."

Had she been contacted by the FBI or any other investigating agency about this?

"No. Not anyone."

Would she talk to the FBI about it?

"I'd talk to anyone, if it'd get these things back."

Would Bruce talk to them? He was never charged with anything.

Instead of answering, she said it would be best if I talked directly to Bruce and handed the phone over to him.

The youngster was angry about the whole affair, but he seemed resigned to the fact that he might never see his equipment again. I asked him to list everything that the sheriff impounded, everything that was in the car at the time of the arrest.

He started listing them immediately. "An $900 Akai reel-to-reel; a Marantz tuner; two recording decks, an eight-track and a cassette; two amplifiers; a Channel Master in a green chest; a bunch of new cassettes; five reel-to-reel tapes; two concert speakers, black, both of them are five feet tall; a Zenith clock; two car speakers; two house stereo speakers; a sea chest; an AM-FM cassette portable radio; a bunch of LPs; a Krager wheel."

"How much was all this worth, in your opinion?"

"At least $7,000, maybe more."

"Tell me about the arrest."

"We were going back up to Arkansas, and for some reason, I don't know why, we were pulled over. Brian got out and walked back there. I found out later he'd been busted for marijuana. There was no dope in the car. They arrested us and impounded the car. They held me there for about a week."

"And what happened when you tried to reclaim your property?"

"All the stereo equipment and recording equipment was gone. Just about everything was missing. The sea chest and a couple of toolboxes were there. That was about all. The wheel was there, too."

"What did they tell you had happened to the rest?"

"They said it was in the evidence room. They said they didn't have a key and couldn't get to it."

"What did you do?"

"I walked in to the sheriff and asked him about it, but he got on the phone and called somebody about his lunch. He said he'd see what he could do about it, and then he scribbled something down on his calendar. . . .. We waited from 8:00 until after 3:00. Then this big fat deputy started cussing us out. He really chewed out my mom."

"Why?"

"He was the one who said we couldn't get any of the stuff back. He said they'd send it back when the cops from Arkansas came to pick up Brian. He made it sound like some of the stuff was gone. . . . What I should've done was load up the wheel and toolboxes and all that right then. One deputy was going to let us have it, but then this fat deputy said we couldn't take any of it."

"What was this fat deputy's name?"

"I don't know. But I'd recognize a picture of him. He was old, about fifty-five or so, and he was fat and short."

"Did the sheriff say anything to you about this?"

"Man, the sheriff didn't even seem interested in it. He just called about his lunch. I remember he told someone to 'hold the carrots' and he also said something about Salisbury steak. He didn't seem to want to know much about any of it."

"Who booked you into the jail when you were arrested?"

"Some jail inmate, a guy wearing white jail clothes. He even read us our rights."

"Who arrested you?"

"Some young cowboy-looking guy. I don't know his name."

"And to this day—four months later—you still have gotten none of your property back from Coldspring?"

"Nothing. Not one thing."

I tried all the following day, Thursday, May 27, to reach Sheriff Parker at his office. Between phone calls I wrote the story, detailing the arrest on Highway 59, the comments from the four county officials who took an inventory of the stereo equipment, the problems the Michaleks had in trying to get the sheriff to return the $7,000 worth of equipment. I briefly connected this Highway 59 arrest to the others that were uncovered in our first three stories, and I mentioned the fact that two separate investigations—one federal and one state—were under way as a result of those stories. Finally, at 6:35 p.m., I reached the sheriff at his home in Shepherd. He didn't sound too pleased to hear from me.

I explained that I had talked to the Michaleks, and that they said the sheriff's department had refused for four months to return $7,000 worth of stereo equipment that belonged to seventeen-year-old Bruce Michalek.

Parker quickly said, "That's not so. . . . When those deputies came down here they would not take it back. They said they weren't about to carry all that crap with them."

"So you still have the equipment, then?"

"It's stored and tagged and all they've got to do is come pick it up. . . . It's all right there in the property room with his name on it."

"They tell me that you haven't responded to a couple of letters asking about it."

"They've called about a dozen times, and Chief John Glover tells them all they got to do is come get it."

"What exactly do you have that belongs to Bruce Michalek?"

"I don't know, four or five suitcases of crap. . . . I don't know what their problem is, 'cause they want us to deliver it to them. And we don't do that."

"But Chief Glover is the person who is handling this matter?"

"Yeah. Some lady has called Glover five or six times. . . . We even got a letter from a lawyer and answered that. We told them to come and get it."

"Then it looks like, from what you're saying, that some wires have been crossed."

"Well, you tell that lady to call me tomorrow and I'll uncross her wires for her." He added again that the property had always been in the property room and "never left it." And he closed with "Sorry about that."

I spent the rest of that night, until almost midnight, on the telephone to Jean O'Dell, Bill Burnett, Mike Jeffrey, and Richard Curry, the four people who took the inventory. O'Dell, Burnett, and Jeffrey said they had been in the property room and sally port several times since Mrs. Michalek had been there on January 26, and they had never seen the equipment that they had inventoried. They said they didn't know where it was, but that it would be interesting to see what would happen if the Michaleks came and tried to reclaim the property.

The next morning I called Mrs. Michalek and Ginger Atkinson and told them of the sheriff's comments. They said they would start making plans for a trip to Coldspring to pick up the equipment. "I just hope it's all there like he says, because I'm sick and tired of trying to deal with this from 350 miles away," Mrs. Michalek said. She denied calling Chief Glover or anyone else in that department more than twice. And Ginger Atkinson said she had not gotten a response from the sheriff's department to her two letters, but she had received a nice letter from Jean O'Dell, who agreed to hand-carry the second letter to Parker.

But there seemed to be a great deal more going on in Coldspring. Judge Jeffrey told me on Friday, May 28, that Doris Yarbrough, the sheriff's secretary, had resigned her post and was going to work for Bill Burnett in the probation office. And Deputy Carl Lee, he said, had told several people he soon would be retiring from the sheriff's department. And last but not least, the judge said that county attorney Robert Atkins had instructed the sheriff to remove his stepdaughter, Sheila Cronin, from the payroll.

As I inserted the sheriff's comments into story number four, I realized it was time to take another trip to San Jacinto County. Douthat, who had done no work on the investigation in about a week, also was ready to go back. Ed reluctantly agreed to let us. The Michalek story ran on an inside page in the second section on Sunday, May 30, and I began planning for the next trip.

· TWENTY-FOUR ·

The first order of business on Tuesday, June 1, was to stop by the courthouse in Coldspring and check in with the county clerk's office. As usual, we had to wait a few minutes until the clerk's office opened up following lunch. Despite Mrs. Imogene Trapp's defeat as clerk on May 1, she apparently was going to stick with her policy of closing the office from 12:00 to 1:00. Some traditions die hard, I suppose. After lunch, I hustled to the criminal dockets to see if the sheriff's department really was filing a bunch of late marijuana possession charges. Within five minutes, I could tell that the rumors were correct.

From my research on the state's law code, I knew that the Speedy Trial Act had a pretty simple formula: if prosecutors were not prepared to go to trial in a misdemeanor case within ninety days after arrest, detention, or release on bond, then all motions for dismissal by the defendant must be granted by the judge. There was no alternative; the judge *had* to dismiss the charges. It didn't seem too complicated.

But my check of the criminal dockets that afternoon showed that Sheriff Parker had filed thirty-three possession charges in which the arrests were more than ninety days old—and all of them had been filed within a ten-day period after our first two stories were published. Twenty-two of those thirty-three arrests had occurred in December 1981, nearly six months before. It appeared that the sheriff had been pretty busy during the ten days after our first stories ran on May 16. And all thirty-three charges, according to the Speedy Trial Act, were no good. Each one contained just as much information as all the others I had checked during the preceding five months—that is, not much information at all. No home towns of defendants, no addresses, no places of arrest, no times of arrest, no arresting officers, no details. But they were all there, big as day, every one of them in violation of the Speedy Trial Act.

I jotted down all the names, docket numbers, dates of filing, and dates of arrest and trotted across the hall to see county attorney Robert Atkins, the official prosecutor on misdemeanor cases in county judge K. P. Bryant's court. I had a few other things to bring up with Atkins, too, including the sheriff's hiring of his stepdaughter, Sheila Cronin. And I hadn't tried to chat with Atkins in several weeks . . . not that he had done much chatting to me before. But what the heck. I walked in on him at 3:45 p.m. and found him doing the same thing he was always doing when I saw him: looking in a law book. I got right to the point and told him I'd just found thirty-three marijuana possession charges across the hall that were more than 90 days old, some of them 180 days old. Was he preparing to prosecute those cases?

"Well, that's a defensive position," he said, pointing out that he was not about to raise the Speedy Trial Act in court, that it would be up to each defendant to bring it up.

And if they didn't bring it up?

"It it's not brought up, then the state will go ahead and prosecute." He said he would place all the cases on the docket and leave it up to Judge Bryant to dismiss them. "We're certainly not going to bring it up," he added. He said he would have no choice but to prosecute the cases since they were filed by the sheriff.

But what if the defendants brought up the Speedy Trial Act in each case?

Then the judge would have no choice but to dismiss the case, he replied.

That sounded like the official county position to me, so I shifted gears and asked about Sheila Cronin. Was he aware that the sheriff had hired his own stepdaughter?

Atkins smiled, the only time I could recall that he had done so, and he said that the matter had been brought to his attention by several members of the commissioners' court whose names he could not repeat. He said the commissioners were not pleased with that type of nepotism.

And what had he done then?

"I called the sheriff and advised him to take her off the payroll . . . because it was my opinion that the relationship was too close."

What happened after that?

"The sheriff said he would take her off, and I assume he did." But he added that he never checked back on it after that. "I told him if he kept her on it would be his problem."

He labeled the Cronin matter as "no big deal."

At 9:30 that night, I reached district judge Joe Ned Dean at his home in Trinity County and asked if he was aware of the thirty-three late possession charges.

"No, I didn't know they'd been filed. Of course, a distict judge normally doesn't know about them until they're indicted."

Would it be considered standard procedure for charges of a misdemeanor nature to be filed in court so long after the arrests?

"It's not standard for them to be that late, no."

And would it be standard procedure for the county attorney to say he wouldn't mention the Speedy Trial Act in court?

"Well, you'd have to expect him to say that," Dean replied. The judge then said he had heard a lot of street talk from Coldspring about the four stories we had published, and he said it might be worth our while to do some more checking on the mysterious burglary of Johnston's Pharmacy back in January, the one in which Gary Parker and Ronnie Greer said they were shot at by the burglars.

I asked if he could tell me anything more about that burglary.

"I feel like that burglary might be taken to the grand jury."

When?

"Probably next month, or within the next sixty days."

Douthat and I spent the first part of the next morning meeting privately in Conroe with district attorney J. H. Keeshan, going over a wide range of problems and cases involving San Jacinto County. Keeshan was impressed with our four stories, but he didn't want anything he told us to get outside his office. His comments, however, were helpful. But I mentioned to him the drugstore burglary and the concerns that had been expressed to me about the fact that the sheriff's son was working as a deputy, and I said several people had told me that he had been involved in the resignation of Gary Parker from the sheriff's department. Could he tell us about that, on the record?

Reluctantly, he agreed, and it was the only on-the-record comment he made to us that morning. Here is what he said:

"The extent of my efforts were to speak with a couple of public officials. Following that, I spoke with one of the sheriff's supporters and I suggested to him that although it wasn't technically nepotism, it didn't look good. And if it's become a type of criticism over there, then it was in the sheriff's interest and the community's interest for Gary not to be a deputy." Following that conversation, Keeshan said, the sheriff called him. "And I suggested directly to him that it might be in his best interests for Gary not to be a deputy."

Did the sheriff agree to take away Gary's badge and gun?

"The indications were it would be done. No promises were made, and no promises sought."

At 11:30 a.m., we met with Kent Morrison in his office in the courthouse. As county treasurer, he was concerned that only $70,000 in fines had been collected and turned in by the sheriff's department so far that year. The sheriff had projected almost $300,000 in fine collections in his budget for 1982. Morrison said the falloff in collections undoubtedly was due to our stories, as well as the presence of the FBI and the task force.

"I'm looking at it this way," Morrison said. "The year is half over, and if you double what has been collected and then double it again, then they're still going to be short. Financially, it's going to be a big problem."

The rest of the afternoon was spent in two places: Judge Jeffrey's boot and saddle shop and the adult probation office where Bill Burnett worked. We went over and over the role each of them had played in the investigation of the drugstore burglary in January, and we searched for something concrete to help us develop the information into a usable story. That was going to be very hard to do. Everyone was concerned about the break-in, and the theft of narcotics, and the reported shooting, and the activities of Gary Parker and Ronnie Greer, but no one had any evidence about anything. We decided at the end of the afternoon to keep the drugstore incident on the back burner for a while.

In the meantime, I had something else planned for that evening. I was driving down to Crosby, Texas, just northeast of Houston, to meet with Cassie Parker and her parents.

Fortunately, the drive from the Holiday Inn in Conroe to Crosby was uneventful; it bypassed most of the Houston traffic, circling to the north of the Intercontinental Airport and to the east of Lake Houston. It was almost 8:30 p.m. when I arrived. The two-story brick house was just as Cassie had described it: "modern, with a stairway leading upstairs in front to the front door." I had no trouble locating the house amid the hundreds of others in this Houston bedroom community.

I was surprised when I saw Cassie for the first time. She looked much younger than I had expected. She was nineteen, but she could have passed for sixteen without any problem whatsoever. She was thin, with close-cut brown hair, and she had the type of eyes that always seem to look sad. She answered the door and invited me downstairs to the den, where her father was waiting. I thought it was a bit odd to have to walk up a flight of stairs to the front door and then walk back down a flight of stairs to the den. But my attention was soon directed elsewhere. Both Cassie and Mr. Kluck were very intense, serious, and concerned; they wanted very much to help me out (they had read all four stories), but they were concerned about being pulled into the FBI investigation. Their reason for this almost immediately crawled over and tugged on my pants leg: curly-haired, two-year-old Courtney. They didn't want to say or do anything that might jeopardize Cassie's custody of the child, they explained. Gary had already filed motions in court to take custody, and they didn't want to say anything that would help his case.

I understood completely. My own daughter was about that age, and I knew how protective a parent can be. I assured them that I would not mention Cassie's name in my stories, and that I wouldn't print anything she said to me without getting confirmation from some other source. But, I said, there probably would come a time when she would have to step forward, either before a grand jury or in court, if everything she had told me on the phone the week before was accurate. I told them that my newspaper's investigation had gotten the FBI and the State of Texas involved in their own criminal investigations, and that those agents seemed to be tracing my stories in an attempt to talk to people that I talked to. And one of the Texas Rangers on the state task force had already approached me about names of people who might help his investigation.

Cassie stared at the floor for a minute and then nodded her head. She said she realized what would happen, that she would probably have to give a statement to the investigators, but she hoped to delay it as long as possible.

Mr. Kluck agreed. He said they had moved out of San Jacinto County earlier in the year hoping to get away from everything that was going on there. But there was too much going on in that county that needed to stop, he said, and if they could help bring it to a stop then they would step forward. But they had to make sure that anything they said or did would be definitive, resulting in absolute action by the FBI or the Texas Rangers.

I said I would do everything I could to respect their privacy, and that I would not give their names to the investigators without first double-checking with them. I hurriedly mentioned that I was under constraints from my editors, and I didn't know how much longer I would be allowed to work on this story. So I was doing something I never before had done as a reporter: I was peripherally cooperating with the task force, mainly by supplying the Texas Rangers with the names and addresses of people I had contacted who had expressed a willingness to testify. And that was it. I was not doing any investigative work for the Rangers or the FBI, and I would never do so. They were conducting their own probes, which just happened to be tagging along behind my own.

With those feeble words of assurance, we sat down in the den and began talking about San Jacinto County, the sheriff's department, Cassie's marriage to Gary, their divorce, and her impressions regarding the drug traffic in that county. We talked until 1:00 a.m. Mrs. Kluck, who was working late as a nurse, joined us a little after 11:00. It was a most enlightening and illuminating interview, even though I knew at the time that my city editor was not going to give me time to follow through on most of the things they were telling me.

The *American-Statesman*, as far as I could tell, was most interested in giving the appearance of being busy, and the way its editors accomplished that was by shuffling reporters from story to story at a rapid rate; by getting them to write short, nonsensical feature stories and butchered daily news stories that usually raised more questions than they answered; and by arranging team reporting assignments that covered preordained areas. Open-ended investigations such as this one were something new to that newspaper. I knew that. Every reporter on the staff knew that. Oh, no editor ever came right out and said, "We don't do that kind of investigating," but their actions confirmed their feelings. Ed didn't have to say anything at all. He just loaded me up with other stories, put me on a few team assignments, juggled my schedule around, assigned me to weekend detail, and effectively and comprehensively started vacuuming up my San Jacinto County story.

The Klucks could not possibly understand this, so I never mentioned it to them. But it was all right there in my mind as we talked for those four and a half hours.

I did learn a great deal about Gary Parker; much of it I was able to confirm later with the Commission on Law Enforcement Officer Standards and Education, the state agency that keeps files on all commissioned law enforcement officers in the state. I learned that Gary had worked for State Representative Jim Browder in Austin from January through May 1977, when he graduated from Shepherd High School, and had joined the San Jacinto County Sheriff's Department in February 1978 at the age of nineteen. He had been appointed a reserve deputy by the county commissioners in April 1979; that summer he completed 70 hours of basic training at the Harris County Sheriff's Academy, being qualified as a marksman by that academy in July 1979. He had joined the state prison system in Huntsville as a corrections officer in August 1979 but left the job nine months later; he left the San Jacinto County Sheriff's Department a day after leaving the prison job and joined the Montgomery County Sheriff's Department one day later than that, on May 1, 1980, as a jailer. He left that job on July 7, 1980. He finished a 240-hour basic course at the East Texas Police Academy in August 1980, then took courses on supervision and basic jail operations in the summer and fall of 1981. In the meantime, his bond was approved by the San Jacinto County commissioners in May 1980, and he applied to the state for a peace officer's commission in June 1980. He filed to run for county Democratic party chairman on January 27, 1982, and was defeated on May 1, 1982.

I also learned a phrase that Cassie said the deputies used for the money taken from Highway 59 victims for bond and towing fees: "breakfast money." She said a lot of breakfast money was made during the time she was around the sheriff's department.

Story number five ran on Sunday, June 6, on the tenth page of the second section. With each passing week, it seemed, our stories were falling deeper and deeper inside the newspaper. This story had a three-column headline that read, "Coldspring Pot Charges Are Filed After Deadline," and it detailed the thirty-three possession charges that were filed after the ninety-day limit set out in the Speedy Trial Act. It included comments from Robert Atkins about the time limitation being a "defensive position" and not his concern. The story also linked the late charges to our first four stories and mentioned that two separate criminal investigations were underway as a result of those stories. The second half of the story told of the resignations, since our investigation began, of one full-time deputy, two reserve deputies, and the sheriff's secretary, and the plans of another deputy to seek retirement. The removal of the sheriff's stepdaughter from his payroll was mentioned briefly. The last four paragraphs were devoted to county treasurer Kent Morrison's comments about the impending financial crunch in the county due to the dramatic falloff of fine collections by the sheriff's department.

With this story behind us, Douthat and I turned our attention to the activities of Ronnie Greer, the twenty-four-year-old reserve deputy with Gary Parker the night of the drugstore burglary.

· TWENTY-FIVE ·

A twenty-two-year-old Shepherd man by the name of Murray Chreene lived way back in the woods in the far south part of San Jacinto County with the rest of his family. It took a good ten minutes on a bumpy dirt road from Highway 59 to get to the Chreene farm. Douthat and I probably would never have driven back there had it not been for justice of the peace Mike Jeffrey. According to the judge, on the night of February 5, 1982, Murray Chreene got himself shot at by a San Jacinto County law officer who was arrested minutes later by a Department of Public Safety trooper, who took the law officer to jail. Everything was fine, according to the judge, except that the sheriff's department declined to file charges on the officer. Which meant that Murray Chreene's assailant was never punished for an allegedly unwarranted shooting. The law officer's name, the judge told us, was Ronnie Greer, and Ronnie Greer also happened to be a friend of Gary Parker's.

It all sounded a little farfetched to us, but the judge's account of the incident was confirmed by Greg Magee and probation officer Bill Burnett. The problem was that none of them had been an eyewitness to the shooting; the only eyewitnesses, according to their story, were Greer and Chreene. But by June 3, a Thursday during a trip to Coldspring, Greer was nowhere to be found. Even his stepfather, Deputy Glenn Snearly, said he didn't know where to find him. That meant we had to talk to Chreene, and also to the arresting DPS trooper, Van Loggins, the next-door neighbor of fellow trooper Red Blanchette.

I spent an hour and a half on the morning of June 3 looking through the criminal charges in the San Jacinto County Courthouse. There was nothing there with Ronnie Greer's name on it, and that applied not only to criminal charges but also to bonds approved by the county commissioners for deputies and reserves; so Greer wasn't actually a law

officer, then. What was he? Everyone we had talked with that week—
Judge Jeffrey, Greg Magee, Bill Burnett, Jean O'Dell, Constable Charles
Clark, Kent Morrison, and a few others—said that Greer regularly
drove a county car, carried a badge and a gun, and conducted himself
as though he were one of the boys at the sheriff's office. He rode on a
regular basis with Gary Parker and often worked the northern stretch
of Highway 59, sometimes by himself, our sources maintained. What
indeed was Greer?

A little before 10:30 that morning, we met just west of Coldspring at
the Y intersection of Highway 150 and FM 2025 with Loggins and
Blanchette. They had been working a roadblock there earlier in the
morning, checking driver's licenses and proofs of liability insurance. I
imagine they wrote a few tickets, too. We spent about thirty minutes
talking to them on the side of the road, going over the events of the
night of February 5. Loggins, who had been on duty that night, was
mad. He felt the sheriff's department was rubbing that whole incident
in his face, and he was on the lookout for Greer.

The tall, slender, dark-haired Loggins said he had been helping the
sheriff's department that night to investigate a reported burglary of a
house in Shepherd, but he got to the scene a bit late because the sheriff's
dispatcher first sent him to the wrong house. Once he got to the proper
location, he learned that Greer was working with the deputies who were
investigating the burglary. But Greer was not there. As he was asking
preliminary questions, the trooper said, he heard that there had been
shots fired a few minutes before at a car wash on Highway 150 in
Shepherd. The shots were reported by one of Chreene's relatives, who
happened to live a couple of blocks behind the car wash.

Loggins said he left the burglary scene and drove past the car wash
to the house behind it, where the complainant about the gunfire was
supposed to be. "I got there just as Greer was driving up," Loggins said,
adding that he had talked to Murray Chreene and learned that Greer
was the one who had done the shooting.

And then, according to Loggins, he had this exchange with Greer:

"I asked him what he was doing with that gun. He said, 'I'm an undercover agent for Sheriff Parker.' I asked him, 'Are you a commissioned
peace officer?' He said, 'I work undercover for the sheriff.' I asked him
again if he was a commissioned officer, and he said he wasn't. So I told
him, 'You're under arrest for carrying a prohibited weapon.' "

The trooper said Greer admitted that he had fired a warning shot at
Chreene, who Greer had thought was a suspect in the burglary. But according to Loggins, all Chreene was doing was sitting in his pickup at
the car wash, minding his own business. Greer was driving a black
Camaro, unmarked, and was reportedly not wearing a badge at the

time. Loggins said Greer apparently never identified himself when he approached Chreene's truck with his .38-caliber revolver drawn. Chreene, according to Loggins, ran when he saw the gun.

What happened next was a little strange. Loggins said he turned Greer over to reserve deputy Ernie Bostic, who transported him to the county jail ten miles away in Coldspring. The trooper said he returned briefly to the scene of the burglary, but then headed for the jail himself about half an hour later.

But as he was driving up Highway 150 to Coldspring to get to the jail, Greer passed him going the other way in the black Camaro.

"I was going to question him, but he was released before I got there." He said he hadn't seen Greer since then.

I confirmed to him that no charges against Greer were on file at the courthouse, and that no record of Greer's ever being commissioned as a peace officer could be found.

"I know. I know," he said.

Later that day, Douthat and I talked with several members of the Chreene family at their farm and learned that Murray Chreene had attended an organizational meeting for a baseball league the night of February 5 and had been killing some time at the car wash before going home. The family was very upset about the shooting, and they said that the day after the incident, February 6, they had filed their own assault charge against Greer. However, no action had ever been taken on those charges, they said.

Douthat reached Murray Chreene by telephone that night, and the twenty-two-year-old said he was sitting in his truck when Greer approached with a drawn .38 and ordered him to get out of the vehicle. "He put the .38 in my back and told me to put my hands on the truck. . . . He didn't tell me his name or nothing. I was scared."

Chreene said he began running from the car wash to the house nearby, where he was going to get his relatives to call for help. While he was running, he said, Greer fired three shots over his head. He had no idea what his pursuer wanted from him; for all he knew, the man was trying to kill him. It was bizarre incident, one that left him shaken and perplexed. But the incident itself didn't stir up his anger as much as Greer's early release and the lack of prosecution.

While Douthat was talking to Chreene, I reached Ernie Bostic, the health clinic administrator and recently resigned reserve sheriff's deputy. Bostic was no more talkative this time than he had been the last, but he denied that he did anything unusual in transporting Greer to jail on the night of February 5. He said he took care of writing up the charges against Greer that night; however, he said, he had no knowledge of the disposition of those charges.

"You may be looking at something that was completely taken care of, in the sense that everybody involved in it had a mutual agreement and did away with it," he said. "I really don't know what happened."

Loggins, meanwhile, said his biggest mistake was "not filing the charges myself and not keeping up with it." He said he had a few things to discuss with Greer the next time he saw him.

The only thing that remained on this weird story was to get the official word from Sheriff Parker on what happened. That was going to be hard, though. I spent the better part of two days trying to reach him at his office and home but got no answer at the latter and no cooperation at the former. A woman who answered the telephone at the sheriff's department said she didn't know when the sheriff would get back, or where he was, or where he was going. I'd have to talk to him about whatever it was that I wanted. Right.

Story number six was punched into the computer on a Friday afternoon. It was shorter than the others, but it dealt only with the Murray Chreene shooting affair. And it ran on the fourteenth page of the second section on Sunday, June 13. The three-column headline said, " 'Agent' Accused, Not Tried, After Shooting." In the original story I turned in, there had been about ten sentences of background information to tie this story in with our investigation of Highway 59 and other law enforcement concerns in San Jacinto County. But by the time the story appeared in print, those five paragraphs had been condensed into two sentences, and no mention remained of Highway 59. The message was loud and clear to me: the *American-Statesman* was getting very tired of this story. And I was getting very tired of the *American-Statesman*.

FBI agent Ed Hartung and Texas Ranger Wesley Styles interviewed Cassie Parker for more than six hours the first Friday in June. They also talked to Greg Magee on more than two occasions, and with Judge Jeffrey and probation officer Bill Burnett. The FBI agent and the Ranger had teamed up. It was now difficult to distinguish where the feds ended and the task force began. But a great part of their questions seemed to center on the drugstore burglary, according to the persons who were interviewed.

On Thursday, June 10, I called Cassie Parker to learn what types of questions had been put to her. "They pretty much put me through the wringer," Cassie said. "They said I could talk to the grand jury if I didn't want to talk to them. They wanted to know about the drugs, the money, the whole bit. They wanted to know it all."

The agents also took a nineteen-inch black and white TV set that Cassie said she got during her marriage to Gary. They told her they wanted to check the serial number. "They had me pretty shook up.

They were just real thorough, and they took a lot of notes." She said they asked her a lot of questions about Ronnie Greer, but she really didn't know a lot about him. "They also told me to keep a low profile, and if anybody said anything threatening to me to call them immediately. Mr. Styles said he'd serve the papers on them himself if that happened."

By the next week, officials in Coldspring were reporting to me almost hourly on the activities of the FBI and DPS. Judge Jeffrey said they went over all the records in the courthouse and in the justice of the peace courts "to see what cases don't go anywhere. . . . They've got an awfully long list, but I don't know where they got their cases. . . . There were two new people, two DPS intelligence officers, I think from Lufkin. They act like they know what they're doing, too."

Burnett, the probation officer, said the various agents were in and out of the county clerk's office nearly every day during the first two weeks in June, and they were making copies of nearly all charges that were entered on the criminal dockets. "They've had four or five people in there, not counting Hartung and Styles, for most of the week," he said. "I think they're really getting serious about all this."

· TWENTY-SIX ·

After five straight weeks of stories on San Jacinto County, we rested. Or rather, our editors at the *American-Statesman* made us rest on that story by loading us up with other goodies. In five weeks, we had written six stories—two lengthy stories on the arrest trap on Highway 59, one on the formation of the state task force and early activity by the FBI, one on the Michaleks' stereo equipment, another on the late filing of marijuana charges, and the last on the Murray Chreene–Ronnie Greer shooting incident. Six articles in five weeks. Not bad. Except that each one was a pain—not to write but to get through the newspaper's strange editing process. Every editor on that paper was encouraged to rewrite stories turned in by reporters, regardless of whether the story needed rewriting. Preferential editing, it was called. Substituting one person's words for another's. Busywork. Time-consuming, pointless, egomaniacal busywork. Some people on that newspaper got a great deal of pleasure out of changing words in a story. Perhaps it made them feel powerful. But the fact remained that most of the copy editors and assistant city editors had far less writing experience than the members of the reporting staff. As Al Pacino said in the great courtroom scene in the movie *And Justice for All:* "Something is *really* wrong here."

I broke out of my doldrums early in the fourth week of June, when three things jarred me into action: first, Judge Jeffrey gave me the name of a Montgomery County man, Al Rachal, who had been trying for more than six months to get Sheriff Parker to return a $500 cash bond he had paid to guarantee his appearance in court on a trespassing charge, and Jeffrey said the man had indeed appeared in court; second, J. E. Foley of Jamestown, Kentucky, called me and said the ACLU had tentatively agreed to file a lawsuit on his behalf against the San Jacinto County Sheriff's Department, charging the department with several counts of civil rights violations; and third, Mrs. Michalek and her son Bruce from Little Rock said they would return to Coldspring that week to try to reclaim their stereo and recording equipment. I had enough new things for Ed to let me go back over there. Douthat, though, was working on other stories and was forced to stay behind. My blood pressure seemed to drop a little, at least for the time being.

Al Rachal, according to Judge Jeffrey, had been arrested by deputies back in December for fishing in the Trinity River too close to the Lake Livingston dam. He was taken to jail, where he paid $500 in cash to the sheriff for his bail bond. On January 13, he appeared in court and paid another $171 after entering a plea of guilty. Jeffrey said his appearance in court meant that his cash bond would have to be returned, but the sheriff for some reason had not returned it.

After driving back to Conroe on Tuesday, June 22, and checking into the Holiday Inn on I-45 in the southern part of town, I began working the phones to see what I could find out about Rachal. Of course, he wasn't in the Conroe telephone directory; nothing is *that* easy. So I ventured on up the road to Coldspring to see what I could find out in the courthouse. I found out plenty.

First, the sheriff hadn't filed any marijuana possession charges in almost a month, not since the batch of late cases filed during the ten days after our first stories ran on May 16. And in the two-week period since my Speedy Trial Act story ran on June 6, eleven cases (six for marijuana possession) were shown on the dockets as having been dismissed for that specific reason. Those eleven Speedy Trial Act dismissals were the only ones I could find over the previous three years. Just a coincidence? Hardly. I just wondered what might have happened over those three years if more Highway 59 arrestees had challenged their charges instead of pleading guilty and paying fines. And what if they had appealed if Judge Bryant had rejected their challenges? Most of those appeals would have gone straight to district judge Joe Ned Dean. If a few people had aggressively fought their arrests, stoppages, searches, bond settings, and all that, perhaps I wouldn't have had anything to write in the first place. But damn, no one ever challenged anything in that county!

Including Al Rachal, apparently. The criminal docket showed that Rachal had pleaded guilty on January 13 and paid a $100 fine plus $71 for court costs. There was no record anywhere in the county clerk's office of his $500 cash bond, however. And that was what was interesting. As usual, the docket and the affidavit of complaint in his case showed no home town or address. I had gotten used to that. But it was still just as aggravating as ever.

I made a few rounds—Bill Burnett, Jean O'Dell, Kent Morrison, Judge Jeffrey—while I was in town, primarily to see what the FBI and Texas

Rangers were up to that day. For they were up to something. I kept bumping into them everywhere I went. As usual, they wanted to know what I was doing over there, and as usual, I told them to read the newspaper and find out. (My cooperation with them went only so far. I could never tell them before I wrote a story what that story was going to say. That smacked of prior restraint, almost, and I feel about prior restraint of the news the way I feel about cancer.) As many as nine federal and state boys were at work in the county that week, by my count. Surely this investigation wouldn't, couldn't, die like the one in 1978. I wouldn't let it.

At 9:30 that night, I reached Al Rachal at his home in Montgomery, a small city about twenty miles west of Conroe on State Highway 105, a city that usually had a radar trap set up just inside its western city limit sign, at least every time I drove through. Rachal sounded a bit surprised to hear from me, as though I shouldn't have been able to contact him by telephone. But as I explained to him, we reporters usually can track down people when it's important. And this was important.

He said he knew it was. He had read a couple of the stories.

I asked him to tell me what happened to him in San Jacinto County back in December 1981.

"I was fishing below the dam there on the Trinity River, and a couple of deputies called me over and said I was under arrest for fishing too close to the cable. They said it was criminal trespass. They made me take my boat out of the water and everything."

And what happened after the arrest?

"Well, it was around noon when they took me in, and at first they were going to lock me up. They said I wouldn't get to see a bondsman until the next day. But I insisted on posting bond that night. They took my $500 and gave me a receipt."

Did he have the money with him?

"Yes, I had it in my pocket."

Did he usually carry that much money with him?

"A lot of the time, yes."

Who set the bond at $500?

"As far as I could tell, it was just one of the deputies."

And then Rachal returned to go to county court?

"Yes. They fined me $171. I pleaded guilty. It really wasn't worth fighting."

And what happened to his $500?

"Well, at first they said they'd mail it to me, but they didn't. I've called and called about it, and nobody seems to know anything about it. I even went up there, and they said they didn't know anything about it.

But they do know about it because it came up in court. And when they took me into the jail I must have filled out about five pages of papers. I thought at first it was just confusion. You know, they said they'd had to change secretaries and all. . . . But no one seems to know anything about anything over there. And all I know is, I'd like to get my $500."

"Who exactly took your $500 and wrote you a receipt?" I asked.

"It was just the sheriff's secretary. . . . I don't remember the name. But I believe it's on the receipt."

Rachal sounded like a credible witness, and his story was backed up by Judge Jeffrey. It would make another decent story, story number seven.

Story number eight was already in the works, and it was going to run as a sidebar to number seven. It was about the Michaleks, the people from Arkansas who were trying to retrieve $7,000 worth of stereo equipment from the sheriff's custody. I had informed them three weeks earlier that the sheriff said he had all their property right there in his office, and that he was just waiting on them to come get it. So the Michaleks were coming to Coldspring to pick up their property.

They arrived on Friday, June 25. The sheriff wasn't around, but Deputy Carl Lee took them to where the equipment was stored. But most of the equipment that was inventoried by the four impartial observers was gone. Despite the sheriff's assurances, the stuff was just flat not there. Mrs. Michalek recovered only two speakers, two toolboxes, the sea chest, and some other personal items. Missing were the $900 Akai reel-to-reel recorder, a $500 amplifier, most of the other recording equipment, forty-nine cassettes, the LP albums, the clocks, and—not the least of these—the inventory list.

"I'm absolutely disgusted by all this," Mrs. Michalek said. "I hope they lock all them up. If this isn't theft, I don't know what is."

Stories seven and eight ran on the third page of the second section on Sunday, June 27. The top story was about Rachal, and it had a head-line over six columns that said, "Inquiry Pursues Claim That San Jacinto Sheriff Withholding Bail." It included two brief comments from the sheriff, whom Douthat had been able to reach at home late Friday, June 25. (Everyone recognized my voice by that time, but no one in the sheriff's family had ever talked to Douthat.) First, Parker said he thought that a secretary in his office had mailed Rachal's money to him the week before, and he attributed the delay to his inability to keep a secretary in his office on a permanent basis. The sheriff's second comment was about the FBI and state investigations. He said he welcomed the probes: "I'm glad to see it. . . . If there is something illegal going on here, hell, I sure want to know it."

Story number eight ran below the Rachal story, and its one-column headline said, "Property Room Missing Items." There was a footnote to that story: Mrs. Michalek said that Deputy Carl Lee had told her that the sheriff's department would pay for the missing stereo equipment.

In the meantime, Mr. Foley was positively ecstatic that the Houston office of the ACLU was interested in filing suit on his behalf against the sheriff's office. "I talked to their lawyer down there, Stefan Presser, and actually he called me. He said they're probably going to take this into federal court down there. I'll tell you what, I'll guarantee that I'll show up for trial. This thing needs to be done; those folks down there have got to be stopped. . . . I know the ACLU's had problems in the past with people filing suit and then not showing up. That kind of thing's been happening all over the country. But I'll be there when the time comes. I won't put up with this kind of so-called law enforcement."

Mr. Foley was aware of the FBI and state investigations, as well as the continuing investigation that I was doing. He was aware of it because I had sent him all my stories. But he said he wanted to take on his own lawsuit against them. "You know, even though there are these other investigations going on, I believe this is the kind of thing I've got to do. I've always believed that a person ought to stand up for what he believes in. And I believe in this. Yes, sir, I surely do."

Another thing popped up during this hectic week: treasurer Kent Morrison said he had received a personal check from Sheila Cronin's mother—the sheriff's wife—in the amount of $1,700. The money, Morrison said, was a reimbursement to San Jacinto County for the salary that the sheriff's stepdaughter had drawn while working in the sheriff's department for ninety days as a dispatcher. They wanted to repay the money, since the young girl had been removed after questions of nepotism were raised. And Morrison mentioned one other thing, a small matter: the state Comptroller's Office had apparently opened its own investigation of San Jacinto County, because two investigators from Austin had shown up to look over the county's criminal justice reports. "I think they want to make sure that the county is sending them all the money we should," he said.

· TWENTY-SEVEN ·

My solo trip to Coldspring the fourth week in June had been productive. It had led directly to two stories, which meant that this investigation had produced eight stories over a six-week period. I had been working in and out of San Jacinto County for a little more than twenty-two weeks; Douthat had been with me off and on for about eleven weeks. But things were still happening: the FBI and the Texas Rangers were scurrying around on a daily basis, the Comptroller's Office was now involved, and a couple of friends of mine at the Internal Revenue Service in Houston were hinting broadly to me about their interest in what was going on. And San Jacinto County was smack in the middle of a financial crisis. Fine collections were about a fourth of what had been projected in the fiscal year budget, and several officials were close to the point of panic. The only recourse, the only way out of the budgetary mess, it appeared, would be wholesale layoffs and cutbacks. The bonanza from Highway 59 was at an end. Everywhere you looked there were men in suits wearing sunglasses and carrying briefcases. The county was in shock. And not one word of any of this had appeared in any newspaper in Houston or Dallas, the state's largest media markets. The Houston news media, in fact, seemed to be consciously ignoring all eight of our stories. Only the Cox chain papers in Texas—Port Arthur, Waco, Lufkin, Longview—picked up our stories. Even the Associated Press seemed reluctant to pick them up. For the first time since I began this investigation, I felt relatively safe from the other media. We now had eight stories under our belts, covering a wide range of topics involving a very small county, and anyone else who wanted to jump into this would have a heck of a lot of catching up to do.

But my frustration with the *American-Statesman* was mounting. I was finding it increasingly difficult to deal with editors whom I no longer respected as professional journalists. Still, there was one last story I wanted to put together before I pulled myself back to watch the progress of the FBI, the DPS, the Texas Rangers, the Comptroller's Office, the IRS, and any other agency in action in San Jacinto County. Too much was happening for those investigators to stop now. My work had brought it all about, and it was only a matter of time until a grand jury was impaneled somewhere, or charges filed. But there was one thing they weren't really zeroing in on: the perplexing activities of Ronnie Greer, nondeputy, undercover agent, alleged assailant of Murray Chreene. Who exactly was Ronnie Greer and how did he manage to get a gun and a badge? Why was he allowed to drive a county car, take part in arrests, carry a loaded weapon, and shoot at people without facing the consequences? Was he the type of man whom Sheriff Parker wanted to enforce the laws in that county? I felt that if I could put together one last investigative story on Greer that would answer some of these questions, then maybe the federal and state boys would take it from there, looking at all the deputies and reserves and everyone else who had a badge and a gun. All I could do was hope. My days on this story were numbered.

One of the things that perplexed me most about San Jacinto County was the incredible number of people who had sheriff's department badges. Greg Magee said he had even stopped cars going through the county and had drivers whom he had never seen present him with departmental badges. He once stopped a middle-aged man for speeding on Highway 156 and asked to see the man's driver's license; instead, the man handed him a badge that identified him as a captain in the San Jacinto County Sheriff's Department. A bit taken aback, Magee could only respond, "I can't arrest you. You outrank me." He said he had never before seen the man.

Judge Jeffrey also had told us of people he knew who were carrying badges—he estimated their numbers in the hundreds. "If you ever collected all of the badges handed out over the past ten years, they would fill up the courthouse."

Constable Charles Clark said the sheriff a few years back had passed out badges "like they were sticks of candy" at a rodeo roundup. "He was shaking hands, slapping people on the back, and giving them a badge," Clark recalled.

Now, sheriffs in Texas are empowered by law to name honorary deputies, sometimes referred to as special deputies, but those deputies have no legal standing whatsoever. They can't go about making arrests, writing tickets, and trying to enforce the laws as they understand them. No, the state Commission on Law Enforcement Officer Standards and Education has elaborate procedures that must be followed before a person can be commissioned as a peace officer. But I was getting the feeling that some people took their honorary badges too seriously; maybe Greer was one of them.

For certain, Greer was not a commissioned officer. And according to probation officer Bill Burnett and Judge Jeffrey, he could never be commissioned because of a criminal record he had in several other counties. Burnett said Greer apparently had been on felony probation at one time, which meant he had been convicted of or pleaded guilty to a felony charge of some type. And the twenty-four-year-old also apparently had been arrested in a couple of other counties nearby. But Burnett had no details.

Judge Jeffrey said Greer had once been arrested in San Jacinto County, too, because he had seen him in the jail wearing jail whites. Greg Magee had also seen him in jail. But Greer apparently had stayed in jail only a few days, because, according to Magee, the next time he saw him out of jail, Greer was wearing a gun, carrying a deputy's badge, and driving a county patrol car. "It was the strangest thing I ever saw," Magee told me. "One day he was in jail and the next he was a deputy. And he took it seriously. He wanted everyone to know that he was a lawman."

Constable Clark confirmed those accounts. "He led everyone to believe he was a police officer. . . . I'll swear to anyone that I saw him with a gun and a badge right there in the sheriff's office."

There was no question in my mind at that point, the last week in June, that Ronnie Greer had operated as a deputy. But I could find no record of his ever having been paid, and neither could Kent Morrison, the county official who wrote out the checks. But according to nearly everyone I had talked with, Greer certainly spent a great deal of time doing his "volunteer work" for the sheriff. He worked many hours of patrol every week on Highway 59, and Greg Magee said that in January Greer had driven a county car down into Montgomery County, where he apprehended a man in connection with a burglary investigation.

All I needed to do was trace Greer's criminal record, and his quick transformation from jail inmate to deputy would make an effective story number nine. Douthat and I talked Ed into letting us make one more trip to Coldspring during the last week in June, only three days after I had returned from the solo trip that resulted in stories seven and eight. Ed had gotten to the point where he wanted us to make out-of-town trips only when we had "sure-thing" stories; he wanted fast results. And he indicated to me that after this trip to pursue the saga of Ronnie Greer, he wanted us to sit back and watch the progress of the state and federal investigations. Which meant, of course, that any future stories would be about those investigations, and not ours. Our investigation would end after this trip. Douthat knew it and so did I.

We left Austin a few minutes before 10:00 on the morning of Monday, June 28. By then I had pieced together a sketchy account of Greer's criminal record in four other counties, in addition to San Jacinto County, and all we had to do was stop by the courthouses in those counties and look up his record.

During the next two days, we were able to put together this account of the criminal record of Ronnie Greer, born January 4, 1958:
• On March 30, 1976, Greer was convicted on a misdemeanor theft charge in Anderson, Texas (Grimes County), was fined a total of $61, and was placed on probation. He served out his probation term and his file was destroyed, according to Grimes County officials. That county does not keep probation records.
• On April 24, 1978, Greer and two other young men were arrested, charged, and later indicted for felony theft by appropriation in connection with the heist of two tires and mag wheels from a car at an apartment complex in Bryan, Texas (Brazos County). The tires were valued at more than $200.
• On June 21, 1978, Greer was charged with misdemeanor possession of marijuana in Conroe, Texas (Montgomery County). The fine was assessed at $200 plus $50 court costs. Greer pleaded guilty in Montgomery County Court-at-Law and paid the $250 by December 18, 1978. The court docket showed Greer posted $500 bail to get out of jail. The date of offense was listed as June 15, 1978.
• On June 23, 1978, Greer pleaded guilty to the felony theft charge in Bryan and was placed on probation for two years. The range of punishment for that offense was two to ten years in prison. He was also fined $174 plus $10 a month for probation expenses.
• On February 16, 1979, Greer was arrested in Cleveland, Texas (Liberty County), for assault, disorderly conduct, and possession of an illegal weapon, a club. He was arrested at 7:22 p.m. by the Cleveland police, and was released from jail at 3:00 p.m. on February 18, two days later. Two Cleveland women called the police to report the assault, but according to police lieutenant Henry Patterson, they never pursued the charges, so those charges were dismissed. Greer was listed in Cleveland records as being five feet nine inches tall and weighing 160 pounds, and he was described as having a scar on the back of his right hand.
• On June 24, 1980, the State of Texas filed a motion in Brazos County to revoke Greer's two-year probation on the felony theft conviction because the young man was delinquent in paying off his fines, court

costs, and probation expenses. The revocation motion meant Greer could have been ordered to the state prison in Huntsville to serve the remainder of his two-year sentence. But the state filed its motion to revoke probation one day too late; Greer's two-year probation period had expired on June 23, 1980. A district judge dismissed the state's motion.

• On October 26, 1981, Greer was charged with theft by check in the amount of $50 in Bryan (Brazos County). The county's justice of the peace docket showed that "restitution was made" to a Bryan grocery store, and the charge was dropped.

• On March 14, 1982, Greer was arrested in Cleveland (Liberty County) on a charge of shoplifting a package of cigarettes from a convenience store. He was booked into the Cleveland jail at 12:25 p.m. and released on $56 bond at 2:59 p.m. His data sheet at the jail indicated he had a scar across his left shoulder. He told the police he lived in Cleveland. Douthat and I went by the address listed in the police files, a mobile home in the eastern end of Cleveland, but got no answer. We called the telephone number listed for that mobile home over a two-day period, and Douthat finally reached a young woman who said Greer no longer lived there; she would answer no other questions about him.

This list of Greer's criminal activity over a six-year period did not include the two charges in San Jacinto County that disappeared—the charge of carrying a prohibited weapon and the aggravated assault charge, both stemming from the shooting incident involving Murray Chreene on the night of February 5, 1982. Those charges, of course, could not be found in the official records at the San Jacinto County Courthouse.

At 9:00 a.m. on Wednesday, June 30, Douthat and I walked into the sheriff's office and told Chief John Glover that we wanted to see Parker. Parker was in his office but was "tied up" with another matter. We said we would wait. At 9:30, we got in to see him. I was taken aback by the sheriff's appearance. He seemed to have lost a great deal of weight and he wasn't nearly as tanned as he had been a month before, when I last saw him in person. I figured he must be ill, or else the activity of the federal and state agents was bothering him.

We asked him to tell us about Deputy Ronnie Greer.

Parker quickly denied that Greer ever worked for him as a deputy. "He was an informant. He closed up a couple of house burglaries, that's all. . . . First off, you couldn't commission him if you wanted to."

"Because of his lengthy criminal record?"

"Yeah."

"A large number of people have told us Greer regularly carried a gun and a badge in this department. . . ."

"Not to my knowledge."

"You mean he never had a badge?"

"Not unless he stole his stepdaddy's [Deputy Glenn Snearly]."

"We've also had people tell us that you hand out a lot of badges to various people."

He shook his head.

"Then where would they be getting these San Jacinto County badges?"

"I guess they go down and get them made, I don't know." He said he had recently gotten a call from a man from California who had run across another man with a San Jacinto County badge. "And I never heard of the son of a bitch," the sheriff said. "It's not hard to get them made."

"Did Ronnie Greer ever work for you as an officer?"

No.

"Did he ever ride with other officers?"

"It's possible he could have ridden. . . . It's not against policy, as long as they're an adult, to let someone ride." But he said Greer never did any police work while riding.

"We were told that Greer also carried a gun. Did you issue him one?"

"I don't have any idea where he would have got it, unless he stole it from his stepdaddy."

"Was Greer ever arrested by your deputies?"

"We picked him up on a Brazos County warrant at one time. I have no idea what ever happened to that." He said officials in Bryan had sent him a teletype message on Greer, who at the time had had car trouble in Humble. He said he sent someone down to Humble to pick him up. That was in 1981, he said.

"Did Greer spend much time in your jail? As a prisoner?"

"I very seldom go into the jail and see what's over there . . . unless some lawyer wants to go in there, okay? . . . I couldn't even tell you how many people are over there right now."

"What ever happened to the charges that came out of the Murray Chreene shooting incident?"

"I don't know."

We then asked a dozen or so questions about the break-in at Johnston's Pharmacy, and about Greer's activities with the sheriff's son that night.

He said Gary and Greer were playing cards at the jail with Robert Rice, a dispatcher, and that the first two decided to leave to return to Shepherd. He said they heard a whooping burglar alarm going off at the drugstore when they walked out of the office. And when they drove over the drugstore, the burglars fired the shots at them and fled.

"Did Ronnie Greer give a statement about that incident?"

"I don't know."

"Do you have that offense report in your office right now? Could we have a copy of it?"

"I think the Rangers picked it up the other day."

"What exactly are the Rangers looking at about the drugstore incident?"

"They're trying to find who in the hell broke in there, the same as we are."

"Do you think there's a possibility they might be looking at Gary and Greer as suspects?"

"I don't know what they're looking for . . . but Greer didn't do it. . . . And you could tell from Gary's voice when he radioed in [about the shooting] that he was scared tee-totally to death."

"Is your investigation of that break-in closed?"

"We don't ever close a case, unless we arrest someone and charge someone. . . . It's an open case."

"Are you assisting the Rangers in their investigation of that case?"

"We're not assisting the Rangers and they're not assisting us."

"Would you personally have any objection to us having a copy of the report Gary filed about the break-in?"

"I don't want to put something in the paper where maybe [the Rangers] are close to busting something. We would love to clear it." He said he would rather check with Ranger Wesley Styles before he released the report to us. "Personally, I have no objection."

Our interview was winding down. We had gotten the information we wanted from him to complete our story about Ronnie Greer. But before we left, I wanted to ask a couple of final questions about the Michaleks and their missing stereo equipment. First of all, I asked him who had the inventory sheet that Mike Jeffrey, Bill Burnett, Jean O'Dell, and Richard Curry had filled out.

"I don't know who has it. . . . I want to see it."

"And last, the property evidently disappeared while in your custody. Are you planning to take any action about it?"

"I will personally reimburse them if it doesn't show up." But, he quickly added, he wanted to see the inventory sheet first.

Story number nine ran on Monday morning, July 5, deep inside the second section of the newspaper. The stacked three-column headline said, "From Jailed to Jailer: Coldspring Inquiry Shows Inmate Got

Power of a Deputy." The twenty-two-paragraph story detailed Ronnie Greer's activities and his six-year criminal history. It included the sheriff's denials that Greer ever served in an official capacity, but the comments to the contrary by Judge Jeffrey, Greg Magee, and Constable Charles Clark were included prominently. As usual, most of the background information about our investigation was cut out of the story during the editing process, as was any mention of Highway 59. It was our last fling, our last independent effort in looking at that county. Ed insisted that it would be best for us to sit back and let the other investigations progress; if anything concrete popped up from those probes, he told us, then we could write some more stories.

So it was over. Nine stories in eight weeks, and only two of them—the first two—appeared on the front page. The other seven were snuggled into the back part of the paper. Still no word of any of it had appeared in Dallas or Houston, even though the FBI, the Texas Rangers, the Comptroller's Office, the Department of Public Safety, and now the ACLU were all conducting their own investigations. And for a week during the middle of July, the Texas Banking Department sent thirteen examiners to the Bank of San Jacinto County to look over the books. Ed wasn't interested because, he said, it would be very difficult to tie that banking investigation to the other ones. I said it would be impossible to tie it to the others while sitting at my desk in Austin, but Ed wasn't receptive to the idea of my making another trip. He was interested in sure-thing stories—lawsuits, charges, indictments—not any further investigative pursuits.

I did confirm the banking probe with Gary Pool, the state's deputy commissioner on banking, and Pool conceded that thirteen examiners constituted "an unusually large number of people" for a small bank like the one in Coldspring. Under further questioning, he conceded further that thirteen people was too many for a routine examination, but he refused to label it as an investigation. "This is a normal examination, a normal procedure," he said.

Fine. And it was just a coincidence that four other investigative agencies were over there at the same time.

Ed wasn't interested. And Douthat was too busy. During a series of changes on the city desk, Douthat was promoted to assistant city editor and ended all his reportorial duties. I spent most of July and August doing daily stories during the day and talking on the phone at night to the people in Coldspring. All the investigations were continuing, with special emphasis placed on the arrest trap on Highway 59, the drugstore break-in, and Ronnie Greer's activities. Wes Styles, the Ranger, kept in touch with me, and he insisted that his work was "moving right along.

We're doing all right." He said he had talked at length with an assistant U.S. attorney in Houston, and that there was a good possibility that a special grand jury would be impaneled sometime in the fall. He said he wanted to get as many names of victims as he could; by the middle of August, he reported that he had more than 150 names.

And on August 31, at 4:45 p.m., the Houston chapter of the American Civil Liberties Union went into U.S. district court and filed a class-action lawsuit against San Jacinto County, Texas, and Sheriff J. C. Parker, charging the county with widespread violations of civil rights stemming from the the marijuana arrest trap on Highway 59. The suit alleged numerous violations of constitutional rights regarding probable cause, due process of law, and illegal search and seizure, as well as improper procedures concerning the setting of bail bonds and fines. "Officials of San Jacinto County have engaged in a systematic conspiracy to indiscriminately detain and arrest motorists; incarcerate them in the county jail; deny them access to counsel; coerce them to plead guilty to dubious criminal charges or deny them the right to trial; extract large fines; and return them to jail when the victims are unable to immediately pay such fines," the first paragraph of the lawsuit contended. The four named plaintiffs in the action—which was seeking an injunction against operation of the alleged conspiracy—were Jeffrey Foley, Patsy DeBorde, J. E. Foley, and Kippy Carr.

I wrote up a story on the lawsuit and turned it in to Ed a little before 6:30 p.m. The story ran at the bottom of the front page on Wednesday, September 1, a day which also happened to be my ninth wedding anniversary and my thirty-fourth week at work at the *American-Statesman*. At 11:00 a.m. on September 1, with a copy of the page one lawsuit story tucked beneath my arm, I walked into Ed's office and gave notice that I was quitting my job in two weeks.

· TWENTY-EIGHT ·

The two Houston newspapers, the *Chronicle* and the *Post*, ran their first stories about the recent problems in San Jacinto County on Thursday, September 2. Both accounts were short—eight paragraphs in the *Post*'s story and twelve paragraphs in the *Chronicle*'s—and both centered on the ACLU lawsuit. Both also got Sheriff Parker's name wrong: they listed him as J. L. Parker, instead of J. C. Parker. And only the *Chronicle* mentioned the investigations by the FBI and the Texas Rangers. Neither went beyond the allegations in the lawsuit about the so-called marijuana arrest trap on Highway 59, a phrase I had first used four months before. Other newspapers around the state picked up the story from the wire services, AP and UPI, but very few ran it on the front page. The *Chronicle*'s story appeared on page nineteen, the *Post*'s on page four.

It wasn't until September 20 that the *Chronicle* ran a front-page story on the San Jacinto County investigations, and that story detailed primarily the November 13, 1981, arrest of Kip Carr. It was a splashy story, complete with a map showing everyone where San Jacinto County was. And it mentioned again the work by the FBI and Texas Rangers.

Then the story disappeared. Not a word was written about the county in Houston or Austin during the rest of 1982. The Texas Rangers and the FBI, to all appearances, had backed off. To all appearances. But that's not what happened. The investigations continued, and in the late fall a squadron of agents descended on the sheriff's department and seized a veritable ton of records, documents, arrest reports, receipt books, and other assorted files and reports. A federal grand jury began looking at the records and listening to some preliminary testimony as the U.S. Attorney's Office in Houston began a strong push to get to the bottom of the mess on Highway 59. I found out about all this when I was contacted by assistant U.S. attorney Scott Woodward, who had been placed in charge of the federal effort and wanted me to help him sort through some of the wild rumors and street talk he'd been hearing. Woodward and I talked on two separate occasions late in the year, with both sessions lasting close to an hour. The Justice Department wanted Woodward to pursue this investigation aggressively, and the prosecutor was interested in hearing my impressions about the Highway 59 operation, the handling of confiscated drugs and property, the setting of bail bonds, and the climate of fear that he felt existed in the county. Woodward had been in contact with Houston lawyer Jeff McClure, who was representing the ACLU in the civil rights lawsuit, and so had I. In fact, I talked with McClure on half a dozen occasions before the end of the year. Everything seemed to be progressing slowly, very slowly.

And the *American-Statesman* was silent.

The federal and state investigations exploded into public view in March 1983. On March 2, the San Jacinto County grand jury indicted Gary Parker and Ronnie Greer for burglary in the January 6, 1982, break-in of Johnston's Pharmacy in Coldspring. The sheriff's son was arrested by Texas Rangers at his home in Shepherd and was released the next day after posting $10,000 bail. Greer was arrested in San Antonio; he was also indicted on a charge of impersonating a peace officer.

District attorney Joe Price of Groveton confirmed to reporters that Gary Parker had filled several prescriptions for painkillers at the pharmacy before January 6, and that after the burglary a garbage bag filled with narcotics had been found by Parker and Greer in the alley behind the store. Price said all the stolen drugs had been recovered except two hundred tablets of the painkiller Demerol.

On March 18, Sheriff Parker went into U.S. district court in Houston and pleaded guilty to a three-count criminal information charge accusing him of using water torture to coerce confessions, of accepting kickbacks from bail bondsmen, and of violating the civil rights of motorists on Highway 59. The guilty plea was part of a plea-bargain arrangement with prosecutors in which the sheriff agreed to serve no more than three years in prison, pay a $15,000 fine, resign his post, and help the U.S. attorney in a continuing investigation. Sentencing was set for Friday, April 8.

The criminal charge carried a maximum possible penalty of forty years in prison and a $30,000 fine. It was filed a mere two hours before the sheriff entered his guilty plea. Parker was charged with ordering his deputies to stop motorists indiscriminately on Highway 59 and shake them down; with extorting one third of all revenues from bail bonds posted by bank president Jim Browder; and with participating in or directing the water torture of as many as fifteen people. The charges held that Parker and several "unnamed co-conspirators" confiscated drugs, guns, and other items from motorists and resold them for their own profit or used them for their own enjoyment. The water tortures were described in this manner: victims, usually jail prisoners, were handcuffed to a chair with their feet shackled, and a towel was placed over their mouths and noses while the chair was tilted backward; water was poured onto the towel until the victims began jerking about, indicating they were ready to talk. The tortures were used to punish the prisoners or to extract confessions, according to the federal charges.

The arrest trap was said to have existed along Highway 59 from September 1980 until April 1982; the bail bond extortion scheme was said to have lasted from September 1980 until December 1981; and the water tortures were described as being used from September 1976 until April 1981.

The same day that the sheriff's guilty plea was entered, March 19, the San Jacinto County commissioners accepted Parker's resignation and appointed retired Houston policeman Bob Brumley—the brother-in-law of newspaper editor Martha Charrey—to take over Parker's unexpired term, which still had another year to run. The sheriff, meanwhile, was freed on $5,000 bail pending the formal sentencing.

On Monday, March 21, Brumley demanded the resignations of four deputies, four dispatchers, one secretary, and eighteen reserve deputies. He said he wanted to "remove all shadow of doubt" that the corruption had come to an end. He also said he wanted to hire his own officers. And until he could do that, DPS troopers and volunteers from the county probation office would patrol the area. The new county judge, Kent Morrison, said he hoped the firings would restore confidence in the sheriff's department.

On April 8, the day of Parker's formal sentencing, U.S. district judge Gabrielle McDonald stunned prosecutors and courtroom observers by refusing to accept the plea-bargain agreement that had resulted in the sheriff's guilty plea two weeks before, the agreement that would have sent Parker to prison for three years. Judge McDonald said the three-year sentence was "most inappropriate" considering the severity of the offenses involved. "The defendant is hereby advised that if he persists in his plea of guilty, the disposition of this case will be considerably less favorable to the defendant," she announced from the bench. Parker's attorney immediately withdrew the guilty plea, and the former sheriff remained free on the $5,000 bond. Parker declined comment about the judge's action.

Kent Morrison, meanwhile, told the *Houston Chronicle* that regardless of the federal judge's rejection of the plea bargain, Parker had still resigned his post. "I don't know about his plea bargain, but I have in my possession a signed letter of resignation, and he is not going to be reinstated."

The explosion of charges and news coverage continued into May. On Wednesday, May 4, 1983, the San Jacinto County grand jury returned state indictments against Humpy Parker and three other former deputies. Parker was charged with misappropriating $2,100 in county funds that were to have been used to pay reserve deputies for their uniforms, with keeping $500 bond money posted by a man who had been arrested for assault, and with keeping $325 that was to have been paid to a savings and loan association as restitution in a forgery case. In addition, Parker and former deputies Floyd Baker, Carl Lee, and Aaron Edwards were charged in a separate two-count indictment with hitting a jail inmate with a flat lead object wrapped with leather and with using water torture to extract a statement from him. The last incident was said to have occurred on September 23, 1980.

Five days after the state indictments, on May 9, a federal grand jury in Houston indicted Humpy Parker on charges of torturing six prisoners with water over a four-year period. In this case, Parker and former deputies Carl Lee, John Glover, and Floyd Baker were accused of trying to suffocate the six prisoners in a water torture scheme to extract confessions. The indictments said the officers and Parker handcuffed the prisoners, struck them, placed towels over their mouths and noses, and poured water onto the towels until the victims began to jerk about, indicating they were drowning. The alleged water torture conspiracy was said to have existed from September 1976 until September 1980. The charges carried possible penalties of ten years in prison and a $10,000 fine, plus additional one-year prison sentences for each incident of water torture. The four defendants were freed on personal recognizance bonds until a trial could be scheduled.

In a period of two months, federal and state criminal charges had been launched at the ex-sheriff and his deputies from several directions. Humpy Parker was hit with water torture indictments in federal and state courts, as well as state charges of mishandling public funds and refusing to refund bond money. Four of his deputies were named in the torture indictments, and two reserve officers—Gary Parker, his son, and Ronnie Greer—were indicted in state court on burglary charges. In addition, by the middle of May 1983, all of them had lost their county jobs. News reporters from all over the country began popping up in Houston to cover the story, as editors and publishers began taking notice of the turmoil in the tiny county just north of Houston. The attorneys involved in the various cases, meanwhile, began preparing to go to trial.

The federal water torture trial was the first to take place. It began the last week in August in U.S. district court in Houston and lasted the better part of three weeks. News coverage of the trial was heavy.

The first witness called by assistant U.S. attorney Scott Woodward was former deputy Greg Magee, who was working at the time as a bank collections officer in Coldspring. Over a three-hour period on Wednesday, August 31, Magee testified that he had witnessed a water torture ordeal in September 1976 in which Sheriff Parker and other deputies took part. He said the incident took place in a small room in the Walker County sheriff's office. He described how the victim, a middle-aged man, was handcuffed to a chair, and how water was poured onto a towel placed around the man's mouth and nose. He said he had just gone to work for San Jacinto County as a deputy, and the torturing of the man, a suspect in a rash of burglaries, left him frightened and confused. "I was scared," he said.

Magee testified that he learned later that the water torture method was favored by Sheriff Parker because it left no marks on the victims. He also said he was instructed that the procedure was an acceptable method of interrogation in the San Jacinto County Sheriff's Department.

The victim of the ordeal Magee described, Vernell Harkless, a fifty-three-year-old bulldozer operator, testified the same day. He also described the incident, but he added that he was tortured two other times over a three-day period in September 1976. He demonstrated how the water tortures were performed and said he had thought the San Jacinto County officers were going to kill him. One of the other incidents had been witnessed by a young inmate in the San Jacinto County Jail, Vernon Perry, also a burglary suspect at the time, who testified that Sheriff Parker was giving instructions to the deputies throughout Harkless' interrogation. Perry testified that Harkless was gasping and struggling while the water was poured over his face, and that at one point the swivel chair collapsed.

Four other victims of water torture in the San Jacinto County Jail testified over the next two days. All described how they were handcuffed and placed in a chair, and how water was poured from a pitcher onto a towel placed on their faces. All said they were roughed up, cursed at, and threatened with further abuses if they failed to confess to criminal acts. All said they decided to cooperate with the officers after being tortured.

On Friday, September 2, two former deputies testified that they had seen jail inmates handcuffed to chairs, with water all over them and the floor, in the San Jacinto County sheriff's office. Neither could identify the victims or the date of the incidents, and neither actually saw the water being poured on the victims. One of the former deputies was Doug Yarbrough, a bank officer in Coldspring and the former partner of Greg Magee in the sheriff's department. Yarbrough testified that he could not recall which deputies were present with the wet prisoner.

Polk County sheriff Ted Everitt testified on Tuesday, September 6, that he watched Sheriff Parker and at least one deputy water-torture two prisoners one night in September 1976. Everitt said he was working as a deputy in Polk County at the time, and that he was in San Jacinto County that night on a burglary investigation. He testified that one of the victims was Vernell Harkless, whom he said he recognized from a construction job in Polk County. He could not identify the other victim. Everitt said he had never seen anything like the water torture method.

The sixth victim of the water torture scheme who was listed in the federal indictment also testified that day. His testimony was backed up by that of a former jail trusty, who said the deputies forced him to try to shackle the victim's legs to the chair. The method described to the jury was the same as that outlined by the others, although the victim also testified that he was beaten several times with a blackjack when he struggled to get out of the chair.

Two of the four defendants testified during the trial. Carl Lee took the stand on Wednesday, September 7, and denied that he had ever abused or tortured jail inmates. Floyd Baker testified the following Monday that he did take part in one incident of water torture, but only when he was ordered to by his supervisors. He also said he had witnessed other incidents of water torture in the jail. Baker said he didn't approve of the water tortures, but he didn't believe the inmates were being injured by them. He said he believed it was his job as a deputy to follow orders.

The federal jury began deliberating the case on Wednesday, September 14, after U.S. district judge James DeAnda declared a mistrial for Baker and ordered that a new trial date be set for him. About six hours later, the jury returned what federal officials called the first major civil rights victory in Houston in several years: Humpy Parker, Carl Lee, and John Glover were found guilty of conspiring to violate the civil rights of the jail inmates involved in the water tortures.

On Tuesday, October 25, 1983, the former sheriff was sentenced to ten years in prison and fined $12,000 for conspiracy to water-torture prisoners. He also was ordered by Judge DeAnda to undergo ninety days of psychiatric evaluation. Former deputy Lee, sixty-three, was sentenced to four years in prison, and former chief deputy Glover, sixty-

five, was sentenced to two years. The federal judge also took the occasion to criticize Parker for what he called the sheriff's "flagrant and un-
forgiveable" conduct. "You ran an operation that would embarrass the
dictator of a primitive country, and you did it over a long period," the
judge scolded the now-forty-eight-year-old Parker. He said the activities
of Parker and the other two deputies "reduced the community to where
law enforcement was in the hands of thugs, pure and simple. . . . What
you saw here is what happens when police start violating the law. . . .
Once they start, they lose sight of what laws to violate."

The situation in San Jacinto County, Judge DeAnda added, "got
totally out of control."

At the conclusion of the sentencing, DeAnda increased Parker's
$10,000 personal recognizance bond to a $150,000 cash appeal bond.
The former sheriff removed his tie, handed it to his wife, Melba, and
was escorted out of the courtroom by federal marshals. Lee later served
notice that he would appeal the verdict, and Glover reported to a
federal prison in mid-December.

Judge DeAnda said he was influenced in his determination for
Parker's ten-year sentence by a report filed with his court by federal
authorities. The report was described as including data about other
offenses, including theft, sales of drugs, abuse of innocent people, and
various civil rights violations.

Afterward, assistant U.S. attorney Woodward said the water torture
scheme did not come to his attention until the investigation of the
Highway 59 operation was well under way. He said it was first mentioned to the grand jury early in 1983. He also said he had seen "no
evidence of remorse" by the former sheriff or his fellow defendants during the trial, "although the lawyers gave lip service to the idea of
remorse."

During the former sheriff's third day in confinement at the Harris
County Jail's rehabilitation unit—according to Woodward and other
law enforcement officials—authorities abruptly became concerned about
Parker's physical and emotional condition and rushed him by plane to
a federal psychiatric center in Springfield, Missouri. Woodward and the
other officials would not explain why they suddenly became concerned
about Parker's health. "The only thing I can say is the fact that his com-
petency to stand trial [in the other cases] became an issue after the water
torture trial," Woodward said, "I can just say that there were certain circumstances during his early part of his confinement that brought that
out."

The fourth defendant in the water torture case, former deputy Floyd
Baker, elected in the meantime to plead guilty to a charge of conspiracy

to violate the civil rights of prisoners rather than stand trial. On Thursday, December 8, 1983, Judge DeAnda sentenced Baker to a four-year prison term and prohibited him from working ever again in law enforcement.

New federal indictments were returned on October 3, 1983, accusing Humpy Parker, his son, Gary, former deputy Robert Rice, and bail bondsmen Herb Atwood and Jim Browder of violating the rights of motorists on Highway 59 by stopping cars without probable cause, conducting illegal searches and strip searches, seizing property without cause, and extracting money under false pretenses. The two Parkers were also indicted separately on charges of attempting to defraud the federal government by submitting falsified documents to investigators. The charges—all centering on the sheriff's department's activities on Highway 59 during an eighteen-month period—confronted the two Parkers with possible sentences of seventy years in prison and $16,000 fines. Federal officials in Houston said the San Jacinto County department operated a "money-making scheme" on Highway 59 that amounted to "highway robbery."

The federal court trial began the last week in November, and the first government witness, once again, was Greg Magee. Woodward said later, "I wanted to lead off as always with my best shot, my best witness."

Magee spent close to eight hours over a two-day period on the witness stand, detailing the illegal stops and searches, the shakedowns in the jail, the trumped-up charges, and the improper seizures of property from motorists. He explained how the deputies would park in the crossover lanes on Highway 59 near the Trinity River bridge, usually on weekend nights, and look for cars carrying young people or blacks or other minorities and for old cars, vans, or vehicles with rock-station bumper stickers. He also testified about the high-speed transporting of arrestees from Highway 59 up State Highway 150 to Coldspring, and about the cooperation among deputies, wrecker drivers, and bail bondsmen.

Another early witness was state district judge Joe Ned Dean, who testified primarily about how the criminal justice system was supposed to work—how charges were supposed to be filed in court, how bonds were supposed to be set, and how cases were supposed to be handled from the point of arrest to the actual disposition of the charge.

And then the victims of the arrest trap took the stand. "We interviewed about two hundred victims across the country, people who had pretty scary stories to tell about their experiences with the San Jacinto County Sheriff's Department," Woodward said later. "We cut that list down to fifty-six that we were going to use, in the trial, and then we cut it down again to thirty. But when we were at the point of going to trial, we cut it down again to fourteen victims. These were the best stories, people who were arrested and never charged, people who were strip-searched, people who had property taken or damaged. We felt like these would be our best witnesses."

One of the first to take the stand, on Friday, December 2, was Baytown tire dealer Kip Carr, who testified about his arrest in November 1981 for having a broom handle in his vehicle. He testified about how the deputy pulled him over for no apparent reason and immediately began searching aggressively through the truck.

A Department of Public Safety trooper and a reserve deputy from another county testified about how they were stopped in San Jacinto County while they were off duty, and about how their vehicles were searched illegally. Three young women also testified to having been stopped on Highway 59 and forcibly searched by deputies for no apparent reason. One of them, a twenty-two-year-old woman, said she was held to the ground by one deputy on the side of the highway while another—whom she identified as Gary Parker—tore her clothes open and began feeling inside her pants. She said that she was not told why she was stopped, but that she asked for a female officer to search her once it was apparent that she was going to be searched. She said the arrest occurred in November 1981.

A common element of the victims' stories was the presence at the jail of bail bondsmen, who collected money supposedly as a fee to post a bail bond. But after the victims related their stories to the jury, all four San Jacinto County justices of the peace, the district court clerk, and the county court clerk testified that they could find no records to indicate that those people had been charged with any crimes. Most of the JPs and clerks spent only a few minutes on the stand, but justice of the peace Mike Jeffrey testified for almost an hour. Jeffrey told the court that it was widely known that most of the arrests would never result in official charges, that any arrest for which an escrow amount was taken from the victim "would never go to trial." Jeffrey also testified about the disappearance of the stereo equipment belonging to Bruce Michalek of Little Rock, Arkansas, and about the detailed inventory list that he and three other county employees prepared and gave to Humpy Parker concerning the stereo equipment. The prosecutors said they wanted this aspect of Jeffrey's testimony to show that property confiscated from Highway 59 victims often wound up being stolen.

Two wrecker drivers, Billy and Jack Fly of Shepherd, testified that they were often instructed by deputies to cut the taillights or license plate wires on the victims' cars, and that they at one point were encouraged to buy more wrecker trucks because the sheriff's department was planning to "step up" its arrests on Highway 59. Other testimony was provided by DPS statistics officials, who gave the jury the staggering numbers of marijuana arrests made in San Jacinto County; by an FBI agent, who summarized the pattern of cases placed on county dockets; by state crime lab officials from Austin and Houston, who testified that no drugs had been submitted from San Jacinto County for analysis; and by district attorneys J. H. Keeshan and Joe Price, who testified about the very small numbers of felony cases submitted to them by the sheriff's department for prosecution.

The trial was in its second week on Tuesday, December 6, with former deputy Doug Yarbrough waiting to testify, when the defendants notified U.S. district judge Robert O'Conor that they wanted to plead guilty to reduced charges in an agreement reached with federal prosecutors. Gary Parker pleaded guilty to one count of conspiracy to deprive motorists of their civil rights, a felony; bail bondsman and former state representative Jim Browder pleaded guilty to a charge of being an accessory after the fact to conspiracy, a felony; and bail bondsman Herb Atwood pleaded guilty to a charge of misprision (concealment) of felony, also a felony charge. Humpy Parker, who was still undergoing psychiatric testing in Missouri, and former deputy Robert Rice, the other defendant in the case, were granted separate trials and would be tried later. Gary Parker faced a maximum sentence of ten years in prison and a fine of $10,000; Browder, a five-year sentence and a $5,000 fine; and Atwood a three-year term and a $500 fine. Sentencing was set for February 17, 1984. In the meantime, Robert Rice also elected to plead guilty to a reduced charge of concealment of a felony, and his sentencing was set for the same day as the others. Rice was also ordered to undergo psychiatric testing.

Afterward, Scott Woodward said he was ecstatic about the guilty pleas. "This is a great victory for the Texas Rangers and the FBI. It also is a very unusual situation in that both of these agencies worked together on the investigation. I don't know if there has been another investigation in which federal and state investigators worked hand in hand like this. All I know is that they really beat the bushes together, and they sure made my job a lot easier."

On February 17, Gary Parker was sentenced to five years in prison, and Atwood, Browder, and Rice were placed on probation.

On Wednesday, December 7, a state district court jury in Coldspring found San Jacinto County constable Rathell Denson guilty of aggravated assault for threatening Highway 59 motorists with a gun, sentenced him to five years in prison, and fined him $2,000. The jury, meeting in district judge Joe Ned Dean's court, deliberated only fifteen minutes before returning the verdict. Testimony showed that two young men from Stephen F. Austin University in Nacogdoches had been driving between Shepherd and Cleveland on Highway 59 when Denson pulled up next to them and threatened them with a pistol. Denson, who had been a constable since 1977, was forced to resign his office.

Meanwhile, former San Jacinto County undercover agent Ronnie Greer pleaded guilty to the charge of burglary in connection with the break-in at Johnston's Pharmacy in Coldspring and was placed on ten years' probation with the stipulation that he cooperate with the state in its prosecution of other San Jacinto County officers. Greer had been subpoenaed by federal prosecutors in the Highway 59 conspiracy trial in Houston, and he was waiting to testify when Gary Parker and the two bail bondsmen pleaded guilty.

The towering pine trees still provide a breathtaking sight on the narrow forest roads leading into Coldspring. The three-story brick courthouse still towers over the small storefront businesses that line the streets to the north and west of the ancient-looking edifice. And the people who work in and around the courthouse still stop and look when an unfamiliar vehicle pulls up to the stop sign at Highway 150 next to a tiny grocery store and land company northwest of the courthouse square. The *San Jacinto News-Times* still comes out once a week with its hodgepodge of weddings, civic news, and short local feature stories. And a political rally—even in the rain—will still draw a good crowd. Coldspring still gives the appearance of a quiet, slow-moving rural county seat. Some things will never change. Others do. Justice of the peace Mike Jeffrey, for example, left his boot and saddle shop to take over the operations of the county's waterworks division, and the store is now used solely as a gunsmith shop. Martha Charrey has begun taking courses in Huntsville and is talking about changing professions. And Greg Magee has left the Bank of San Jacinto County, where he worked as a collections officer after resigning his deputy's commission in disgust in July 1982.

But even in a town like Coldspring, beset for more than two years with investigations, indictments, convictions, and turmoil, the more things change, the more they stay the same. A few minutes before 10:00 p.m. on the night of Tuesday, October 18, 1983, Greg Magee walked into the Public Safety Building just off the courthouse square. The new sheriff, Bob Brumley, had assembled an entirely new department, purging the ranks of all who had worked under Humpy Parker, right down to secretaries and dispatchers. Magee had worked for Parker almost seven years before going voluntarily before the FBI and Texas Rangers to detail the atrocities that had gone on in the department. But on this night he was going back to work. Sheriff Brumley had called Magee and asked him to come back as a deputy.